The Life And Martyrdom Of Saint Thomas Becket, Archbishop Of Canterbury, Part 2

John Morris

ROEHAMPTON:
PRINTED BY JAMES STANLEY.

THE

LIFE AND MARTYRDOM

OF

SAINT THOMAS BECKET,

ARCHBISHOP OF CANTERBURY.

SECOND AND ENLARGED EDITION.

BY

JOHN MORRIS,

PRIEST OF THE SOCIETY OF JESUS.

PART II.

BURNS AND OATES,

LONDON:
GRANVILLE MANSIONS,
ORCHARD STREET, W.

NEW YORK:
CATHOLIC PUBLICATION SOCIETY CO.
BARCLAY STREET.

1885.

CONTENTS.

PAGE

CONTENTS.

CHAPTER XXVI.

CLAIRVAUX.

1169.

At Clairvaux on Palm Sunday St. Thomas excommunicates the Bishop of London and others—these sentences generally disregarded at Court—publication of the Bishop's excommunication in St. Paul's on Ascension Day—the danger run by the Archbishop's messengers—the King's violence when angry—Gilbert Foliot's appeal in Lent—meeting of Bishops at Northampton on Trinity Sunday—King Henry's letter to Foliot — further excommunications on Ascension Day — courageous conduct of the Bishop of Worcester—the Pope requests St. Thomas to suspend the censures for a time.

ST. THOMAS was now in a better position than he had yet been. King Louis was more firmly his friend than ever, and his powers were now fully restored to him, both by the lapse of the term for which they had been suspended, and by the publication of the Pope's second letter to the King.

At last the blow, long merited and long delayed, fell on the head of Gilbert Foliot, Bishop of London. The Bishop knew perfectly well that the sentence was pending, although the citations could not, in consequence of the severity of the watch that was kept, be legally and formally delivered. He wrote to Jocelin of Salisbury, to warn him that he was to be included in the coming censure; and at the beginning of Lent they both appealed to the Pope, naming as the term of the appeal the 9th of February, 1170. This they certified to St. Thomas.[1] It was, however, the opinion of the canonists who advised the Saint that the appeal was invalid, as being captiously made in order to avoid justice : on Palm Sunday,[2] therefore, April 13, 1169, at Clairvaux, he excommunicated Gilbert Foliot; and in the document [3] which announced it to the Dean and clergy of London he threatened, unless satisfaction was made by them in the interval, on Ascension Day to excommunicate also Geoffrey Ridel, the Archdeacon of Canterbury, and Robert his vicar, Richard of Ilchester, Richard de Luci, William Giffard, Adam of Charing, and all who should have either usurped Church property or urged the King to injure the Church or banish the innocent, and all who should have injured the Pope's messengers or his own. The names were added of all who were excommunicated at the same time with the Bishop of London : they were, the Bishop of Salisbury; Hugh Earl of Norfolk; Randulf de Broc; Thomas Fitz-Bernard; Robert de Broc, a cleric; Hugh of St. Clair; Letard of Northfleet, a cleric; Nigel de Sackville; and Richard the brother of William of Hastings, a cleric, who had usurped the Church of Monkton. There are several names found here which are amongst the excommunicates of Vezelay, which is accounted for by the

[1] *Materials*, vi. pp. 534, 539, 540.
[2] *Ibid.* p. 451.   [3] *Ibid.* p. 558.

rumour which reached the Archbishop, that John of Oxford had obtained their absolution. He had, in truth, as we have seen, obtained but a very conditional one, which was very freely interpreted; for Alan de Neville had been absolved on the plea that he was going to Jerusalem, and several others at Holy Trinity in London, under pretext that they were in danger of death, as they were about to join the war against the Welsh.

The Archbishop's letters excommunicating the Bishop of London were carried by two messengers, whose names were Berengar and William Bonhart, the latter of whom has described to us their delivery.[4] On Ascension Day, May 29, 1169, they went together to St. Paul's Cathedral, at the high altar of which a priest named Vitalis was singing Mass. At the offertory, Berengar went up to the altar, and kneeling down placed the Archbishop's letters in the priest's hands, who turned to receive them, thinking them an offering. Berengar then held his hands firmly, until he had bidden him in the name of the Pope and the Archbishop, to give one copy to the Bishop, and the other to the Dean; and he commanded him not to proceed with the Mass, nor William of Nordhall[5] the deacon, nor W. Hog the subdeacon, whom he called as witnesses, to continue to assist at it, until the letters were read aloud. Berengar then turned to the people, and said in a loud voice, "Take notice, that Gilbert the Bishop of

4 *Materials*, vi. p. 603.
5 William was Bishop of Worcester from 1186 to 1190.

London has been excommunicated by Thomas the Archbishop of Canterbury and Legate of the Apostolic See." When the people heard this, some tried to stop Berengar, others insulted him; but William Bonhart covered him with his cloak, and, mingling with the crowd[6] who poured out of the church, they got safe to their lodgings. Some of the people nearest the altar asked the priest whether the city was placed under an interdict; and on learning that it was not, they asked no more questions. Vitalis did not wish to continue the Mass until the letters were read; but the deacon went to Nicholas the Archdeacon, who said, "Would the priest stop his dinner if a messenger were to bid him cease to eat, in the Archbishop's name?" They continued the Mass, the letters being only read privately. The King's officials instituted a strict search for Berengar both in the city and the country, but without success. He afterwards went to York, bearing letters from the Pope; and he managed to escape arrest.

The danger which Berengar ran was very serious. He was a layman, and not literate; but he is described as a young man who would expose himself to peril, and who was not afraid even to die for God's sake. A very strict watch

6 Fitzstephen (p. 90) says, that people who had heard Mass in their parish church in the morning were in the habit of leaving the cathedral after the Gospel, probably having attended the sermon. Bonhart thought this escape so wonderful that in writing to St. Thomas he says that he has, as witnesses of the fact, Berengar himself, Richard the nephew of William de Capes, and the son of William Wannoc.

was kept up along the coast, so that the chance of escaping detection was but small; and when taken, the Archbishop's messenger had to expect not only the severe penalties of high treason, but also whatever else Henry's irascible temper might choose to order on the spur of the moment. An extract from a letter,[7] showing what the great Henry Plantagenet could become in a paroxysm of rage, will not be out of place here. " Richard de Humet ventured to say something that seemed like favouring the Scotch; and the King broke out into open abuse, calling him a traitor outright. In his fit of passion he flung down his cap, undid his belt, threw from him his cloak and robes, tore the silk covering off his couch, and, sitting down as if on a dunghill, began to chew stalks of straw." The same writer says, "It was at Toucques that his lordship the Pope's messenger was taken; he is still imprisoned and in chains. Here, too, the Lord saved Master Herbert out of the hand of his pursuers. Surely he should not have exposed himself so on a matter of such little consequence." Another specimen of the King's temper is given us in the fate of a bearer of a letter to the King. "You know, I conclude," writes Nicholas,[8] Prior of the Hospital of Mont-St. Jacques, near Rouen, "in what a strait the messenger was who delivered the letter to the King. His fingers were

7 *Materials*, vi. p. 71. This Richard de Humet was Justiciary of Normandy; so that Henry could not restrain his violence, even against a great nobleman and high officer of State.

8 *Ibid*. p. 76.

thrust into his eyes, as if to tear them out, till the blood flowed ; and hot water was forced down his throat, till he confessed that the letter came from Master Herbert. He is not yet released from prison ; though the King has received an order to that effect from his mother."

The fear of being subjected to violent usage was, under such circumstances, quite enough to deter people from carrying the Archbishop's letters ; and the wonder is, rather how so many reached their destination in safety, than how in some cases no one could be found to take them. This would also account for the three warnings which the canon law requires not being served on the Bishop of London previous to his excommunication, and for the formal notice of it being after such an interval. He had, however, known of it long before the Archbishop's letter was published in London. Early in Lent (March 18, 1169) Gilbert Foliot had appealed at St. Paul's in the presence of many abbots, priors, archdeacons, and clerics ;[9] and, about the same time, he had assembled[10] at Westminster the Bishops of Exeter and Salisbury, Richard of Ilchester, Laurence the Abbot of Westminster, Guy Rufus the Dean of Waltham, and the Barons of the Exchequer. The Bishop of Exeter sent him a preliminary message that he must not offer him the usual salutation of a kiss ; but on their meeting, and Gilbert offering it, Bartholomew did not refuse it. The object of the Bishop of London was to try and induce his

9 *Materials*, vi. pp. 614, 619.   10 *Ibid*. p. 606.

brother of Exeter to join him in an appeal;
but he did not succeed. Jocelin of Salisbury,
in the course of the proceedings, made use of
the insulting phrase, in reference to the sentence
passed upon him, "If Buinard the Archbishop, or
any fool of an archbishop of mine, were to order
me to do anything that I ought not to do, do
you think I should do it?"

The Bishop of London was in the country, at
a place called Stubbehuthe (Stepney), when he
learnt what had happened in his cathedral.[11]   On
the Saturday following (May 31, 1169) he met
the Chapter, which had been summoned for that
day; and after much conference, Vitalis was
ordered to produce the letters, which he did,
giving the Bishop and the Dean those respectively
intended for them. The Bishop read his aloud,
knitting his eyebrows, and pronouncing the words
with difficulty through vexation. When he had
finished the letter, he began to argue against it
under the following heads:

"The first head is from the Old Testament.
Adam sinned in Paradise. God did not sentence
him at once, but suffered him to depart; then
cited him, saying, 'Adam!' then rebuked him,
saying, 'Where art thou?'

"The second head from the New Testament.
It is said to Peter in the Gospel, 'If thy brother
sin against thee, rebuke him in private;' afterwards, 'before two or three;' thirdly, 'tell it to
the Church;' then, lastly, reckon him incorrigible,
'let him be to thee as a heathen and a publican.'

[11] *Ibid.* p. 604.

"It will not do for the Archbishop to say, ' I could not cite the Bishop of London.'   It appears he could: if he could do the greater, that is, excommunicate, he could do the less, that is, cite.

"Not to be appealed from is the privilege only of the Pope.   I am safe, therefore, by my appeal; and in the sacred name of the Most Holy Trinity, I dash this deed of his to pieces against the rock on which the Church is founded.

"In all criminal cases, four persons are necessary,—the accuser, the accused, the witnesses, the judge; these he confounds in his eagerness against me, accusing, witnessing, judging all himself.   Hence it is clear that, if he could, he would be executioner too.

"He puts his sickle into another man's harvest; for he has no power over my person or my church: over my person, because I never made profession of obedience to him, nor yet obeyed him, nor yet made profession to the Church of Canterbury in the name of this Church of London; over my Church, because the Church of London reasserts the right which was only taken from it by a Pagan invasion,—that is, of being the archiepiscopal see.   This I am prepared to prove, and on this ground I renew my appeal.

"If it is true, as he says, that he holds his power from the Pope as legate, neither will that assist him; for he is not yet within the limits for which his commission is granted."

The Dean, Archdeacon, and all the canons

and priests of St. Paul's joined the appeal;[12] but the canons of St. Bartholomew's, St. Martin's, and Holy Trinity refused. Finally, the Dean caused the letter sent to him to be read.[13]

Whatever validity there may be in canon law in the other points of the Bishop's appeal, one of those above mentioned was particularly disgraceful. When he was translated from Hereford to London, he refused to make a fresh profession of obedience, on the express plea that it was not requisite, since that made by him on his promotion to Hereford was still in force. St. Thomas carried the question with him to Pope Alexander when they both went to the Council of Tours; and, with the express provision that it should be no prejudice to the Archbishop or his Church, Alexander decided the cause in Gilbert's favour. It was, therefore, literally true that he had not personally made any profession to St. Thomas, for when made Bishop of Hereford, his profession was made to Theobald; nor had he in the name of the Church of London professed obedience to Canterbury; but he had been exempted from both on the express condition that he should not claim the exemption which he now pretended.

The Bishops on Trinity Sunday held a meeting at Northampton.[14] The object was to induce them to renew the appeal which the

[12] *Materials*, vi. pp. 606, 618. The Abbots of Westminster, Ramsey, Chertsey, Reading, and Stratford, the Archbishop of Rouen, and the Bishop of Lisieux, all wrote to the Pope on behalf of the Bishop of London (*Ibid.* pp. 621—639).

[13] *Ibid.* p. 558.

[14] Ep. Gilb. Fol. ii. p. 268; Ep. S. Tho. i. p. 328.

Bishops of London and Salisbury had made at the beginning of Lent. When the Bishop of Durham, who sat first, was asked, he answered that he had not been present when the appeal was made, nor had he received any citation; that he would, however, consult his metropolitan, the Archbishop of York; and after due deliberation, he would do whatever he might, saving God's honour and his own. The evasion was highly approved by the other Bishops, who were unwilling to take a bolder part than they were forced into against St. Thomas. They were also probably deterred by the pretensions to independence of Canterbury, which Gilbert had mixed up with his appeal, and which, especially on the Continent, excited the liveliest indignation. The Archbishop of Sens, and the Bishops of Auxerre, Thérouanne, Noyon, Paris, and Troyes all wrote[15] on the subject.

The Bishop of Exeter was next asked what he thought; and he replied, that his brother Bishops had made the appeal without his knowledge; that if they appealed, they would be uniting themselves with excommunicated persons; and that if the Pope should confirm the sentence, there was great danger, which nothing should induce him to encounter. If, however, it were for the good of the Church, and if by the King's favour he might leave the kingdom, he would appeal against any fresh injury which might be feared, but not against any already

[15] Ep. S. Tho. ii. p. 154; Ep. Gilb. Fol. ii. pp. 205, 224, 228, 235, 267.

inflicted. For his part, if any sentence of his superior directed against himself were to come to his knowledge, he would bear it obediently. This answer strongly excited the ridicule of Gilbert Foliot.

The Bishop of Winchester was requested to send an answer to Northampton to these same points that were proposed to his brethren. His reply was this: "The Divine law binds a man who is summoned to a higher judge not to appeal to an inferior; and he who appeals, is in duty bound to carry on his cause. Now I, who am worn out by sickness and old age, am summoned by the Lord, and am therefore unfit for appeals to an earthly tribunal. I pray you to excuse my joining in appeals which may bring me under an anathema." Roger of Worcester, who was himself on St. Thomas's side, records these proceedings; and adds, that these two Bishops, Bartholomew of Exeter and Henry of Winchester, incurred by their answers the suspicions of the King's party, and were for the future excluded from their cabals. Going further still than this in the direction of obedience, four bishops published [16] the letters proclaiming Gilbert's excommunication, the Bishop of Norwich in his first synod, and the Bishops of Lichfield, Winchester, and Chichester, on the day after they received them.

Though Gilbert was unsuccessful with his fellow-Bishops, he had recourse to the King, who wrote [17] him a letter from St. Macaire on the

[16] Ep. S. Tho. i. p. 328.   [17] *Materials*, vi. pp. 598, 599.

Garonne, in Gascony, giving him leave to appeal. "I have heard of the grievance which that Thomas my traitor and enemy has inflicted upon you and other persons of my kingdom; and I bear it with not less vexation in your case, than I should if he had vomited forth his venom against my own proper person." Henry also wrote the Pope in his behalf, of which letter the following is an extract: "I cannot adequately marvel that your wisdom should hand me over to what I consider most injurious molestation, who am a devoted son of the Church of Rome, ever ready to submit to justice. Now he who desists not to afflict the innocent, has added a fresh injury to the multitudes that preceded it. Supported, as he says, by your Holiness's authority, he has just now excommunicated the Bishops of London and Salisbury, unconvicted, uncited, unadmonished, and while an appeal was pending; and to several of my friends he holds out a threat of the same treatment, without any reasonable provocation. At all this I am not less indignant than if I had been the object of his sentence myself. It seems to me that your fatherly goodness has, as it were, cast me off; that you have ceased to regard the sufferings of your son, and will permit my wicked adversary to proceed against me as he pleases."

The further excommunications, threatened at Clairvaux on Palm Sunday, were carried into effect on Ascension Day. The persons censured were Geoffrey Ridel, Archdeacon of Canterbury, Robert his vicar, Richard of Ilchester, Richard

de Luci, William Giffard, and Adam of Charing.
It is to be feared that much attention was not
paid to these sentences; so that the contagion
spread in such a way that we are told, that in the
King's chapel hardly any one was to be found to
give him the *pax*, except persons under either the
major or minor excommunication,—the first incurred by sentences passed upon them by name,
and the second by communicating with those
who were excommunicated. Fitzstephen notes
that Robert and Nigel de Sackville, the King's
sealbearers, who had been excommunicated at
Vezelay, died young; and that Robert the vice-
archdeacon of Canterbury and the priest of
Thierlewde (Throwley) died of such grievous
ulcers, that they seemed stricken by the hand of
God.

The sentence on Geoffrey Ridel gave one of
the bishops whom St. Thomas had consecrated
an opportunity of showing his sense of duty.
Roger, the son of the Earl of Gloucester, a near
relation of the King, was Bishop of Worcester;
and to him has been attributed the glory of being
the only Bishop who was willing to be banished
for St. Thomas's sake. Geoffrey Ridel retained
his place in the chapel-royal, notwithstanding
his excommunication. The Bishop of Worcester
happened to go to Court, where he was well
received by the King; who was content to listen
to his remonstrances, though he would not be
guided by them. One day they entered the
chapel, where the King was about to hear Mass.
The Bishop was in his place, when he saw the

V

Archdeacon of Canterbury come in; on which
he immediately left the chapel. Henry was
astonished and angry; yet, though he knew the
motive well enough, he sent a messenger to him,
to bid him come back and explain why he had
gone away. Roger sent him the cause for answer; when he received another message from
the King, to bid him leave the kingdom with all
speed. The Bishop sent for his retinue, and
ordered them to follow him, which they did as
soon as they could get their baggage together;
and he then sent word to the King that he
already had his foot in his stirrup,[18] and that he
would leave the country directly. After a while,
the King broke out into insults and threats; on
which one of those about him mustered courage
enough to expostulate: "My lord, what have
you done? You have banished a Bishop who is
closely united to you in faith and blood. If I
might say so, you have not done well. Besides,
you have given the Archbishop what will please
him best; and the Pope, who has had no reason
for blaming you yet, will now have a cause to
do so, placed in his way by yourself. You grieve
your friends, and rejoice your enemies, by banish-
ing an innocent man, not to say a bishop." The
King was moved, and sent a horseman after the
Bishop; who, however, refused to return. He
then sent others, and finally, a party mounted
on fleet horses, with an earl at their head, with

[18] "In *strepa* vel orbe tenente pedem seu quo alio dignatur
nomine" (Fitzstephen, p. 86). "*Stirrup* put for *sty-rope*, a rope
to mount by, from A. S. *stigen*, pp. of *stigan*, to mount" (Skeat).

orders to bring the Bishop back, whether he would or no. Roger returned, and spoke in plain terms to the King; and ever after, while the Bishop was there, the Archdeacon never entered the chapel nor the King's presence.

The Pope sent the following letter[19] to St. Thomas on the subject of the excommunications, dated from Benevento the 19th of June: "We marvel greatly that, at the time when your envoys and others from our well-beloved son in Christ, Henry the illustrious King of England, were still present at our Court and waiting our determination, you should have thought fit, ourself not consulted, to utter any sentence against the dignitaries of the realm. Moreover, although we doubt not your general prudence and circumspection, yet it often happens that persons see less clearly in their own cause than in the cause of others; and for this reason, as we are unwilling that your sentence should be revoked but by your own deed, we advise, counsel, and exhort you, as a beloved brother, that in order to mitigate the King's displeasure, you of your own will suspend it, till such time as you learn from our envoys whether the said King is willing to be reconciled, and to realize the promise of your recall.

"It becomes ourself and you to wait with patience, and to tolerate him with all gentleness of spirit, for the space of two or three months, that we may leave him without excuse. If you do not think fit to accede to this our request, and things

[19] Ep. S. Tho. ii. p. 22; Froude, p. 429.

turn out not according to your wish and expecta-
tion, but, which God avert, to the contrary, you
must attribute the result to yourself, and not to
us.   But if, according to our wish and suggestion,
you suspend the sentence till the arrival of our
envoys, and the King still persists in his obstinacy, in that case, before the departure of the
envoys, you shall be at liberty unhesitatingly to
revive the sentence without incurring the risk of
our displeasure.   Yea, rather you may look to
us for every support and assistance."

This letter seems to take for granted the
validity of the censures in spite of the want of
the three canonical citations or monitions, probably from the notoriety of the offences and the
impossibility of serving the warnings.

CHAPTER XXVII.

THE POPE'S ENVOYS.

1169—1170.

King Henry tries bribery on a large scale—has recourse to the
King of Sicily—Gratian and Vivian appointed Envoys by
the Pope—their interviews with Henry—Gratian returns to
the Pope with the Archbishop of Sens—St. Thomas threatens
an interdict, if the King does not repent—the King imposes a
new oath on his subjects, and obtains a conference with King
Louis by a pilgrimage to St. Denys—at Vivian's request
St. Thomas comes to Montmartre and terms are agreed on
by Henry, who however refuses to ratify them by a kiss, and
retires to Mantes—St. Thomas lodged in the Temple—the
English Bishops resist the King—Henry returns to England.

IT was mentioned that King Henry sent other
messengers to the Pope, when Bernard de la
Coudre told him the contents of the second
commonitory letter. It was their business[1] to
see what money could effect in his favour. The
Emperor Frederic Barbarossa had been so unsuccessful in his invasion of Italy, that the threat
to join the Antipope was now less likely to be
carried out than it had been. Henry's present
object was to see what advocacy his money could
buy. He offered the Milanese three thousand
marks and a thorough repair of their fortifications, if they would join the other states, which

[1] Ep. Jo. Sar. ii. p. 208 ; Froude, p. 435.

he was attempting to corrupt, in prevailing on
the Holy See to depose or translate the Archbishop of Canterbury.   On the same conditions
he promised the citizens of Cremona two thousand, and those of Parma and Bologna one
thousand each.   To the Pope he offered a re-
lease from all the demands the Romans made
on him, and ten thousand marks besides; and
to allow him to appoint what pastors he would,
as well in the Church of Canterbury, as in all
other sees now vacant in England.   A letter[2] of
the Saint's of this date shows what dioceses
were in this condition.   " He has now for five
years," he writes, "held the revenues of our see
and all our goods, besides the bishoprics of Lincoln, Bath, Hereford, and Ely.   The possessions
of Llandaff he has squandered on his knights;
the Bishop of Bangor he will not suffer to be
consecrated, and that see has been ten years
without a Bishop."

On all his offers proving ineffectual, he tried
next what the power of the King of Sicily could
do for him ; but neither the Bishop of Syracuse
with all his efforts, nor yet the labours of Robert
Count of Basseville, and the other host of inter-
cessors, nor the great power, weight, and influence which that King possessed with the Pope, in
consequence of the generous way in which he
had helped the Holy Father in his late troubles
at Rome, could effect his wishes.   His envoys
were at last dismissed in disappointment, having
obtained nothing but a promise that the Pope

2 Ep. S. Tho. i. p. 121.

would send fresh envoys to mediate a peace. The
· persons selected were very acceptable to St.
Thomas, being Gratian, a subdeacon and notary
of the Holy See, a nephew of Pope Eugenius III.,
and Vivian Archdeacon of Orvieto,[3] and advocate
in the Roman courts. They were bound by an
oath to abide by prescribed terms of peace, which
they were on no account to exceed. It was also
in their instructions that their expenses should
not be defrayed by the King, unless peace were
granted ; nor were they to remain a day beyond
the time appointed them. These precautions
against bribery were, at least in the case of
Gratian, perfectly successful ; for, when his mission was over, he returned with the highest reputation for integrity.[4]

On the feast of the Assumption, August 15th,
1169, the letters of the new envoys reached the
King at Argentan. He was much troubled on
reading them ; and on the following day he sent
John of Oxford and Reginald, the one the Dean,
the other the Archdeacon, of Salisbury, to meet
the envoys, who on the 23rd of August reached
Domfront. On hearing of their arrival, two excommunicates of the King's party, Geoffrey
Ridel and Nigel de Sackville, left the town in
haste, doubtless fearing lest they should be
treated as such by Gratian and Vivian. That
very day, late in the evening, King Henry returned from the forest, and visited the envoys

3 "Urbis veteris," which Mr. Froude has translated, "of the
ancient city."
4 Ep. S. Tho. ii. p. 277 ; Froude, p. 437.

before he went to his own house. He behaved towards them with all honour, reverence, and humility. While they were exchanging their first compliments, Prince Henry, who had been hunting with his father, arrived with his youthful train blowing their hunting-horns, and bringing the stag they had killed as a present to the envoys.

The next morning, at about six, the King again waited on them, and they attended him to the apartments of the Bishops of Séez and Rennes. After some delay, John Dean of Salisbury and Reginald the Archdeacon were admitted, and soon after the Archdeacon of Llandaff. These remained in conversation together till three in the afternoon: they were standing, and spoke sometimes gently, sometimes loudly and angrily. The King's object was to obtain the absolution of the excommunicate clerics, without their taking the oath. Just before sunset the King came out, very wroth, complaining bitterly that the Pope had never listened to his requests in anything, and said with defiance, "By God's eyes, I will do something else." Gratian answered mildly, "Threaten not, my lord; we fear no threats, for we come from a Court which is accustomed to dictate to emperors and kings." Then a convocation was held of all the barons and white monks that were in attendance, and nearly all the chapel-royal; and the King called on them to witness the greatness of the offers he had made, namely, the restitution of the archbishopric, and the restoration of peace. At last he left them somewhat pacified, and he appointed that day week for giving a definite answer.

On the day named, August 31, the Archbishops of Rouen, Bourdeaux, and all the Bishops of Normandy, met by appointment at Bayeux, and the Bishop of Le Mans accidentally joined them. The Bishop of Worcester arrived on the following day; the Bishop of Poitiers excused himself, as he was holding a synod, but promised to come when it was over. The envoys presented the Pope's letters praying for the Archbishop's return and reconciliation. After a tirade against the Saint, which was the King's only reply, he concluded by saying, " If I grant any of his lordship the Pope's requests for that person, I shall deserve many thanks for it."

The day following, the Bishops met the envoys at the King's palace, called Bur, near Bayeux. Immediately on their arrival, they all entered the park together. The King began by a demand, in private, for the absolution of his clerics, without their taking the oath. This the envoys positively refused; on which Henry immediately mounted his horse, and swore in the hearing of all, that never again would he listen to the Pope or any one else in behalf of the Archbishop. The prelates who were present entreated the envoys, for the love of God, to concede this point; which they accordingly did, though most reluctantly. The King then again dismounted. Soon after, when all in the park were collected, Henry remarked, that he wished them all to know that it had not been through him that the Archbishop

had left England, and that he had often recalled
him, that he might explain his conduct, but he
had always refused; in the present instance, however, in compliance with the Pope's prayers and
commands, he would restore his archbishopric to
him in peace, and allow all to return that had
been banished on his account. This concession
he made about three o'clock in the afternoon,
and afterwards was very cheerful and went
through much other business.

Later on he returned to the envoys, requesting
that they would go to England to absolve the
excommunicates who were in that country. Their
refusal made him angry, but he urged one of
them at least to go, or to commission one of their
clerics, and he would pay their expenses himself.
This too Gratian refused, and the King shouted
angrily, " Do what you will, I care not for you
or your excommunication one egg." He then
mounted his horse and rode off; but on the Archbishops and Bishops following him and remon-
strating, he once more returned. The sum of
their deliberations was, that the Bishops should
write to the Pope, testifying that in their presence
the King had offered the Archbishop peace, and
that he was ready to comply with every command
of his Holiness, but that the difficulty was raised
on the part of the envoys. Much time was wasted
in the composition of the letter, and at last the
King determined to leave them, quite out of
patience. The Bishops then informed him that
the envoys had previously shown them a mandate
from the Pope, commanding every one to obey

whatever they might decree. The King answered, "I know, I know, they will interdict my kingdom; but shall not I, who can take a strong castle a day, be able to take one cleric, if he publishes the sentence?" However, on one or two points being conceded, the storm blew over, and Henry said, "Unless you make peace this night, you will never get to this point again;" and then calling all together, "It behoves me to do much at the request of my lord the Pope, who is my lord and father, and therefore I restore his see to the Archbishop, as well as my favour to him, and to all who are banished on his account." The envoys and all the others returned thanks, and the King added, "If I have been deficient in anything to-day, I will make it up to-morrow."

The next day, September 1, they met at the same place at noon, and after a long discussion about the absolution of the excommunicates, whether they should or should not take the oath, it was at last agreed that Geoffrey Ridel, Nigel de Sackville, and Thomas Fitz-Bernard should place their hands on the Gospels, and declare in the word of truth that they would obey the instructions of the envoys. A request was then made that all the Church property which the King had alienated might remain with its new holders. This was, however, refused. Then it was proposed that the Bishops should draw up in writing the terms of peace to which the King had consented. The King had insisted on the expression being allowed, "that the Archbishop should hold his Church to the honour of the King and his posterity;" and this the envoys had thought unobjectionable. But on the conference breaking up, about nine o'clock at night, the King insisted that there should be inserted in the terms, " saving the dignity of his kingdom;" but Gratian refused to consent to this on any con-dition whatsoever. It was, in fact, the introduc-tion of the Constitutions of Clarendon into the negotiation, which we should have said had been as yet unmentioned, were it not that, by sug-gesting the change, the King showed what mean-ing he had attached to the apparently simple and innocent phrase which the envoys had allowed.

On the 8th of September, the envoys retired to Caen, whence they sent to the King to say that they would permit the clause he had requested, if "saving the dignity of the Church" were also introduced. This was refused; and Henry charged them with inconsistency for rejecting a qualification which, he maintained, they had in the first instance admitted. They then gave the King a month for consideration, warning him that at the expiration of that time, the sentence of the Archbishop would be again put in force with respect to the persons whom they had absolved. The month passed, and affairs being thus restored to their former state, Gratian returned, leaving Vivian behind. The Archbishop of Sens accompanied him to the Pope, which frightened King Henry much, as he regarded these two dignitaries as his most powerful opponents. He accordingly despatched other messengers in his own behalf to the Holy Father.

The Archbishop of Rouen wrote to complain of the envoys, and so also did some of the Bishops of Normandy, who seem to have become more strongly partisans of the King, as those of England returned to some sense of their duty.

For the greater part of a year all restriction had been taken off from the exercise of the highest ecclesiastical power which St. Thomas could use ; he was, moreover, Legate of the Holy See; but he had been very patient, and had waited until all hope of the King's repentance was gone. He felt that the time was now come ; so he issued letters[5] to the principal religious houses in England, and to the Bishops or other officials of the different dioceses, ordering them by his own authority and that of the Apostolic See, if the King should not repent and make amends to the Church by the feast of Our Lady's Purification, February 2nd, 1170, to publish the interdict he laid upon them. By this sentence all sacraments and rites of religion of every kind were prohibited, save only baptism for infants, and penance and the Holy Viaticum for the dying; Low Mass would be permitted for the consecration of the Blessed Sacrament for the sick, but the doors were to be closed, the laity excluded, and no bells rung. The religious would also be at liberty to recite the Divine Office in a low voice, under similar restrictions. The same letters, besides denouncing those who were actually excommunicated, pronounced a similar sentence, to date from Christmas, unless before that

5 Ep. S. Tho. i. pp. 199, 200, 207, 267, 335, 346.

time they had given satisfaction, against John of
Oxford Dean of Salisbury, Guy Dean of Waltham, John Cumin, Ralph Archdeacon of Llandaff, and Wimar, a priest attached to the person
of Earl Hugh. Other letters[6] of a somewhat
similar tenour, but declaring the interdict to begin
fifteen days after their publication, were intrusted
to some of the French Bishops, but they never
were actually published.

The King did his utmost to prevent their admission into England, threatening those who
introduced them with the severest punishments.
He decreed[7] that if the bearer were a regular, his
feet should be cut off; if a cleric, he should be
blinded and mutilated; if a layman, he should
be hanged; and if a leper, be burned. He caused
an iniquitous oath to be administered throughout
the country, that the letters of the Pope and the
Archbishop should not be received, nor their
commands obeyed. Maud, Countess of Devonshire,[8] the daughter of Baldwin de Redvers, is
recorded as having refused to take any such oath,
or to permit any of her vassals to do so. The
Archbishop of York also resisted it; but the other
Bishops were weak enough to permit it to be
administered in their dioceses. St. Thomas sent
secretly to absolve from the obligation of observing it all who had been forced into taking it.

6 Ep. S. Tho. i. pp. 201, 209, 229, 297, 344, 347.
7 *Ibid.* p. 252.
8 Fitzstephen, p. 102. Thomas of Froimont gives a curious
account of how his father avoided taking the oath by stooping
and mingling with the crowd of those who had taken it (*Anecd.
Bed.* p. 256).

The presence of Gratian, and of William Archbishop of Sens, at Rome at the same time, and
the conduct of St. Thomas, frightened the King.
The course adopted by the Saint probably had
not the same effect as the issuing of actual letters
of interdict, as, at the very least, when the term
named had expired, a declaratory sentence would
be necessary to prove that the King had remained
contumacious; but it was certainly a warmer
earnest of what would surely follow than anything that had as yet happened. If Henry asked
for another interview with the King of France, he
could hardly hope it would be granted; he therefore determined on a measure which would bring
about a conference, even unsolicited. He entered
the territories of King Louis in the guise of a
pilgrim to the shrine of the glorious martyr
St. Denys, which he declared would be an opportunity of seeing, for the first time, the young
prince, Philip; as it was not right that he should
be a stranger to the son of his feudal lord, the
King of France. His scheme completely succeeded; for Louis hastened at once to Paris to
entertain him; Henry having also pretended that,
if he had an opportunity, he would intrust Prince
Richard to his guardianship. Henry at the same
time consented to terms which satisfied Vivian,[9]
and led him to urge St. Thomas very warmly to
join the conference of the Kings to be held at
St. Denys, on Sunday, November 16th, assuring
him that he would be met with the hymn, "Glory
to God in the highest, and on earth peace to my

9 Ep. S. Tho. i. p. 253; Ep. Gilb. Fol. ii. p. 299.

lord of Canterbury."[10]   King Louis preferring a similar request, St. Thomas consented, and promised to meet Vivian at Corbeil on the Friday.

When the King of England had visited the shrine of St. Denys, on the 18th of November, where he made an offering of a magnificent cope, and four-and-twenty gold pieces, Vivian, in a preliminary interview, tried to obtain from him a ratification of the promise which he had just made of the terms on which he would now consent to a reconciliation.[11]   The King, however, behaved in so unsatisfactory a manner, that Vivian complained openly both before his face and to St. Thomas of his evasive conduct, declaring that he had never met with such a liar; or, as he expressed it in writing to the Pope,[12] "He is sophistical and captious in every word he says about the Church."   As Vivian had shown himself the most favourable to the King of the last two envoys, this strong declaration of his was counted of some importance.

At the foot of the hill of Montmartre, between Paris and St. Denys, was a chapel called the Holy Martyrdom, marking the spot where St. Denys was put to death.   Here St. Thomas was praying, as King Henry returned from St. Denys. A messenger came to hurry him, saying that the two Kings and Prince Philip were waiting in the plain near the chapel.   His reply was, that it was becoming in a priest to proceed with gravity.

[10] *Ibid.* ii. p. 216; i. p. 357.
[11] Ep. S. Tho. i. p. 254; Froude, p. 455.
[12] Ep. S. Tho. ii. p. 221.

St. Thomas [13] advanced his petition through the Archbishop of Rouen, the Bishop of Séez, and Vivian, that the King would restore his royal favour to him and his, together with their possessions and goods which had been seized; offering in turn to show him every kind of deference which is due from an Archbishop to a King. The prelates who were mediating required that the Saint should expressly name all such possessions of the see of Canterbury as he required to be restored. Length of absence, and the great difficulty of intercourse with England, rendered it impossible for him to say what the King and his officials had alienated; the Saint therefore demanded the restoration of every thing which Theobald had held, and all which he had himself possessed at the time he attended the Council of Tours. Three things, however, in particular he named: first, those lands which Henry of Essex had held under the Archbishop, on the plea that the King, as his feudal lord, having resumed the lands which that nobleman had held under the crown on the occasion of his attainder, the same proceeding ought to be extended to the archbishopric. The fief of William de Ros the King had usurped, contrary to his royal oaths; and of this St. Thomas demanded restitution, as well as of the Church property bestowed upon John the Marshal, whose name appeared so prominently at the beginning of the Council of Northampton. The mediators expressed their confidence of being able to obtain this from the King, without

[13] Ep. S. Tho. i. p. 219.

W

which St. Thomas declared his determination to remain in exile, disdaining, as he said, to purchase peace for himself with the goods of the Church. Of obtaining restitution of the revenue and movable property of which the King had possessed himself they were less sanguine, amounting, as it was calculated to do, to thirty thousand marks; though some of them thought that perhaps a thousand marks might be paid, to enable the Archbishop and his companions to meet the expenses of their return. Urged especially by the King of France not to permit a money question of a personal character to hinder a reconciliation between himself and his King, the Saint said that he would be contented with a part only of what was due to him.

King Henry, on his part, declared that he readily forgave all the offences of which he had complained, and that in the matters now proposed he was willing to abide by the decision of the King of France, or of the clergy of France, or the University of Paris. On hearing this, the Saint professed himself satisfied; but he stated at the same time, that he would rather settle the affair amicably than by litigation, and he therefore made his petition in writing, to prevent future misunderstanding and evasion, framing it in such moderate terms, "that it was obvious to all that he would refuse no conditions of peace which were not absolutely intolerable for the Church."[14]

Some time before, the Saint, foreseeing the

[14] Ep. S. Tho. i. p. 382; ii. p. 220.

probability of negotiations being ultimately successful, and of the King finally consenting to such
terms as he could accept, had consulted the Holy
Father what pledge or guarantee he ought in
such a case to require. The Pope had advised
him to ask the King for the kiss of peace,
thinking it unbecoming for a priest to require an
oath from his own sovereign. St. Thomas, therefore, now sent to ask Henry to ratify his good
intentions towards him by the kiss. The King's
message in reply was brought without remark by
the mediators to St. Thomas, who was still in the
chapel, that he would have done so with pleasure,
· if he had not one day in a rage publicly sworn
never to admit the Archbishop to the kiss again,
even if he should be reconciled to him ; and that
this oath was now his sole reason for refusing,
not that he retained any ill-will whatever. His
reply to the written petition was, that the Archbishop should enjoy in peace all that *his predecessors* had enjoyed, as well as all *his own* possessions ; by which phrase he seemed, to those who
were not familiar with the circumstances, to
concede everything, while in fact, it was intended
not to include the Church property which St.
Thomas had himself recovered, soon after his
consecration, as well as the benefices which had
fallen vacant during his exile. King Louis said,
before Vivian and many others, that unless the
kiss were granted, he would not advise our Saint
to put foot in England, though Henry should
give him a sum of gold equal to a King's ransom ;
and Count Theobald added, that to do so would

be mere folly.   King Henry did not wait for any reply, but set off abruptly for Mantes, about twelve leagues from Paris, during the whole of which ride that evening he uttered frequent reproaches against the Archbishop.   Prince Philip met him on the road, but their interview was far from cordial ; and King Louis, who accompanied him to Mantes, was offended that he had not received charge of Prince Richard, afterwards our Cœur de Lion, which had been the pretext of their meeting.   Henry was not, however, content to break off the negotiations ; so, as a bribe to induce him still to try to bring about some arrangement, he sent Vivian twenty marks, which were scornfully rejected.   Gilo Archdeacon of Rouen, John of Oxford, and John of Séez, went to the Pope to endeavour to prevent the measure so much dreaded by Henry, of legatine power over his Continental dominions being conferred upon the Archbishop of Sens.

St. Thomas again lodged in the Temple, the very place where he had lived when he visited Paris in all his magnificence as Chancellor.   In the evening of the Conference, as he was leaving the chapel where it had been held, one of his party came up to him and said, " To-day we have treated of the peace of the Church in the Martyrdom, and I believe that by your martyrdom only will the Church attain peace."   The Saint briefly answered, " Would that even by my blood she might be freed ! "

After Matins that night in the Templars' Choir, the companions of the Saint came to expostulate

with him on the present state of his affairs.
While any thing vital had been at stake, they
said, they had been proud to bear their share
of his confessorship; but now the King had
withdrawn his demand for any oath, without the
usual *salvo* of God's honour and the Church's
dignity; he had now consented to make restitution of all Church property; and there was
nothing to be exiled for, since his refusal to give
the kiss of peace might fairly be accounted a
personal matter, like the repayment of the stolen
revenue, which the Archbishop had consented to
forego.

While these matters were going on, which at
length rendered a reconciliation probable, news
came from England that the Bishops were beginning to act a more manly part.[15] Geoffrey Ridel
the Archdeacon of Canterbury, together with
Richard Archdeacon of Poitiers, and other officials, summoned all the Bishops and abbots to
London in the King's name, to give security that
they would observe the new edict, and receive no
messenger from the Pope or the Archbishop without the royal permission ; nor obey any interdict,
if such should be promulgated, nor pronounce an
anathema against any of the King's subjects.
However, none of the Bishops, nor any abbot,
except Clarembald, the intruded Abbot of St.
Augustine's, chose to obey the summons. The
Bishop of Winchester publicly protested, and
declared that while he lived he would, at all
costs, obey the Apostolic decrees, and those of

15 Ep. S. Tho. i. p. 219; Froude, p. 458.

the Church of Canterbury, to which he had professed his fealty and obedience; and the noble old man charged all his clergy to do likewise. The Bishop of Exeter followed his example, prepared to obey in all things; and he took refuge in a religious house till the storm should pass over. The Bishop of Norwich, though expressly forbidden in the King's name, excommunicated Earl Hugh and some others, according to the instructions he had received, even in the presence of the royal officials. On descending from the pulpit, he placed his pastoral staff upon the altar, saying that he would see who dared to extend a hand against the Church and its possessions. He also entered a religious house, to live with the community. The Bishop of Lichfield declared his readiness to execute all the orders of his ecclesiastical superiors; and, to secure himself from the officers, he took refuge in the Welsh part of his diocese.

Fresh messengers were now sent by King Henry to the Pope,[16] to retract all that had been before demanded, and instructed to leave the arrangement of the terms of reconciliation entirely to the judgment of the Holy Father. The Bishop of Auxerre, and other Norman Bishops, took the opportunity of trying to bring about another interview between the King and the Archbishop.[17] St. Thomas was accordingly on his way to the place of meeting, and had reached Pontisare with his companions, when they were

[16] Ep. Jo. Sar. ii. p. 224.
[17] Ep. S. Tho. i. p. 259; Froude, p. 463.

informed that the King had abruptly broken his engagement, and would wait no longer at the place of conference. This sudden change was brought about by the return of some of the King's messengers from Rome, asserting, though untruly as it turned out, at least in the manner they reported, that the Holy Father had consented to the absolution of the Bishop of London, and the other excommunicates. The King was so elated, that he left, declaring that he was going to make arrangements for the coronation of his son. Accordingly, in March, 1170, he returned to England.

CHAPTER XXVIII.

OUTRAGE AND ·PEACE.

1170.

The Archbishop of Rouen and the Bishop of Nevers receive authority from the Pope—they absolve the persons excommunicated—St. Thomas's letter to Cardinal Albert—coronation of Prince Henry by the Archbishop of York—courage of the Bishop of Worcester—the Pope repeats the threat of an interdict—Henry's insincerity—conference in Traitors' Meadow—reconciliation.

THE report of the absolution of the excommunicates which King Henry's messengers had brought him, and which served so completely to unmask his insincerity in the late negotiations, was not altogether without foundation. The Pope, probably giving credence to Henry's last expressions of submission, and wishing to conciliate him still further, selected two of the Norman Bishops, who had shown themselves of late to be his friends, the Archbishop of Rouen and the Bishop of Nevers; and to them he intrusted the care of concluding the negotiations, and of absolving the excommunicates. From this last power, however, the case of the Bishop of London was excepted; and in the other cases two conditions were required for its lawful exercise, the *certain hope* of reconciliation, and the exaction of the usual oaths. These two Bishops were instructed by the Pope to urge upon the King the immediate fulfilment of the offers made by him at the late conference; and on his refusal, they were ordered, after a notice of forty days, to lay the kingdom under an interdict.

St. Thomas warned the Bishop of Nevers,[1] that Henry's first object would be to obtain the absolutions; and that when he had once gained his point thus far, they would be unable to make any further progress with him. The two Bishops, when urged by Henry, neglected the condition imposed upon them by the Pope, which made a certain hope or immediate prospect of reconciliation a necessary preliminary, and complied with the King's request. Meanwhile Gilbert Foliot had been pleading his own cause with the Pope in person; and he was so far successful, that the Holy Father removed the exception in his case, which had prevented him from benefiting by the powers conferred on the two Bishops. He hastened to the Archbishop of Rouen, by whom he was at once absolved, without the presence of the Bishop of Nevers, as the Pope's letter required, and that with all publicity, on Easter Day, 1170. Foliot regarded it as a great triumph; and by way of showing this openly, he even celebrated pontifically with all solemnity in St. Thomas's own Church of Canterbury.[2] These

[1] Ep. S. Tho. i. p. 302; Froude, p. 467.
[2] *Ibid.* i. p. 250.

events drew the following letter[3] from St. Thomas, addressed to one of the Cardinals.

"I would, my beloved, that your ears were within hearing of my countrymen, and that you knew the contemptuous sayings against the Church of Rome which are being chanted in the street of Ascalon!

"I know not by what fortune it has come to pass, that the side of the Lord is always sacrificed at the Court of Rome: Barabbas escapes, and Christ is crucified. By the authority of the Court, our exile, and the sufferings of the Church, have been protracted to the end of the sixth year. Your lordships have condemned the wretched and homeless, and for no other reason, I speak it from my conscience, than because they are feeble and Christ's little ones, and will not recede from the justice of the Lord; on the other hand, you have absolved the sacrilegious, the murderer, the robber, persons who have not repented, and whose absolution, I say it freely, Christ being my authority, would not hold in the sight of God, though it were St. Peter that pronounced it. In St. Luke's Gospel our Lord commands, that 'if thy brother sin against thee, rebuke him; and *if he is penitent*, forgive it him; and if seven times a day he sin against thee, and seven times a day he turn to thee, *saying, I repent*, forgive it him.' Think you the words of Christ are idle where He says, 'if he is peni-

3 Ep. S. Tho. i. p. 95; Froude, p. 478. This was addressed to Cardinal Albert, who was one of the Legates sent after his death by the Pope to the King.

tent,' and 'if he turn to thee, saying, I repent?'
Surely in the Day of Judgment.He will not admit
that His words were idle; nor will He pass over
those uncondemned, who, against the form He
prescribes, presume, by vain absolution, to justify
the wicked, without confession or penance, and
to save alive the souls that should not live.

"And now I have done. For the rest I com-
mit to God His own cause, that God for Whom
I am proscribed and exiled. Let Him act by
me as He sees best. It is my intention to give
the Court no further trouble in this matter. Let
those seek its protection who are strong in their
iniquity, and who, after trampling justice under
foot and leading innocence captive, return glory-
ing in the shame of the Church."

The words of this letter breathe in every line
the same ardent soul that led him when a boy
to leap into the brook after his hawk, or in later
times taught him to put on the terrible hair-shirt,
and to bear severe scourgings three or four times
in the day. Ever in earnest, there is still the
same impatience of obstacles that hinder the
end he has in view, as when he buckled on his
armour and laid lance in rest for his earthly
master's cause. That cause ever became his
own: his Master now is God, and God's cause
is his cause; he looks singly to its attainment,
and with apostolic liberty he speaks; for "where
the Spirit of God is, there is liberty."

The King's threat that he would go to England
and hasten the coronation of the Prince, was
not an idle one. . For some time past he had

entertained this wish, apparently with the view
of hindering, in some degree, the effect of per-.
sonal sentence of excommunication against himself. His difficulty in this project was, that the
coronation of the Sovereign was one of the un-
doubted prerogatives of the see of Canterbury.
Reginald of Salisbury advised him to request
the Pope to empower some other Bishop to perform the ceremony;[4] and on his replying that he
believed it to be impossible to obtain such a
favour, Reginald answered, "Our lord the Pope
will act like a dolt and a fool, if he does not
grant your petition."   The request may have
been made and have met with success; for two
letters of Alexander's are still extant,[5] empower-
ing Roger, the Archbishop of York, to crown the
young Prince. Their genuineness, however, is
very questionable. The plea which Henry urged
in his own excuse afterwards, and which doubtless was the pretext used at the time to justify
the usurpation, St. Thomas[6] learned from the
King's own lips, and he related it to the Pope.
It would seem, then, that after Theobald's death,
while Canterbury was vacant and St. Thomas
still Chancellor, Henry had entertained the wish
that his son might be crowned, though he was
then a child but six or seven years old. Roger
de Pont l'Eveque was in such disfavour that

4 Ep. S. Tho. i. p. 226.
5 Ep. S. Tho. ii. pp. 43, 45. It was reported, so the Bishops
of Noyon and Paris wrote to the Pope.(Ep. Gilb. Fol. ii. p. 230),
on the return of Richard Barre and Ralph Archdeacon of
Llandaff, that such a power had been granted.
6 Ep. S. Tho. i. p. 70.

St. Thomas was able to remind Henry that he
had said, that he would rather his son were
beheaded, than that he should have Roger's
" heretical hands " laid upon him.   In order
to prevent any claim on the part of the Archbishop of York to exercise this great function
during the vacancy of the see of Canterbury,
Henry applied to the Pope that his son might
be crowned by any bishop whom he might
choose.   This faculty he now brought forward
in favour of the very Prelate whom it had been
obtained to exclude.   St. Thomas, on the other
hand, previous to the negotiations respecting
the absolution of the Bishop of London, had
received from the Holy Father letters,[7] dated
February 26th, and still earlier from Anagni, in
November, others again from the Lateran, April
5th, forbidding any one but the Archbishop of
Canterbury to perform the ceremony. St. Thomas
did his best to send these letters into England;
but the watch that was kept up was so vigilant,
that it would appear that no copy escaped until
the very Saturday before the coronation. They
were then delivered[8] to the Archbishop of York

[7] Rymer's *Fœdera*, i. p. 29. St. Thomas's own letters to the
Bishops (Ep. S. Tho. i. pp. 190, 227).

[8] Fitzstephen (p. 103) says so expressly. St. Thomas asked
the King why he had driven Roger and the other Bishops into
disobedience; " for *they had received* the prohibition of our lord
the Pope that they should not presume to do this in any way in
our absence" (Ep. S. Tho. i. p. 70). Roger of York took oath
after the martyrdom, that he had not received them (Diceto,
p. 558). One set of letters was certainly destroyed (Ep. S. Tho.
ii. p. 288).

and the Bishop of London, only to be entirely disregarded.

After the return of St. Thomas to the Abbey of St. Columba, near Sens, he told Herbert one morning that he was convinced that Prince Henry would not live long; for as he lay sleepless, after Matins, thinking of the King, his greatness and wonderful prosperity, and while musing especially over what might be the future fate of Prince Henry, his former pupil, to whom he was much attached, and of one of his brothers, either Richard or Geoffrey,—as he was dropping off to sleep, he heard a voice which said,

Mors tulit una duos, tulit altera sed male patrem.

Herbert says that St. Thomas never wrote a line in his life, never having been taught to versify when young; and he adds, that he thought he had lived to see the fulfilment of the verse. The story is interesting, as showing the feelings of affection the Saint still entertained for the Prince, whom he calls "our Henry," notwithstanding the ceremony which was then being performed at Westminster, of which that Prince was the central figure.

The King summoned the Bishops and barons to meet in London on Sunday, June 14th.[9] The Queen was not to leave Normandy, and for some unexplained reason the Princess Margaret was to remain with her; but Richard of Ilchester was sent to hasten the Prince's movements, as his father was waiting for him on the English

9 Ep. S. Tho. ii. pp. 64, 287, 299.

coast; and he speedily crossed the Channel, attended by the Bishops of Bayeux and Séez. When the Sunday came, Prince Henry, who had been previously knighted by the King, was crowned by the Archbishop of York; and, as if to render the outrage more flagrant, not only was the usual coronation oath to maintain the liberty of the Church omitted, but another was substituted in its place, to observe the royal customs.[10]

Immediately afterwards, Henry returned to Normandy. Before he had left for England, he had ordered the Bishop of Worcester to be present at the coronation; the Bishop accordingly went to Dieppe. The King had crossed, when the Queen, who remained at Caen with Richard de Humet, the Justiciary of Normandy, fearing lest he should interfere with the coming invasion of the Archbishop's rights, sent him fresh directions not to cross the Channel; and she ordered the provost of Dieppe and the ship-owners not to permit his passage. When Henry, on his return, was approaching Falaise, the Bishop went out three miles to meet him. The King began at once to insult him: "Now you are plainly a traitor. I myself ordered you to be present at my son's coronation; and, though I named the day, you have chosen to be absent: you have shown plainly enough that you have no love for me, nor for my son's promotion. Now I see that you favour my enemy, and hate me and mine: but you shall no longer

[10] Ep. S. Tho. ii. pp. 33, 50, 84.

have the revenues of your bishopric; I will take
them away from you, for you have shown yourself unworthy of bishopric or benefice. Truly
you never were the son of the good Earl Roger,
my uncle, who brought you and me up together
in that castle, and had us there taught our
letters and our manners." The Bishop, in reply,
mentioned the simple fact of the prohibition
which he had received when in the port; but
the King would not believe him, and said, still
in a violent passion, "The Queen is in the castle
at Falaise, and Richard de Humet is not far
off; do you quote them as your authorities?"
"Certainly not the Queen," said the Bishop;
"for if, through fear of you, she should suppress
the truth, you would be in a greater rage with
me; and if she were to confess it, you would be
shamefully mad with that noble lady. I am not
of sufficient consequence that for my sake she
should hear one rough word from you. It is
well I was not present at that coronation, which
was offensive to God, not on the Prince's account,
but on the prelate's; and if I had been there, I
would not have suffered it to be performed.
You say that I am not the son of Earl Roger.
Whether I am or not, I cannot tell; but you
do not show by your gratitude that that same
Earl Roger, my father, was your uncle, who
brought you up as became your birth, and after
fighting your battles, offensive and defensive, with
King Stephen for sixteen years, was at last taken
prisoner on your account. If you had thought
of these things, you never would have reduced

my brothers as you have. You have reduced
the tenure and honour of a thousand men, which
your grandfather the great King Henry gave to
my father, to a fief of two hundred and forty,
and thus injured my brother the earl. Then
my younger brother, who has the reputation of a
brave soldier, you have suffered to fall into such
poverty, that on that account he has left secular
life and service, and has taken the perpetual
vow, with the ensign and habit of the Hospital
of Jerusalem. These are the advantages you
confer on your relations and friends: thus you
requite those who deserve well of you. As for
your threat of taking away the revenues of my
bishopric,—take them, if you are not satisfied
with those of the archbishopric and six vacant
sees, and many abbeys, which you receive to
the peril of your soul, and turn to secular uses,
the alms of your fathers, the good kings, and
the patrimony of Jesus Christ." These words,
and more of the same sort, were said in the
hearing of all who were riding with the King.
A knight of Aquitaine, who did not know the
Bishop, asked who was speaking; and on being
told who it was, he said, "It is lucky for him
that he is a churchman; if he were a soldier,
the King would not leave him two acres." Another, thinking to please Henry, reprcached the
Bishop bitterly; but the King, turning to him
in indignation, loaded him with the foulest abuse,
saying, among other things, "You vile fellow,
do you think that because I say what I like to
my cousin the Bishop, you or any other person

X

may insult or threaten him? I can scarcely keep my hands off your eyes; it is too bad for you and the others to abuse a Bishop." They arrived at their resting-place; and after dinner the King and the Bishop talked apart amicably on the subject of a reconciliation with St. Thomas. To the honour of the Bishop of Worcester be it recorded, that he took every opportunity of sending assistance to our Saint; and while the justiciaries made this a frequent pretext for persecuting abbots and other ecclesiastics, they never dared to molest the Bishop on that account.

All this time, the Archbishop of Rouen and the Bishop of Nevers were doing nothing to bring Henry to terms, in conformity with the Pope's instructions. They had been ordered to follow a monition of an interdict by the sentence itself within forty days, if the King did not ratify his former proposals; and the very power of absolving the excommunicates, which they had used, was only conferred to be employed in case of the certain hope of reconciliation. The Archbishop of Sens wrote to the Pope to complain of their dilatoriness; and in consequence, fresh letters came from the Holy Father, ordering them to bring the King to a conference within twenty days, and then, within forty more, to lay the kingdom under interdict. These letters were sent, in the first instance, to St. Thomas, who, for reasons which have not come down to us, delayed to forward them. The two Bishops made a faint and ineffectual attempt to cross the Channel while the King was in England;

but on his return, they had the conference with him which the Pope required. It seems singular that the coronation of the Prince is nowhere spoken of as an offence committed *by the King* against the Archbishop's rights; but, as will be subsequently seen, the prelates who performed it were alone punished as guilty. Henry consented at once to all the terms which had been proposed at Montmartre, repeating, however, his refusal to take or give the kiss of peace. The Pope had suggested that in this case the Archbishop might receive the kiss from Prince Henry, or, as he is henceforward called, the young King; but St. Thomas did not ultimately press for that sign of amity in the subsequent negotiations.

From this moment the question arises, which is of such vital consequence to the character of King Henry II., and on which his personal responsibility for the martyrdom of St. Thomas really depends, whether, that is, he was sincere in his desire for a reconciliation, and in the arrangements which he now concluded. It must be acknowledged, that his refusal to give the kiss is not the only suspicious circumstance which leads us to doubt how the oath, which he took before his absolution, after the martyrdom, could have been sincere. Fitzstephen tells us that "some one wrote to the King to ask, 'Why is the Archbishop kept out of the kingdom? He had far better be kept in than kept out.' The hint was given to one who understood it. The King forthwith arranged a conference to treat of a peace, and there conceded everything which

before he had refused." Then, beyond doubt,
the *apparent* object of the coronation of his son
is precisely that which is suggested by the same
writer: "But first he caused his son to be
crowned with all despatch, on account of a
certain result which might possibly take place;
so that, if a crime were committed, the kingdom
could not be punished on his account, seeing
that he would be no longer the King of it." [11]

On the 16th of July, the Archbishop of Rouen
and the Bishop of Nevers went to inform St.
Thomas, who was still at Sens, of Henry's readiness to comply with the terms which were required of him. The Kings of England and
France held a conference on the 20th and 21st,
in a plain between the two castles of Viefui and
Freitval, on their borders; which plain the poor
exiles afterwards learnt was called by the inhabitants Traitors' Meadow. The Archbishop of
Sens had pressed St. Thomas to attend this
conference, in company with himself and the
two Bishops, adding, that a peace could never
be effected between them while they kept aloof
from one another. The Saint was, in the first
instance, very unwilling to attend unbidden; but
at last he acquiesced. The Kings settled their
affairs without making any mention of the Archbishop of Canterbury; so that, after their second
day's conference, his clerics returned to him,
bringing news that the business was over, and
the Kings on the point of retiring; and it was
greatly feared that they, who had attended un-

[11] Ep. S. Tho. ii. p. 301; Froude, p. 498.

invited, would retire disgraced. In the interval, however, the Bishops, who had accompanied the Saint, had been interceding with the King, who consented to an interview on the following day, which was the feast of St. Mary Magdalen. He promised to abide by the Pope's commands in every point, excepting the matter of the kiss, adding, on his oath, that if he refused, it was not from any design against St. Thomas: and, calling God to witness this, he prevailed on the Archbishop of Sens to pledge himself for its truth. He even said, that he would yield in this point, however reluctantly, rather than part finally at variance. The Archbishop of Sens returned to the Saint, and told him how gracious the King had seemed both in his manner and words; and intreated him not to mar the prospect of returning kindness by insisting on the kiss; adding that Henry had promised publicly, that, on returning to his own dominions, he would receive him with the kiss, and every demonstration of gratitude. The Saint "was prepared even to lay down his life for his sheep," —a phrase used in a letter describing these circumstances, which shows how little credit St. Thomas's friends attached to the King's protestations; and he therefore yielded to the advice of the Archbishop of Sens, and late in the evening his answer was laid before Henry.[12]

[12] St. Thomas was entertained at the time of his reconciliation to the King, by Emmeline, a lady of Chaumont, who years after pointed out the place where his bed was laid to Ralph, a priest of Angers, by whose advice, as she was old and ill and could not undertake a pilgrimage to Canterbury, she slept on the same spot and was cured (Will. Cant. p. 450).

That night the King of England was the guest of the King of France. The following allusion to the coming day was heard to pass between them : " To-morrow," said King Henry, "that thief of yours shall have peace, and a good one too." "What thief, pray," replied Louis, "by the saints of France ? " "That Archbishop of Canterbury of ours," was the answer. King Louis rejoined, " I wish he were ours as well as yours; you will please God and man if you make a good peace with him, and I shall be ever grateful to you."[13]

On the morning of the feast, July 22, at dawn of day, the King, with a vast multitude in his train, set out for the spot which had been agreed on by himself and the King of France for the interview. King Louis was not himself present. St. Thomas arrived rather later, attended by the Archbishop of Sens and Count Theobald. The other French also, who had attended the conference between the Kings, crowded to the spectacle in great numbers. At the first sight that Henry caught of the Saint's approach, he darted forward from the midst of his party, and made straight up to him with his head uncovered, in order to be the first to give the salutation. They exchanged greetings, offered right hands, and embraced; so that some thought the King had broken the oath which they had heard him swear, that he would not admit the Archbishop to the kiss. Henry then retired with the two Archbishops; and St. Thomas addressed him respect-

[13] Ep. S. Tho. i. p. 65; Froude, p. 503.

ing the injuries done to himself and the Church, in a discourse which the Archbishop of Sens declared was most moving and pertinent. After this, the King and the Saint conversed together for the greater part of the day, so long, indeed, as to weary out all who were in attendance. The anxiety and attention with which they were watched by the bystanders may be gathered from the fact, that it was remarked that St. Thomas shifted frequently from side to side in the saddle, which they afterwards knew to have been caused by the irritation occasioned by the hair-drawers that he wore. At length, however, a sight was seen which struck all with amazement. St. Thomas, on a sudden, dismounted, and knelt at the King's feet; the King sprung from his horse in haste, and taking hold of the stirrup, obliged the Saint to remount, saying with emotion, " My Lord Archbishop, what more? Let us renew our old intimacy; let us henceforth be friends, and forget our past enmity. Only, I beg of you, give me honour in the sight of those who are standing by."

He then passed over to his party, and said, " Now that the Archbishop has shown such good intentions, if I, in my turn, did not show as good, I should indeed be the worst of men, and should verify all the evil that has been said of me. I believe I can do nothing wiser or better than try to surpass the Archbishop in kindness, charity, and good offices." It is only just to Henry's impulsive character to believe him to have been in earnest for the moment.

The King then withdrew, and St. Thomas was able to explain to his friends what had caused so striking a termination of the conference. After the other subjects had been spoken of, St. Thomas said, that it was necessary for the King's own welfare and that of his children, as well as for the preservation of the power which God had given him, that he should make formal reparation to his mother, the Church of Canterbury, for his late most grievous injustice to her, in having, by an enormous violation of her most ancient privilege, and contrary to the Pope's letter, caused his son to be crowned by the hands of the Archbishop of York; a prelate, blind, headstrong, and presumptuous enough to perform that rite in another Archbishop's province. For some time the King showed a reluctance to admit this charge, and said, though not, he protested, in any spirit of contention, that an Archbishop of York had crowned William the Conqueror, and a Bishop of Hereford had done the same for King Henry his grandfather, so that he might conclude that it was open to a king to choose the prelate who should crown him. The Saint showed in reply, that, in the first instance, Stigand, the Archbishop of Canterbury, had never received the pallium, so that the see was, to all intents and purposes, vacant; and that, in the second case, Archbishop St. Anselm being in exile, the Bishop of Hereford was his deputy, and the Archbishop of York had made no claim. And further, that on the return of St. Anselm, his royal grandfather had acknowledged the rights of Canterbury by requesting to be crowned anew by him. Henry rejoined, that he had had leave from the Pope to choose any Bishop for the ceremony; but St. Thomas reminded him that when that leave was granted, there was 'no Archbishop of Canterbury, that its object had been to exclude this very Roger, and that, at any rate, the later prohibitions of the Pope revoked the former concessions. He did not say these things from any wish to lower or disgrace the Prince, whose success and glory, on the contrary, he desired, and would endeavour to promote by every means in the Lord, as in Stephen's time he had laboured hard to maintain the King's own right to the crown.

Henry, with a look of good humour, and in a cheerful tone, replied, " You have a double right to love my son; for I made you his father, as you may remember, and gave him into your hands. And his love for you is such, that he cannot endure the sight of any of your enemies. He would have used coercion to them before now, only his reverence and dread of me prevented him. But as soon as he has the opportunity, I know he will take vengeance, and a severer one even than he ought. I doubt not that the Church of Canterbury is the noblest of all the Churches of the west; she consecrated me; and so far from wishing to deprive her of her rights, I will in this instance, as you advise, take measures for her relief, and restoration to her ancient dignity. But as for those who up to this time have betrayed the interests of both of us, I will, with God's help, answer them as traitors deserve." He added, that St. Thomas should crown Margaret, his son's wife, and as an acknowledgment of the rights of his Church, he should repeat the coronation of the young King. This it was which made the Saint leap from his horse; there was apparently no longer anything to separate him from his flock.

Those who were present were called together, and before them Henry declared that he restored to the Archbishop his royal favour, together with his Church, and all its possessions entire. It was arranged that one of the Saint's clerics should go to the King before long for a letter to his son, which should empower and command a full restitution; and Herbert was the one to whom this matter was confided. As many of the co-exiles of the Saint as were there then came forward, and did obeisance at the King's feet; and he promised to reinstate them all.

After consulting with the Archbishop of Sens and his other friends, St. Thomas drew up a memorial recounting the points to which the King had consented, amongst which the case of the coronation was particularly specified. This was presented through the Archbishop of Sens, and was ratified by the King. That Henry expressly and publicly consented to the punishment of the Bishops, who had merely executed his will, is perfectly certain; but as it is a point of the very greatest consequence, since the anger that led to the martyrdom was excited by the course here agreed to by the King himself, and as just

before his death, St. Thomas solemnly reminded
Fitz-Urse of this very consent, it will be well to
insert the words of another witness.[14] " I was
present," writes Theobald Count of Blois to the
Pope, " I was present when the King of England
received the Archbishop of Canterbury with every
sign of peace and good-will.   In my presence his
lordship of Canterbury complained to the King
of the coronation of his son; and as he was
conscious that he had inflicted an injury, he promised satisfaction.   Complaint was then made
of the Bishops who had dared to place the new
King on the throne, against the right and honour
of the Church of Canterbury; and the King gave
him free and lawful power over them, that, at
your Holiness's pleasure or at his, sentence might
be pronounced against them.   These things I
saw and heard, and I am ready to attest and
confirm them by an oath, or in whatever other
mode you may prefer."

St. Thomas and the King, when these concessions had been publicly made, conversed together
alone till evening, as familiarly as in the days of
their friendship; and it was agreed on parting,
that the Saint should return to pay a visit of
thanks to the King of France and his other
benefactors, and to arrange his affairs; and then
go and stay with Henry, previous to embarking
for England, to show how perfectly their intimacy
was restored. St. Thomas, however, subsequently
determined to wait in France till he heard from
the envoys he was about to send that restitution

[14] Ep. S. Tho. ii. p. 211.

was actually made; for as long as the King retained a foot of Church land, he could not trust his sincerity.

As he was leaving, the Bishop of Lisieux openly said that, as the King had taken his followers into favour again, the Saint ought to adopt a similar course towards all who had opposed him. He answered that the cases could not be classed together, but that, as far it was possible, he wished to be in peace and charity with all; and, having first consulted with the King, he would endeavour that every thing should be so arranged with reference to the honour of God and the Church, that if any failed in obtaining absolution (which God forbid), the blame would be chargeable upon themselves only. Geoffrey Ridel Archdeacon of Canterbury stepped in, and began some swelling reply, when the King, to prevent any revival of old animosities, drew the Saint out of the crowd, begging him not to mind what such persons said. He then asked the Archbishop's blessing, which concluded the conference.

CHAPTER XXIX.

DISAPPOINTMENT.

1170.

King Henry does not keep his engagements—St. Thomas has various interviews with the King—the Pope's action—the Saint prepares to return to England—the King's leave to excommunicate the Bishops concerned in the coronation—indications of coming danger—last words with the King—John of Salisbury precedes the Saint, who leaves Sens, and passes through Flanders—from Wissant he sends the Pope's letters of censure to three Bishops in England—further indications of danger—St. Thomas crosses from Wissant to Sandwich—his reception and entrance into Canterbury.

St. Thomas[1] wrote at once to inform the Pope and Cardinals of the reconciliation which had taken place. It is a striking proof how well King Henry was understood by them, that their joy was mingled with mistrust. As Cardinal Albert expressed it,[2] "the Ethiopian does not easily change his skin, nor the leopard his spots." Events soon showed that Henry was determined to be consistent with himself, and violate his engagements, however recent and however solemn.

Messengers were sent over into England by St. Thomas, carrying letters from the King to his

[1] Ep. S. Tho. i. p. 65; Froude, p. 503.
[2] Ep. Gilb. Fol. ii. p. 119; Froude, p. 519.

justices, ordering restitution to be made of the
Church property. Such benefices as had fallen
vacant during the exile of the Saint had been
given away. In the first instance, Henry's nomi-
nees were ejected, and the clerics appointed by
St. Thomas obtained possession; but they were
soon dispossessed again, and the intruders rein-
stated. It was also remarked by thoughtful
observers, as an important sign of the King's
intentions, that the Archbishop's Michaelmas
rents were received by the royal officers as before.
The messengers of the Saint[3] wrote to him from
England, to the effect that all his friends whom
they had met despaired so completely, that even
when they showed them the King's letters, with
his great seal hanging to them, and declared that
they had themselves been present at the reconciliation, and even stated this on oath, they could
hardly obtain credence. The only person whom
they could get to co-operate with them was
Robert, the Sacristan of Canterbury. They had
had interviews with the young King, but without
any satisfactory result. The date of this letter is
in the first week of October.[4] It was forwarded
by St. Thomas to the Pope, with the complaint
that nothing had yet been gained from Henry but
bare words. John of Salisbury and Herbert of
Bosham had previously been sent to the King
himself. They had found him in Normandy;
but as he was suffering from a tertian fever, it
was long before they could see him on the sub-

3 Ep. S. Tho. ii. p. 306; Froude, p. 512.
4 Ep. S. Tho. i. p. 77; Froude, p. 516.

ject. At their last interview, Henry said to John of Salisbury, " O, John, I will never give you the castle, unless I see you behave to me differently than you have yet behaved." This was an application either for Rochester Castle, or for Salt-wood, the fief of Henry of Essex, which Randulf de Broc occupied.[5]

When St. Thomas heard that the King was about to give an interview to one of his firm friends, Theobald Count of Blois, he determined to be present. It took place at Tours, on the 12th of November. The evening before, the Archbishop arrived ; but it was noticed that though the King came out to meet him, he did not look kindly upon him or his companions. Nigel de Sackville, whose name had figured in some of the lists of the excommunicated, was the King's seal-bearer and one of his clerics, and had received from his master the Church of Harrow, which was one of the vacant benefices. Fearful of being obliged to restore it, he was not over-anxious for peace. The King thought that he should have some difficulty the next morning in refusing the kiss of peace to the Archbishop, if they should hear the same Mass ; but Nigel de Sackville relieved him of his difficulty, by recommending him to have a black Mass celebrated, in which the *Pax* is not given. After Mass, as usual, the *Salve Sancta Parens* was said in honour of our ever-blessed Lady; after which the priest kissed the text of the Gospel, and carried it to the Archbishop, and then to the King, for them to kiss.

5 Ep. S. Tho. ii. pp. 185, 262.

St. Thomas then said, " My lord, I have come to you in your own dominions, now give me the kiss according to your promise." The King said, " Another time you shall have enough."

On another occasion, the Saint met the King at a castle near Blois, in order that he might carry out the advice of the envoys, and see as much of him as possible, in order to confirm the reconciliation. In the course of familiar and cheerful conversation, Henry said to him, " Oh, why do you not do my will? I certainly would put every thing into your hands." When St. Thomas repeated this to Herbert, he told him that it reminded him of the saying in the Gospel, " All this will I give Thee, if Thou wilt fall down and worship me."

Even before St. Thomas's last letter reached the Pope, his Holiness was determined to enforce the terms of the reconciliation which had been concluded. On the 9th of October, he issued from Anagni[6] letters to the Archbishops of Rouen and Sens, and the Bishop of Nevers, enjoining them to threaten the King with an immediate interdict; and all occupiers of Church lands were ordered to make restitution forthwith, under pain of excommunication. Full powers, dated Segni, October 13,[7] excepting only the persons of the King, the Queen, and the Princes, were lodged in the Saint's hands, as Apostolic Legate. Sentence of suspension had been pronounced by the Pope at Veroli, on the 10th of September,[8]

6 Ep. S. Tho. ii. pp. 63, 72.   7 Ibid. ii. p. 29.
8 Ibid. ii. pp. 32, 48, 82.

against the Archbishop of York and the other
Bishops who were present at the coronation;
while the Bishops of London and Salisbury, by
letters dated Ferentino, September 16, were
replaced under the excommunication from which
they had been absolved. In these letters the
substitution by the Bishops, on that occasion,
of the Constitutions of Clarendon for the Coronation Oath was naturally dwelt on by the Pope
as an additional cause for the punishment
which was inflicted; for several of those Constitutions had been condemned by him. St.
Thomas, in his letter of complaint against the
King,[9] requested the Pope to withdraw the mention of the Constitutions, as being particularly
calculated to irritate him; while the part taken
by the Bishops in the young King's coronation
was abundantly sufficient cause for their censure,
and one in which Henry had acquiesced. He
also begged that the sentences of all the Bishops,
but that of the Archbishop of York, might be
intrusted to his discretion. The Pope consented,[10]
writing from Frascati on the 24th of November,
and as he urged St. Thomas to return to England,
in spite of the King's non-fulfilment of his
engagements, the Saint now prepared for his
departure.

The French nobles provided him and his companions with everything that was necessary, with
such liberality, that when he actually started
there were more than a hundred horses in his

9 Ep. S. Tho. i. p. 77; Froude, p. 524.
10 Ep. S. Tho. ii. p. 85.

Y

train.   His farewell visit to King Louis was very
affectionate and moving.   He must indeed have
found it difficult to express his gratitude for the
truly royal treatment he had received from him.
In their conversation, the Archbishop showed his
sense of the danger to which he was now ex-
posing himself.   "We are going to England,"
he said, "to play for heads."   "So it seems to
me," said Louis.   "My Lord Archbishop, if you
followed my advice, you would not trust yourself
to your King, as long as he refuses the kiss of
peace.   Remain ; and as long as King Louis lives,
the wine, the food, and the wealth of France
shall never fail you."   The Saint answered,
"God's will be done ;"   and they parted with
tears, to meet again, we may hope, in that land
where even a cup of cold water given in the name
of a disciple does not lose its reward.

The parting words of St. Thomas to the Bishop
of Paris were: " I am going to England to die."
And, indeed, stories were afterwards told which
showed that some people believed that such
a fate was deliberately prepared for him.   A
priest, named Richard de Halliwell, was told by
one of the sergeants of the King's Court, that he
had with his own hands sealed the letters which
were sent to England to command the death of
the Archbishop, and that Nigel de Sackville had
written them ;   and he added, that he had confessed this before to an English Bishop and
asked for a penance, but the Bishop had said,
"What for ? you did your lord's command ;"
and, as if he had done no harm, enjoined him

nothing. Another anecdote is also very significant. Reginald de Warrenne one day entered the chapter of the Canons of Southwark, with whom he was very intimate, and said to them, " Pray heartily to God for me, for I have great need of it. Soon, perhaps, you will hear that something has been done in England, such as never before has been heard of: as far as I am concerned, it is quite against my will, but I am not my own master."

The Saint wrote to Henry in the following terms,[11] expressive of the same tone of mind as that which pervaded his farewell to King Louis. After showing what procrastination there had been in making restitution, he said, " Meantime, Randulf violently outrages the property of the Church, collects our stores into the castle at Saltwood, and, as we have been informed by those who can prove it, has, in the hearing of many, boasted that we shall not long enjoy our peace; 'for that, before we have eaten a loaf of bread in England, he will take away our life.' Your highness knows that voluntarily to overlook a wrong is to participate in the guilt. Yet this Randulf is plainly relying on your countenance and authority; for how else could he venture so far? What was the answer he returned to your son's letters? We leave this for your discretion to reflect upon, when you are informed of it.

" Forasmuch, however, as there are plain indications that, through hatred of our person, the mother of the British Churches is in danger of

[11] Ep. S. Tho. i. p. 380; Froude, p. 526.

perishing, we, in order to save her from this fate, are prepared, God willing, to surrender our life into the hands of Randulf and his accomplices in persecution ; yea, and to die a thousand deaths for Christ's sake, if His grace enables us.   I had intended, my lord, ere now to have returned to you, but the necessities of the afflicted Church draw me to her side.   With your favour and permission, I purpose returning to her ; perhaps, unless your timely pity ordain it otherwise, to die for her.   Yours, whether we live or die, now and ever in the Lord."

When the part that was actually taken by Randulf de Broc in the martyrdom is remembered, this letter cannot but be regarded as very remarkable.   His parting with King Henry is thus told.   "Go in peace," said the King ; " I will see you at Rouen or in England as soon as I can."   St. Thomas said, "My lord, my heart tells me that you will never see me again alive." " Do you think I am a traitor ? " " No, my lord," was the simple answer.   The Saint then went to Rouen at the King's request.

John of Salisbury went before him into England, where he landed on the 12th of November.[12] Three days before, a mark had been set on all the Archbishop's effects, and his officials had been excluded from all share in the administration of the property.   Also, an edict had been published in all the ports, forbidding any of the Archbishop's friends to leave England, under penalty of exile and proscription.   John of Salis-

[12] Ep. Jo. Sar. ii. p. 240 ; Froude, p. 256.

bury was received by both clergy and people of Canterbury with great honour, and presided, in the Archbishop's name, over a synod which was held there on the 18th of November, a few days after his arrival. He had a gracious audience of the young King; but he saw too many signs of the insincerity of the reconciliation which had been made, not to believe the general report that the rancour against them, which had been nominally softened, was in reality more vigorous than ever. The Christmas rents followed those of Michaelmas into the King's coffers.[13]

The pretext which Henry alleged for not meeting St. Thomas at Rouen was, that the men of Auvergne had sent to request succour to repel an attack which they expected from the King of France. He sent in his stead the notorious John of Oxford. When St. Thomas saw him, he said that times were indeed changed when the Archbishop of Canterbury was to receive protection from him. The Archbishop of Rouen said that he had received no instructions from the King to accompany him, and that as all was safe enough, it was not necessary. He also gave him three hundred pounds as a gift. The King urged his immediate departure by letter. " Inasmuch as many things are told me respecting your lordship's delay, which perhaps are not true, I think it expedient for you to take your departure for England with all speed." He had also received letters from the Pope, exhorting him to return fearlessly to his church, and fulfil his ministry.

[13] Ep. Gilb. Fol. ii. p. 300.

They left Sens on the feast of All Saints, with which day the seventh year of their exile began.[14]

St. Thomas and his fellow-travellers were escorted through Flanders by Philip Count of Flanders, and at his request the Saint consecrated for him a chapel at Male, a country-seat belonging to the Count.[15] Our Saint once more received hospitality at the great Abbey of St. Bertin at St. Omer, and was conducted thence to the fort of the Count of Guisnes by Peter Abbot of Ardres. As they passed the Abbey of Ardres on the west and there was not time enough to spare for a visit to it, at the Abbot's request St. Thomas raised his right hand and blessed it; and that blessing the chronicler[16] of the abbey says, rested upon it " with blessings of sweetness." Baldwin, Count of Guisnes, who had been knighted by him when he was Chancellor, received him with every mark of honour. The next morning the Saint had recourse to the ministry of Gusfrid, the Count's chaplain, and made his confession to him in his chapel before making his way to the sea.

They chose the port of Witsand or Wissant, in the territory of Boulogne, for their embarkation. From this place he forwarded the Pope's letters[17] of censure to the Bishops by a person named Osbern, but that for the Archbishop of York was intrusted to a nun named Idonea, doubtless as

[14] Ep. Gilb. Fol. ii. p. 239.

[15] Martene, *Thes. Nov. Anecd.* iii. 657 ; *Materials*, iv. p. 262.

[16] D'Achery, *Spicilegium*, ii. p. 812 ; *Materials*, iv. p. 263.

[17] Ep. S. Tho. ii. pp. 48, 82.

a messenger less likely to be suspected. The letter[18] which St. Thomas wrote to her on the subject is well worthy of insertion.

"God hath chosen the weak things of the world to confound the mighty. The pride of Holofernes, which exalted itself against God, when the warriors and priests failed, was extinguished by the valour of a woman: when Apostles fled and denied their Lord, women attended Him in His sufferings, followed Him after His death, and received the first-fruits of the Resurrection. You, my daughter, are animated with their zeal; God grant that you may pass into their society. The spirit of love hath cast out fear from your heart, and will bring it to pass that the things which the necessity of the Church demands of you, arduous though they be, shall appear not only possible but easy.

"Having this hope, therefore, of your zeal in the Lord, I command you, and for the remission of your sins enjoin on you, that you deliver the letters which I send you from his Holiness the Pope to our venerable brother Roger Archbishop of York, in the presence, if possible, of our brethren and fellow Bishops; and if not, in the face of all who happen to be present. Moreover, lest by any collusion the original instrument should be suppressed, deliver a transcript of it to be read by the by-standers; and open to them its intention, as the messenger will instruct you.

"My daughter, a great prize is offered for your

18 Ep. S. Tho. i. p. 399; Froude, p. 53.

toil; remission of sins, a fruit that perisheth not, —the crown of glory, which, in spite of all the sins of their past lives, the blessed sinners of Magdala and Egypt have received from Christ their Lord. The Lady of Mercies will attend on you, and will entreat her Son, Whom she bore for the sins of the world, God and Man, to be the guide, guard, and companion of your steps. He, Who burst the bonds of death, and curbed the violence of devils, is not unable to restrain the impious hand that will be raised against you. Farewell, bride of Christ, and ever think on His presence with you."

The Bishops were found by the messengers at Canterbury, preparing to cross the sea; and they submitted to the sentences which were thus pronounced against them, the Archbishop of York of suspension, and the Bishops of London and Salisbury of excommunication. To his very great satisfaction, the news of their having received the letters was brought to St. Thomas while he was waiting at Wissant for a fair wind.

One day they walked down to the beach to see the ships in which they were to cross, when a vessel arrived from England. They asked the sailors what was there said about the Archbishop's return? They were told, that every one was much pleased. But Herbert was taken aside by one of them, whom he thought was the captain, who said: " Wretched people, what are you doing? Where are you going? Certainly to your death; so say all who know any thing about it, and everybody expects it: and, besides, there are soldiers in the very port where you are going to land, waiting to take the Archbishop, and those who are with him." Herbert told St. Thomas what he had heard; and the Saint took counsel of his companions. Gunter of Winton, a good and simple soul, who had been very faithful to the Archbishop, recommended that they should wait until the storm caused by the suspensions passed over, saying, "If the country is moved by it now, what will it be when the King has heard of it?" Herbert's opinion was, that it was impossible to go back again into Flanders; and he said, that a death in such a cause would be a glorious martyrdom. St. Thomas briefly answered him, "Your speech seems faithful; but it is hard, and who shall fulfil it?" He then said, "Truly, Gunter, I see the land; and, by God's help I will enter the land, though I know for certain that my death awaits me." To a similar warning, given him by Milo Dean of Boulogne, in the name of his lord the Count of Boulogne, he replied, "Did you tell me I were to be torn limb from limb, I would not regard it; for I am resolved that nothing shall hinder my return. Seven years are long enough for a pastor to have been absent from the Lord's sorrowing flock. I will only ask my friends (and a *last* request *should* be attended to), that if I cannot return to my church alive, they will carry me into it dead." He added that he hoped that the library which he had thought of leaving on the Continent, but which the uncertainty of public affairs had made him resolve to take with him, would make his monks willing to give him a burial-place in exchange.

On another occasion, when one of his clerics asked him what they were waiting for, and why they did not embark, he said, "Forty days will not pass after your entrance into the country, that you will not wish you were any where in the world rather than in England."

Robert, the keeper of the treasures of the Cathedral of Canterbury, was sent over by St. Thomas the day before he sailed, that he might make some preparation for the reception of the exiles. On his landing at Dover he was seized and made to take oath that he would return as soon as the wind permitted. Nothing was alleged against him except that he had no passport from the King.

On Tuesday the 1st of December, very early in the morning, the Saint embarked. Knowing that Dover was beset with soldiers, he ordered the vessel to be steered for Sandwich, a fief of his own, and the very port from which he had sailed on All Souls' Day, 1164. His ship could be distinguished from the others by the archiepiscopal cross, which was erected as he approached the shore. The poor people [19] caught sight of it,

[19] Among them was a youth called George, who afterwards in a storm invoked the martyr thus: "Save thy servants, O martyr Thomas, who of old were subjects of yours and were ready to defend you when you came back and made us happy. The officers were preparing their arms, but your devoted people were on the watch for you. We did what we could and what we were bound to do, and we make no boast of it, but now that we have fallen into trouble for our sins, help us" (Will. Cant. p. 325).

and collected in great numbers: some ran into the water to receive him; others knelt for his blessing; many wept; and some cried out, "Blessed is he that cometh in the name of the Lord, the father of the orphans, and the judge of the widows."

The retainers of the three Bishops, under the command of Randulf de Broc, Reginald de Warrenne, and Gervase of Cornhill, the sheriff of Kent, who had been awaiting his arrival at Dover, soon heard of his landing; and hastening to Sandwich, with scarce a salutation to the Archbishop, began to demand why, on his very first entrance, he had begun by suspending and excommunicating the King's Bishops. The Saint answered quietly, that the King would not be offended by it; for he had received his permission to punish the injury to his Church, which those Bishops had committèd. On hearing that the King had known of what he had done, they became a little more moderate; but they demanded the absolution of the Bishops. St. Thomas postponed the matter till he reached Canterbury; and John of Oxford protesting in the King's name against all violence, the soldiers, who had their armour on under their capes and tunics, retired. However, before they left, Reginald demanded that, if there were any foreigner among them, he should take the oath of allegiance to the King, which was exacted in the case of those who were suspected to be spies. It happened that Simon, the Archdeacon of Sens, was in the Archbishop's company; but as the oath made no mention of the Pope, and was not usually imposed upon the clergy, the Saint would not suffer it; and the sensation caused by his arrival prevented them from enforcing it.

The six miles which he had to go from Sandwich to Canterbury were passed over in a sort of triumphal procession, owing to the vast crowds, especially of the poor, who thronged the roads to welcome him. Some threw their garments in the way, crying, " Blessed is he who cometh in the name of the Lord." The parish priests led out their parishioners in procession to meet him, with the Cross preceding them ; and they knelt for his blessing, while the air resounded with the same joyful cry. Though the distance was short, the concourse was so great, that they were late in reaching Canterbury.

CHAPTER XXX.

THE RETURN.

1170.

Joy in Canterbury at the Saint's return—the three Bishops demand absolution in vain, and then cross the sea—Prior Richard sent to the young King at Winchester—St. Thomas goes to Rochester and Southwark—a servant sent to the Earl of Cornwall, who returns with a warning—St. Thomas meets the Abbot of St. Alban's at Harrow—outrages of Randulf de Broc—return to Canterbury—William the poor priest of Chidingstone—Confirmations by the way—the Saint enters Canterbury—holds an ordination—Prior Odo—interview between the three Bishops and the King—his anger—four knights leave Normandy for Saltwood Castle—St. Thomas at Canterbury on Christmas Day—his last letter to the Pope—the knights come to Canterbury.

THE Saint entered into his cathedral city amidst every sign of rejoicing. The bells were ringing merry peals; the cathedral was decked out; the inhabitants, from the highest to the lowest, dressed themselves in their silks and gayest clothing; a public entertainment was prepared for great numbers; a numerous procession, with his own conventual chapter, attended him into the town; the churches resounded with the sound of the organs, chants, and hymns, and the halls with trumpets; and the whole place was overflowing with joy. He entered the city by the gate that led to the cemetery belonging to the

Cathedral, passing barefoot through the streets straightway into the church; and people remarked that his face shone as he did so with an outward splendour, as his heart was on fire with a holy gladness. He went to his episcopal throne, and there received the religious to the kiss of peace. This he was able to do, though there were many among the monks of Christchurch who during his absence had incurred censure by communicating with Gilbert Foliot and other excommunicated persons, for he had sent about a month before his return faculties by John of Salisbury to Brother Thomas of Maidstone to absolve and reconcile them all. The past was therefore forgotten in this happy moment. Men were crying with joy all around; and Herbert went up to him, and said, "My lord, we do not now mind when you may have to leave the world; for this day the Church, the spouse of Christ, has conquered in you." He made no answer, but simply looked at Herbert. In the chapter-house, he preached a beautiful sermon on the text, "We have here no abiding city, but seek one to come;" he then entered his palace, after a day of great solemnity.

The next morning, the King's officials came, accompanied by the chaplains of the three Bishops, to ask for absolution from the censures. "He had not come," they said, "in peace, but with fire and sword; treading his fellow-Bishops under foot, and treating them as his footstool, uncited, unheard, unjudged." They said too, "that his suffragans had gone to the sea, that they might receive him in the procession with the Church of Canterbury; but that they had unexpectedly and undeservedly found themselves dressed in certain black garments, of which, if his lordship pleased, they must be ridded before they could present themselves." He answered that "the peace of sinners was no peace; for there was no true peace except to men of goodwill. Jerusalem, abounding in luxury and self-indulgence, said to herself, 'It is peace;' but the Lord in His pity wept over it, because the vengeance of God hung over it and was hidden from its eyes." With regard to their objections against the sentence, they must remember that it was passed by the Pope, and that it was not for them to call the acts of his Holiness in question. "I understand the meaning of this application: if I have not the power of absolving them, they will consider me a Legate with curtailed powers; if I have the power, they will try by secular violence to extort absolution from me. I am setting no snares for them." As, however, they were very urgent for the absolution, the Saint finally promised that, after ascertaining the King's wishes, and consulting the Bishop of Winton and others of his brethren, he would consent for the sake of peace to accept their oath to obey the judgment of the Pope, and would take on himself the responsibility of doing what he could, subject, of course, to his Holiness's approbation; and that he would receive them as brothers, with Christian love.

The Bishops objected to this proposal, as unconstitutional, and derogating from the dignity of the crown; but on its being represented to them that the Pope himself had required a similar oath from them on their former absolution, the Bishops of London and Salisbury were prepared to give way; but the Archbishop of York persuaded them to throw themselves on the King's patronage, and excite the jealousy of the young King, as though it were the Saint's object to effect his deposition. The Archdeacons of Canterbury and Poitiers were on the point of crossing; but the former was now left behind to repair to the new King, and, as far as possible, poison his mind against his former guardian. The Bishops crossed the Channel; and, at their suggestion, six of the dignified clergy from each vacant see in the province were summoned to attend the King on the Continent, and go through the forms of an election before him, which it is unnecessary to say, would be invalid and uncanonical. This scheme, of which St. Thomas had been informed by his messengers in England while he was yet abroad, was frustrated by his martyrdom.

When the Archbishop had been eight days at Canterbury, he sent Richard, the Prior of St. Martin's at Dover, who was his immediate successor in the archbishopric, to the young King at Winchester, to say that he was about to come to pay his homage to him as his new Sovereign. He was thus prompt because he was anxious immediately after this visit to begin his visitation of the diocese, from which he had been so long separated. He took with him three magnificent high-stepping chargers, richly caparisoned, as a present for his young lord.

Prior Richard was met on his arrival at Winchester by the young King's guardians, William St. John, William Fitz-Adeline, Hugh de Gondreville and Randulf Fitzstephen, who made difficulties about admitting him into the young King's presence. When assured that the message that he bore was one of peace, they allowed him access to the young King. The message of which he was the bearer from the Archbishop was, that through the merits of the saints of Canterbury and the prayers of the faithful, God in His mercy had reconciled him to the King; that he had therefore returned to England, which reconciliation and return he wished the young King to learn from himself; that he knew that enemies of his were misrepresenting him to the young King, and that he called God to witness that he held him to be his lord and king; but that as it had not been by his, the Archbishop's, hand that the coronation had been performed, he begged for a conference with him on this subject. The young King's answer was discourteous to St. Thomas, though civil in form to Prior Richard, saying to him that he owed him no favour for his present errand but that his thanks were due to the Prior for hospitality shown by him of old to his mother Queen Eleanor and for marrying his sister the Princess Matilda to Duke Henry of Saxony. Prior Richard was told to leave, for the young King would answer the Archbishop by his own messengers.

z

St. Thomas began his visitation by going to London, hoping there to receive an invitation to meet the young King. On the way the Bishop of Rochester, his old friend Walter, Archbishop Theobald's brother, met him in procession with his chapter and clergy. As he entered London, he was conducted by another procession to St. Mary's, Southwark, a church of canons regular. The multitude of people of every class who came out to meet him was incalculable. The poor scholars and clerics of the city went out for about three miles; and when he came in sight, their *Te Deum* rent the air. The Saint, who scattered his alms freely on the way, was lodged in the palace of the Bishop of Winchester by the riverside in Southwark. The canons received him at the door of St. Mary's; and intoning the *Benedictus Dominus Deus Israel*, the vast multitude took up the chant and continued the canticle. A crazy woman named Matilda, amidst the general joy, called out repeatedly, "Archbishop, beware of the knife."

The next day, the young King's promised messengers came, Jocelin of Louvain, younger brother of Adeliza, the Queen of Henry I., with a knight called Thomas of Turnebuhe, but they were the bearers of an order to him to return at once to Canterbury. The Archbishop asked if it was the King's intention to exclude him from his presence and confidence. "His commands were what I told you," Jocelin replied, and left him haughtily. As he was passing out, he met a rich citizen of London whom he knew, to whom he said, "And are you come to the King's enemy? I advise you to go home quickly." He made answer, "We do not know whether you reckon him the King's enemy; but we have heard and seen the letters of the King, who is over the water, respecting the reconciliation;[1] if there is anything more behind, we know nothing about it."

Reginald of Dunstanville, Earl of Cornwall, whose conduct to St. Thomas at Northampton had not been unfriendly, now advised the young King to give him the audience he asked for. This may have come to the Saint's knowledge, or else he trusted to the Earl's comparative friendliness, and he resolved to send a confidential servant to stay with the Earl, in the hope that thus he might have speedy information of what was said or done in the young King's Court. The Earl was at Breamore, near Fordingbridge, suffering from a fistula, and nothing could more strongly show the hostility of the Court than the fact that St. Thomas's messenger could get. access to the Earl or hope to remain in his household only by pretending to be a physician come to cure him. However he was soon recognized. The very next day the young King came to see his uncle,[2] bringing him some game. The King's servant who brought the game, standing watching the serving and the guests, said, "Is not that William

[1] That to the Bishop of Exeter is given in Ep. Jo. Sar. ii p. 266.

[2] Reginald was a natural son of Henry I., created Earl of Cornwall 1140, ob. 1175.

I see there, from the household of Archbishop Thomas?" On this the Earl said to his physician, "Return in all haste to the Archbishop, and tell him from me that he must look to himself. Nothing is safe. And let John of Salisbury know, and John of Canterbury, and Gunter, and Alexander the Welshman, that wherever they are, they will be killed by the sword." The messenger started that night, and making all haste, delivered the Earl's warning to his master at Canterbury, in the presence of John of Salisbury only, in all probability on Sunday, the feast of St. John. The Archbishop then made use of a gesture and a phrase that he repeated later, "Here, here," said he, striking himself a light blow on the neck, "the varlets (*garciones*) will find me."

About the feast[3] of St. Lucy, December 13, the Saint was at Harrow, his own manor, which Nigel de Sackville had usurped. He sent from thence to his friend Simon the Abbot of Alban's, closing his letter with the words, "that he never had needed consolation so much as then." The Abbot came to him, and was most affectionately received. After they had talked over all that the Saint had undergone abroad, the Abbot said, "By God's grace, it is all now happily ended." St. Thomas sighed; and taking the Abbot's hand under his cappa, and pressing it, he said, "My friend, my friend, I will tell you my case as to another self: things are very different with me

3 Matthew Paris (a monk of St. Alban's) inter vitas xxiii. S. Albani Abbatum, de Abbate Simone, ed. Wats, p. 60.

to what men think. New persecutions are beginning. The King and his son (who is my only
hope) are devising fresh injuries." The Abbot
said, "How can this be, holy Father?" With a
deep sigh, and looking up, the Saint answered,
"Well enough, well enough I know to what
matters are tending." When they parted, St.
Thomas bade the Abbot pray for him to his
holy martyr-patron, and promised to remember
him in his prayers. "I will go," he added, "and
celebrate such a feast in my church as the Lord
shall provide me."

A messenger came from Canterbury, to say
that Randulf de Broc had laid hands on a
ship of his, laden with wine, and had cut the
cables, carried off the anchors, killed some of
the sailors, and imprisoned the others in Peven-
sey Castle. The Saint immediately sent the
Abbot of St. Alban's and the Prior of Dover to
complain of this outrage to the young King;
and, at his command, the ship was ordered to
be restored.

The Archbishop was accompanied by five
mounted soldiers as an escort, on account of
the unsafe state of the roads. It was reported
to King Henry, that he was marching about
England with a great army, besieging the towns,
and intending to drive the young King out of
the country.

At Wrotham, on the first evening of his return
towards Canterbury, a poor priest named William,
who said Mass at Chidingstone, came to him, and
in a private audience, which he had requested,

said, "My lord, I bring you some relics of St. Laurence, St. Vincent, and St. Cecilia, as St. Laurence told me to do in a vision."

St. Thomas. "Brother, how do you know that they are the relics of those saints?"

William. "My lord, in my vision I asked St. Laurence for some sign, for I said that otherwise you would not believe me; and St. Laurence told me that you lately put your hand to your breast, and found the hair-shirt torn which you wear next your skin; and while you were deliberating whether you should have that one repaired or a new one made, you soon put your hand in again, and found it whole."

St. Thomas. "In virtue of obedience, I command you to tell nobody, as long as I live."

William. "So be it;" and he added, "I am a poor man, and I serve in another man's church; think of me."

St. Thomas. "Come to me four days after Christmas, and I will provide for you." He then went away.

Randulf de Broc and Gervase of Cornhill, who had privately had the names reported to them of some of those who had gone in procession to meet the Archbishop, summoned the priors and more distinguished citizens. They pretended that the King commanded that they should give bail to appear when called upon, to answer for having gone out to meet a traitor. The priors and ecclesiastics would not attend; but many citizens did. They replied, that they had not seen any letters from the King, nor even from the justices; and that they were the King's liege men, and responsible to him alone, and not to them.

The De Broc family, in order to provoke him, hunted[4] in a chase of his without permission, and killed a stag; they also carried off several of his dogs and kept them. One day before Christmas, Robert de Broc, who had been a cleric, and then a white monk, and had apostatized and returned to the world, waylaid a train of the Archbishop's pack-horses, and set a nephew of his, John de Broc, to cut off the tail of one of them, on the King's highway. The poor mutilated beast was brought for the Archbishop to see.

All along the road which he had travelled, miracles were wrought after his martyrdom, more particularly in the places where he had stopped to give Confirmation to children, to mark which spots crosses were erected. The most famous was at Newington, a manor belonging to Richard de Luci, and Benedict[5] remarks that for the Saint to work wonders on his property, was to heap coals of fire on the head of an ancient adversary.

As soon as he arrived at Canterbury he dismissed his five soldiers. His last journey was over and he was once more in his Church on his birthday, the feast of St. Thomas the Apostle,

---

4 This was forbidden by King Henry in an instrument which St. Thomas witnessed when Chancellor (Rymer's Fœdera, i. p. 40).

5 Benedict, p. 164.

when he began his fifty-third year. The feast
of his patron saint fell on a Monday. He had
reached Canterbury in time to hold an ordination
in his Cathedral on the previous Saturday in
Ember week, December 19. Many were ordained
from other monasteries and churches of the province, but of Christ Church monks he only ordained five, one subdeacon, one deacon, and
three priests. The deacon was William of Canterbury, who records the fact. The ordination
of some other monks of Christ Church the Saint
postponed, as they had been irregularly received
in his absence, and he caused them to be excluded
from the Chapter, but just before Christmas he
allowed them to renew their petition for admission, and he granted it, sobbing as he uttered an
admonition to them to remember the indulgence
that he had shown them.

Amongst those intruded during his absence
was Odo,[6] the prior of the monastery. St. Thomas
therefore regarded the office of prior as vacant,
and he had summoned the Abbot of Boxley and
the Prior of Dover to advise him in the choice

6 Prior Wibert died September 27, 1167, and John of Salisbury
wrote a strong remonstrance to the Convent for applying to the
King on the occurrence of the vacancy (*Materials*, vi. p. 301).
The Pope in a letter dated May 16, 1168, ordered the Convent to
receive a Prior of the Archbishop's appointing only (*Ibid*. p. 418).
St. Thomas did not recognize the intruder, but when he wrote
in the following year, he addressed his letter "Wilhelmo Sup-
priori et Odoni et cœteris fratribus" (*Ibid*. p. 589). We learn
from William of Canterbury (p. 542) that some of the monks
were troubled at Odo's continuing in office. On the other hand,
others wanted him to be St. Thomas's successor as Archbishop
(*Materials*, iv. p. 177).

of one of his monks to fill the post, but the appointment was prevented by his death, and Odo continued to hold the place of prior, till in 1175 he was made Abbot of Battle.

The three Bishops who had crossed the sea found the King at his palace, called Bur, near Bayeux. When counsel was asked of them, Roger of York said, "Ask your barons and soldiers; it is not for us to say what ought to be done." At last some one said, "My lord, as long as Thomas lives, you will not have good days, nor peaceful kingdom, nor quiet times." The Bishops complaining that it was a shame to the King and his realm, that they should be so suspended from their offices that they were hardly allowed to bless their food, and declaring that if the King did not put a stop to the Archbishop's presumption, it would grow much worse, Henry fell into one of his terrible fits of rage, so that he was scarcely conscious of what he said. He repeated again and again, "What slothful wretches I have brought up in my kingdom, who have no more loyalty to their King than to suffer him to be so disgracefully mocked by this low-born cleric!" So saying he left the council-chamber.

Four knights immediately departed together. Their names were, Reginald Fitz-Urse, William de Tracy, Hugh de Moreville, and Richard Brito, or Le Breton. After swearing to carry out the end of their conspiracy, they separated in the night of Christmas eve; and it was remarked, that though they left different ports of France, and entered England at different places, they arrived at the same hour at Saltwood Castle. The King, after their departure, summoned the barons into his chamber, to complain that the Archbishop had entered his country like an invader; that he had suspended the Archbishop of York and the Bishops, and excommunicated others, for their services to himself; that he had disturbed the whole kingdom, and intended to deprive him and his son of their crowns; and that he had obtained from the Pope a privilege giving him and the Bishops the disposal of benefices, without regarding the advowsons of the earls or barons, or even of the King. The Earl of Leicester was the first to speak: "My lord, the Archbishop and the Earl, my father, were intimate friends; but be assured that, from the time he took himself out of your kingdom and favour, he has not seen a messenger from me, nor I from him." Engelger de Bohun, the uncle of the Bishop of Salisbury, and himself excommunicate, said, "I do not know what you can do with such a man, except you bind him with a wicker rope, and hang him on a cross." William Malvoisin, nephew of Eudes Count of Brittany, was the third speaker: "Some time ago," he said, "I was at Rome, on my return from Jerusalem. On questioning my host concerning the Popes, I learnt that a Pope had once been killed for his intolerable haughtiness and insolence."

As soon as this debate was ended, the King sent William de Mandeville Earl of Essex, Seyer de Quincy, and Richard de Humet, in search of the four who had left. The report was, that they were to seize the Archbishop. Earl William and Seyer went as far as the coast, but did not cross. Richard went to another port and crossed. The young King was at Winton. Richard sent to Hugh de Gondreville and William St. John, his guardians, to come without his knowledge to Canterbury, with the troops of the royal household. He himself lay in wait on the coast, that the Archbishop might be taken, if he attempted to fly; and the Earl of Essex and Seyer did the same on the other side of the Channel.

The four knights reached Saltwood on Monday the 28th. We must therefore now return to St. Thomas, whom we have accompanied to Canterbury. On Christmas night he sang the Gospel of the Nativity after Matins, according to the rite still in use in the Benedictine Order; and he celebrated the midnight Mass himself. He also sang the High Mass on the festival, and before it he preached a beautiful sermon on the text which so much occupied his thoughts: "On earth peace to men of good will." When he came to speak of the holy Fathers of the Church of Canterbury, the confessors who were there, he said that they had one Archbishop who was a martyr, St. Elphege; and that "it was possible that they might soon have another." The tears burst from his eyes, and his sobs interrupted his words. All in the church were deeply moved; sobs and groans of sorrow were heard, and amongst them a low murmur, "Father, why do

you desert us so soon? To whom do you leave
us desolate?" Checking his tears, the Saint in
a loud clear voice excommunicated Robert de
Broc, whom he had summoned by a messenger
to do penance; but the contumacious sinner had
sent for answer, by a soldier named David of
Rumnel [Romney], that if he were excommunicate, he would act as such. He involved in the
same sentence the usurpers of his two churches,
Harrow and Thierlewde or Throwley.

Christmas Day in that year fell upon Friday;
and St. Thomas, proceeding from the church to
the refectory, thought it more religious to eat
meat than to abstain, in honour of the joy of
Christmas, for which alone the Church suspends
the precept of abstinence. On both the following
feasts of St. Stephen and St. John the Saint sang
Mass. On the former day he sent off three of
his attendants, Herbert of Bosham, Alexander
"the Welshman," as they called him, his cross-
bearer, and Gilbert de Glanville, who had not
been very long in his service. Herbert was sent
to the King of France, the Archbishop of Sens,
and others of the Saint's friends. He left at
night through fear of treachery, with many tears;
his own conviction being confirmed by the Saint's
words, that he, who had borne so much with his
master, would never see that master's face again
upon earth. The others were the bearers of a
letter[7] to the Pope, the last its writer ever sent
to the Holy See, of which he had been the un-
flinching champion. In it he told the Pope of

7 Ep. S. Tho. i. p. 81; Froude, p. 539.

all that had lately taken place; and he added, that a plan was in progress, of which he had had some notice from his messengers before he returned to England; that six dignitaries of each vacant Church had been summoned before the King to go through the form of election of their Bishops, whom he would be obliged to refuse to consecrate; and thus a pretext would evidently be furnished for rekindling animosities. The concluding words of the letter were, " May your Holiness fare well for ever, dearest Father!" Two other messengers also left him, Richard his chaplain, and John Planeta, who had been with him at Northampton, with instructions to the Bishop of Norwich to absolve the priests on the domains of Earl Hugh Bigod,[8] who had incurred the lesser excommunication by their intercourse with excommunicated persons. They were to take oath to send, within a year, two of their number to the Pope, in their name, to accept their penance from his Holiness.

The Saint did not forget the poor priest William, who had come to him at Wrotham. He sent William Beivin, who knew him, in search of him, to see whether he had arrived at Canterbury. As he was not found, the Saint gave to William Beivin, to be given to the priest, a deed, conferring upon him the chapel of Penshurst, to which he had added an excommunication against any one who should dare to hinder its fulfilment. In virtue of this deed, the priest received the

[8] Hugh Bigod, Earl of Norfolk, was excommunicated by the Pope himself for usurping the property of the Canons of Pentney. See Note G.

benefice after the martyrdom; the young King saying, when he heard of the miracle, that he would not incur the Saint's excommunication.

On this Sunday, St. John's day, St. Thomas received a letter from a friend of his among the courtiers, bidding him beware of his coming fate. This was probably the outspoken warning of Reginald Earl of Cornwall, already mentioned. He hid the letter within his hair-shirt, where it was found after his death.

On the Monday a monk of Westminster, who was at Canterbury on business, asked St. Thomas whether he remembered a message St. Godric,[9] the hermit of Finchale, had sent him years before. " Right well do I remember it," he said, " but he has passed from this world to our Lord, and it is some time since we sung our funeral Mass for him. I know that he did not need our help, for he is happily reigning with Christ in Heaven. The message that he sent me by you, came to pass as he said, for I went into exile only Archbishop of Canterbury, and now I have returned Legate of all England."

Another message from St. Godric foretold his martyrdom to St. Thomas. " Tell him not to be troubled," said St. Godric while St. Thomas was still in exile, " if for a little while he will have much to suffer; but the longer the trial is, the fuller will be the crown, and the light burden of this tribulation will bring forth an increase of everlasting beatitude. For within six months peace by word of mouth will be made between

9 See Note H.

him and the King, but Godric will not then be living here : and within nine months his honours and possessions will be restored to him, and he will return to his see in Kent, where not long after, an end shall come to him altogether and of all things—an end that shall be for his saving good, his joy and perfection ; and to many men a remedy of salvation, a help and consolation." [10]

The soldiers of the castles round Canterbury, Dover, Rochester, Saltwood, and Bletchingley, were on the alert, and the castles put into a state of defence ; perhaps to prevent any vengeance being taken by the people for what was now about to happen.   It was on the 28th of December that the four conspirators reached Saltwood, where they would learn from their host that Robert de Broc, the apostate monk, had been solemnly excommunicated on Christmas Day.   They spent the long winter night in concerting their scheme ; and early in the morning of the next most memorable day, which after ages were to know as the Feast of the Holy Martyr St. Thomas, they set out with the De Brocs for Canterbury.   They went to St. Augustine's Abbey, outside the walls, the intruded abbot of which, Clarembald,[11] who had been a

---

[10] *Libellus de vita et miraculis S. Godrici*, auctore Reginaldo monacho Dunelmensi.   Surtees Society, 1845, pp. 236, 297.

[11] The Papal commission of inquiry into the character of the abbot-elect of St. Augustine's informed the Pope that they had absolved some of Clarembald's attendants, who, through the fear of the Abbot and the King, had communicated with the murderers of St. Thomas on their return from their crime (Ep. Jo. Sar. ii. p. 272).

constant enemy of the Saint's ever since his refusal to bless him in his abbacy, received them.
They remained there all the morning. They
had sent, at an early hour, to collect as many
soldiers as they could from the castles and the
neighbourhood. With about a dozen men-at-
arms, they rode from St. Augustine's to the Archbishop's palace; others being dispersed about the
town, with orders, in the name of the King, to
summon all the soldiers they might find, and to
command all other persons not to stir from their
houses nor to move, happen what might. Their
place of rendezvous was the house of one Gilbert,
not far from the gate of the palace, where they
ultimately assembled.

A soldier, who was sworn to the conspiracy,
told Richard, one of the cellarers or bursars of
the monastery, that the Saint would not see
Tuesday night. Richard repeated what he had
heard to St. Thomas, who smiled and said,
"They are threats." Reginald, a citizen of
Canterbury, also told him that the murderers
had landed and were making their preparations.
The Saint shed tears, and said, "They will find
me ready to die; let them do what they like.
I know, my son, and am certain that I shall die
a violent death; but they will not kill me outside
my church."

It was about four o'clock in the afternoon
when the four conspirators, with their small troop
of soldiers, reached the palace. Before another
hour and a half had elapsed, the soul of St.
Thomas of Canterbury was safe in Heaven.

CHAPTER XXXI.

THE BIRTHDAY.

1170.

The last morning—Matins—the thought of flight—Mass—spiritual conference and confession—dinner—the coming of the four knights—the interview—the knights call to arms—John of Salisbury's remonstrance—the panic of the monks—the Saint enters the church—the knights follow through the cloister—the Saint's last words—the martyrdom.

THE Saint had spent his last morning well. His Matins[1] he had recited at midnight in his room, with several of his clerics and of the monks; and when the Divine Office was over, he opened a window, and stood for a long time silently looking out into the night. At length he suddenly turned to his companions, and asked what o'clock it was, and whether it would be possible to reach Sandwich before daybreak. They replied, that it was yet very early, and that there was time to go a great deal further than that, which was but seven miles. On this they heard him say to himself, "God's will be done in me: Thomas will wait for whatever God has in store for him, in the church over which he presides."

He had assisted at Mass in the Cathedral; he visited all the altars, which was a customary devotion of his, and the shrines of the saints;

[1] Girald. Cambr. *Angl. Sacr.* Lond. 1691, ii. pp. 423, 424.

AA

and he remained several hours in the chapter-house, in close spiritual conference with two of the monks, who were remarkable for their piety. He went to confession to one of the religious whom he was accustomed to call "a man after his own heart," Dom Thomas of Maidstone,[2] and his great contrition, and his obedience in the fulfilment of his penance, were deemed worthy of record.   Three times on that day he received the discipline : his foreknowledge of his martyrdom probably leading him to anticipate the amount of mortification of this severe kind which he was accustomed to inflict upon himself every day. He dined at three o'clock in the afternoon ; and doubtless there was that day a double tenderness in his large clear eye as it roamed over the hall to see what was needed, whether by his clerics on one side of him, or his monks on the other. Amongst these were John of Salisbury, and William Fitzstephen ; and probably with them the visitor Edward Grim, a cleric of Cambridge. With the monks were Benedict, afterwards Abbot of Peterborough, and Gervase the historian. Doubtless his former confessor and early in-structor, Robert, the Prior of Merton, had an honourable place.   His dinner consisted of a pheasant : and one of the monks said to him, "Thank God, I see you dine more heartily and cheerfully to-day than usual."   His answer was, "A man must be cheerful who is going to his Master."

When dinner was over, and the grace chanted,

2 Will. Cant. pp. 102, 509, 510.

the Saint retired to his private room to hold his usual conference with his friends; for evidently he had resumed all the routine of his life, as he used to practise it at Canterbury, before his exile. He sat upon the bed, and his clerics and some of the monks were on either side of him. The crowd of persons, principally the poor, who had as usual dined with him, were still waiting about in the courtyard. Those who had served at the Archbishop's dinner were themselves dining, when the four knights, followed by one attendant, Randulf, an archer, entered by the open and hospitable doors. William Fitznigel, the Archbishop's seneschal, who was about to leave his service, and in the end acted a very unfaithful part, met and recognized them, and showed them the way to the room in which the Archbishop was. As they passed through the hall, the servers invited them to dine; but they declined. Fitznigel, entering the Archbishop's room, told him that four of the King's household knights were without, wishing to speak with him. " Let them come in," was the answer of the Saint, who continued his conversation with the monk he was talking to, without looking towards them. As they entered, those who were nearest to the door saluted them as usual; and they returned the salutation in a low tone of voice. They went close up to the Archbishop, and seated themselves on the floor at his feet, without offering him any salutation, either in their own or the King's name. Randulf, the archer, sat on the floor behind them.

After a pause, which drew the attention of all,

the Saint quietly saluted them, calling William de Tracy alone by his name. They took no notice of the salutation, but looked at one another in silence; until at length Fitzurse contemptuously said, "God help you." The colour rose in the Saint's face; and Fitzurse continued, while his companions still held silence, the play of their countenances showing what was passing in their minds, " We are come to you with the commands of the King over the water; say whether you will receive them in private, or in the hearing of all?" "As you wish," said the Archbishop. "No; as you wish," rejoined Fitzurse. The Saint ordered all to leave the room, at Fitzurse's ultimate request. The door-keeper ran up, and opened the door, so that those who were in the next room could see both the Archbishop and the knights. As soon as Fitzurse had begun to speak of the absolution of the Bishops, the Saint said, "These are not things to be kept secret;" and, not wishing to place himself in their power, called the door-keeper, and ordered him to send in the clerics and monks, but not to admit any lay persons. The knights afterwards confessed, that while they were in the room with him alone, they had thought of killing him with his archiepiscopal cross, which stood by, as there was no other weapon at hand. When his friends re-entered the room, the Saint said to the knights, "Now you may tell your lord's will, in their presence." Reginald Fitzurse answered, "As you have chosen to make these things public, instead of private, we can satisfy you, and tell these people. My

lord the King says, that he made peace with you
in all cordiality; but that you have not kept it.
He has heard that you have gone through his
cities with bands of armed men; and you have
excommunicated the Archbishop of York and the
other Bishops, for crowning the young King.
You must go to Winton, and do your duty to
your lord and King." "And what am I to do?"
said the Saint. "You ought to know better than
we," was the answer. "If I knew, I would not
say I did not know; but I believe that I have
done my duty towards him." "By no means,"
retorted Reginald; "there is much to do, much
to mend. The King's commands are, that you
go to the young King, and take the oath of fealty,
and swear to make amends for your treason."
The Saint said, "What am I to swear fealty
for? And what is my treason?" Neglecting
the latter question, Fitzurse answered the former.
"The oath of fealty is for the barony which you
hold of the King; and all your foreign priests,
too, must take the same oath of allegiance." St.
Thomas answered, "For my barony I will do my
duty; but know that neither I nor my clerics will
swear any more oaths. There are enough per-
jured and censured already. But, thank God, I
have already absolved many, and I hope, by
God's help, to free the rest." Reginald replied,
"We see that you will not do anything we propose. The King further orders you to absolve
the Bishops." "I did not suspend nor excommunicate them," said the Saint; "but it was
done by the Pope. You must go to him." "But,"

said Reginald, "whether you did it or no, it was done through you." St. Thomas answered, "I confess I was not sorry that the Pope punished the offence against my Church. As to my suffragans of London and Salisbury, I have already sent them word that I would absolve them, on their oath to observe the judgment of the Church; but they have refused. The same I am now ready to do. All that was done, was under the King's permission, which he gave me on the day of our reconciliation. I was on my way to the young King when I received his orders to return, for which I was sorry. So far from wishing to uncrown him, I would gladly give him three crowns, and broad realms."

Fitzurse became still more insulting. "What is that you say? It is an unexampled and unheard-of treachery, if the King has given any leave to suspend the Bishops, who were only present at the coronation at his own command. It never came into his mind. Yours is an awful crime, in feigning such treachery of our lord the King." "Reginald, Reginald," said the Archbishop, "I do not accuse the King of treachery. Our reconciliation was not so secretly done; for Archbishops and Bishops, many men of rank, and many religious, and more than five hundred knights were there, and heard it; and you yourself, Sir Reginald, were there." "I was not there;" he said; "I neither saw nor heard it." The Saint answered in a quiet tone of voice, "God knows it; for I am certain that I saw you there." He swore he was not there; and re-

peated that it was indeed a strange and unheard-
of thing for him to accuse the King of treachery.
"This cannot be borne any longer; and we, the
King's liegemen, will not bear it any more."
The other knights then broke silence for the first
time, swearing again and again, by God's
wounds, that they had borne with him far too
long already.

John of Salisbury said, "My lord, speak in
private about this." "There is no use," said the
Archbishop: "they propose and demand things
that I neither can nor ought to do."

Fitzurse. "From whom do you hold your archbishopric?"

St. Thomas. "Its spiritualities from God and
my lord the Pope, its temporalities and possessions from the King."

Fitzurse. "Do you not acknowledge that you
have it all from the King?"

St. Thomas. "By no means; but we must give
what is the King's to the King, and what is God's
to God." This made them the more angry.
St. Thomas continued: "Since I have landed
under the King's safe-conduct, I have suffered
many threats, insults, and losses. For instance,
my men have been made prisoners, and their
property taken from them: Robert de Broc has
mutilated one of my horses, and Randulf de
Broc has violently detained my wine, which the
King himself sent to England through his continental dominions. And now you come to
threaten me. I must say I think it very hard."
Hugh de Moreville said, "If the King's men have

injured you or yours, why did you not tell the King, and not excommunicate them on your own authority?"

St. Thomas. "Hugh, how you hold up your head! If any one injures the rights of the Church and refuses to make satisfaction, I shall wait for no one's leave to do justice."

Fitzurse. "These threats are too much." Another shouted, "Threats, threats; will he put the whole land under an interdict, and excommunicate us all?" And another followed: "God be propitious to me, he shall not do it; he has excommunicated too many already." They leapt up, twisted their gloves, flung their arms about in a state of the wildest excitement, and altogether behaved like madmen. One rushed up to him and said, "We warn you, that you have spoken to the peril of your life." Reginald said, "Thomas, in the King's name, I defy you." The Saint answered, "I know that you have come to kill me; but I make God my shield. You threaten me in vain. If all the swords in England were pointed against my head, your terrors could not move me from the observance of God's justice, and the obedience of our lord the Pope. Foot to foot you will find me in the battle of the Lord. Once I went away like a timid priest: I have come back by the advice and command of the Pope; I will never leave again. If I may fulfil my priestly office in peace, it is well for me: if I may not, God's will be done. Besides this, you know what there is between me and you; so I am the more astonished that you should threaten the Archbishop in his own house." He said this to remind Reginald Fitzurse, William de Tracy, and Hugh de Moreville, that they had sworn fealty to him on their knees when he was Chancellor. They shouted out, "There is nothing between us against the King." Reginald Fitzurse added, "We can well threaten the Archbishop, we can do more: let us go."

A great number of persons had now collected besides the ecclesiastics, especially some of the soldiers of the Archbishop's household, attracted by the loudness of the voices. Reginald turned to them and said, "We enjoin you in the King's name, whose liegemen and subjects you are, to leave this man." Finding that they did not move, he said, "We command you to keep him in safe custody, and produce him again when the King shall please." "I am easy to keep," said the Saint; "I shall not go away. I will not fly for the King, nor for any living man." He followed them to the door, saying, as he placed his hand upon his head, the very place where he afterwards received his death-wound, "Here, here, you will find me." He called to Hugh de Moreville, who was the gentlest of the party, to come back, that he wanted to speak to him; but he would not listen. As they went out, they seized on the seneschal, William Fitznigel, saying, "Come with us." Fitznigel called out to the Archbishop, "Do you see, my lord, what they are doing to me?" He answered, "I see: this is their strength, and the power of darkness." The

Saint then followed them a few steps from the room, asking them quietly to let Fitznigel go, but without effect. They also, as they went, seized on another soldier of the Archbishop's, called Ralph Morin. They passed through the hall and the court to the house of Gilbert, where their followers were, calling out loudly, with violent and threatening gesticulations, "Arms, men, arms!" Some of their soldiers had removed the Archbishop's porter from the great door, and placed one of their own men there, so that when they came pouring out, shouting, "The King's soldiers, the King's, the King's!" the great door was opened for them, and immediately afterwards it was shut. The wicket was left open, and William Fitznigel, and Simon de Crioil, a soldier of Clarembald, the Abbot of St. Augustine's, kept guard on horseback in the court.

The Saint, on failing in his attempt to recall Hugh de Moreville, returned to his room, and sat down again on the bed. John of Salisbury said to him, "My lord, it is a wonderful thing that you will take no one's counsel. What need was there for a man of your station to make them more angry by rising and following them to the door?"

St. Thomas. "What would you have me do, Dom John?"

John of Salisbury. "You ought to have called your council, and given them a milder answer. They only try to make you angry, to take you in your speech; for they seek nothing but your death."

St. Thomas. "Counsel is already taken. I know well enough what I ought to do."

John of Salisbury. "By God's blessing, I hope it is a good counsel."

St. Thomas. "We must all die, and the fear of death must not turn us from justice; I am more ready to die for God and justice, and the liberty of God's Church, than they are to inflict it on me."

John of Salisbury. "We are sinners, and not ready for death; and I see no one who purposely wishes to die but you."

St. Thomas. "God's will be done."

Some said, that there was nothing to fear, that it was Christmas and they were drunk, and would have behaved differently if they had not dined: "besides, the King has made his peace with us." Others, however, thought that they would surely fulfil their threat. Some people rushed in, saying, "My lord, my lord, they are arming." He answered, "What matter? Let them arm." They could also hear the sound of wailing in the church, from a number of persons who had heard the proclamation to the soldiers to arm and hasten to the palace. The domestics ran down the stairs and across the hall towards the church, to get out of the way of the soldiers. The panic of most of them was complete, when they heard the noise of the crashing of a door and window in a passage which led from the orchard to one of the outer rooms. "My lord, go into the church," said the monks. "No," he replied, "do not fear; monks are too timid and

cowardly." Some tried to drag him there. Others
said that Vespers were being sung in the choir,
and he should go and assist at them. When he
had moved a few steps, he stopped, because he
saw that his cross was not borne before him as
usual: and Henry of Auxerre then supplied the
place of his absent cross-bearer. He made them
all precede him; and once he looked round to
the right, either to see whether the soldiers
were following, or whether any one had been
left behind. They could not go the usual way to
the church, so they turned down a passage which
had long been closed. One of the monks ran on
before to try and force the door open, of which
they had not got the key, when the two cellarers
or bursars of the monastery, Richard and William, came up through the monks' cloister, into
which the passage led, and tore off the bolt, and
so opened the door. So unexpected an interference seemed quite like a miracle. The door was
shut behind them, which the Saint did not much
like. Twice he paused in the cloister, and once
in the chapter-house, trying to compose his companions and overcome their panic.

When the monks in the choir heard the armed
men, and saw two terrified boys who rushed in
among them, they were thrown into confusion.
Some continued the Office, while others fled to
the door by which the Archbishop was entering.
Not knowing what might have happened, they
were overjoyed to see him; and said, "Come in,
father, come in, that we may suffer together and
be glorified together. Console us by your

presence." He answered, "Go on with the Divine Office." As they still remained about the door, he said, "As long as you keep in the entrance, I will not enter." They gave way, and the people who were crowding forward being pushed back, he said on the threshold, "What are these people afraid of?" They answered, "Armed men in the cloister." He replied, "I will go out to them." As he looked round, they begged him to go into the church and up to the sanctuary, that he might be defended by the sanctity of the place. This he refused to do. Some of the monks brought an iron bar to fasten the door. He said, "Go away, cowards; let the blind wretches rage: I order you, in virtue of obedience, not to shut the door: a church ought not to be fortified like a castle." The monks, however, drew him in, and tried to fasten it. He immediately went to the door, saying, "Let my own people in;" and moving away those who were close to it, he opened it, and drawing in with his own hands those who were outside, he said, "Come in, come in quickly." He was now urged away by those around him; the door was, however, left open, opposing no barrier to the entrance of the soldiers, who were close at hand.

When the knights had first entered the Arch-bishop's room, they had on their capes and tunics over their coats-of-mail. These they took off under a large mulberry-tree in the garden, and put on their swords. Fitzurse armed himself in the porch before the hall, making Robert Tibia, the Archbishop's shield-bearer, help him. Osbert

and Algar, and others of the Archbishop's servants, seeing the soldiers making these preparations, shut the hall-doors, and fastened them
securely.   The knights were not able to force
them open; but Robert de Broc, the cleric, who
had become familiar with the place during its
usurpation by Randulf, called out, "Follow me;
I will take you in another way."   He led them
through the orchard, and tried to go straight by
that entrance to the Archbishop's room.   Not
succeeding in this, he led them through the
ambulatory, the wooden steps of which were
under repair, that he might open the hall-door.
The carpenters' tools were lying about, and Fitzurse seized an axe and the others hatchets.
Breaking a door and a window, they got into the
hall, and after severely wounding the servants
who had closed the doors, they re-opened them.
They then rushed over the palace, and not finding
the Archbishop in his room, they followed him
rapidly through the cloister to the church.   Fitzurse entered on the right hand, the other three
on the left; they all had their swords drawn,
while in their left hands they held the carpenters'
tools they had picked up.   They were so covered
with their armour, their vizors being down, that
nothing was visible of their persons but their
eyes.   Fitzurse shouted, "This way to me, king's
men!"   They were followed by a number of their
soldiers with weapons, though not in armour,
and some of the townsmen of Canterbury, whom
they had forced to join them.

It was about five o'clock on an evening in mid-winter, and almost dark. If the Saint had chosen, he could have easily concealed himself, and so have escaped his death. But he had already said that the time for flight was past; so that he did not avail himself of the neighbouring crypt, nor of the hiding-places in the very accessible roof. John of Salisbury and the other clerics fled away, and hid themselves behind the altars, and where-ever they could find refuge, leaving him with only three, Robert the Prior of Merton, William Fitz-stephen, and Edward Grim. A little later the first two followed the others, leaving Grim alone with him. Whether this faithful cleric carried his cross at this time is not recorded, but the tradition, especially in pictures of the event, is so uniform, that it is not improbable that he took it from Henry of Auxerre, when the panic seized him.

The three who remained with him urged him up the steps which led from the transept towards the choir. The Saint said to them, "Leave hold of me, and go away; there is nothing for you to do here; let God dispose of me according to His will." On the entrance of the soldiers into the church, one of them called to the monks who were with him, "Do not move." Another cried out, "Where is Thomas Becket, the traitor to the King?" To this no answer was returned. Fitzurse, who was on the right hand of the knights, said to one against whom he had run, "Where is the Archbishop?" The Saint instantly answered, having first made a slight motion of his head to the monks, "Here I am; no traitor,

but the Archbishop." He came down the steps
which he had ascended, and turned to the right,
under the column by which he had been hidden
from the knights on their first entrance. He now
had a statue of our Blessed Lady before him,[3]
with her altar in the nave beyond it; on his right
was the altar of St. Benedict, and on his left his
cross. His back was to the wall. Some one
struck him on the shoulders with the flat of his
sword, saying, "Fly, or you are a dead man."
He answered, "I will not fly." The four knights
now came up, with Hugh of Horsea, a subdeacon, named Mauclerc, calling out, "Absolve
the Bishops immediately, whom you have excommunicated." He said, "I will do nothing more
than I have already said and done."

The Saint then turned to Fitzurse, "Reginald,
Reginald, I have done you many favours; do
you come against me in arms?" "You shall
know it," he said; and added, "Are you not a
traitor?" The Saint replied, "I do not fear your
threats, for I am prepared to die for God; but let
my people go, and do not touch them." Fitzurse
laid hold of his robe, knocking off his cap with
his sword, saying, "Come, you are my prisoner."
The Saint answered, "Do with me *here* what you
will;" and he pulled the border of his cappa
from his hand. They then tried to put him on
William de Tracy's shoulders, and carry him out
of the church; but he stood firmly in his place,
keeping fast hold of the column in the middle of
the transept, and Edward Grim assisted him. One

3 See Note I.

of his assailants, probably Fitzurse, he laid hold of by his coat-of-mail, and nearly threw him down on the pavement, calling him by a name[4] which reproached him for the immorality of his life, and adding, " You shall not touch me, Reginald ; you are my man, and owe me fealty and submission." Fitzurse answered, " I owe you neither fealty nor homage, contrary to my fealty to the King."

Fitzurse, seeing that they could not drag him away, and beginning to be afraid of the interference of the people, who were assembled in the church for Vespers, flung down the two-edged axe which he had brought to force the door, and which was found there after the martyrdom, and waved his sword, crying out, " Strike, strike." When the Saint saw that the blow was coming, he joined his hands, and covered his eyes with them, and bowing his head, said, " I commend myself to God, to holy Mary, to blessed Denys, and St. Elphege." The first severe blow was a slanting one. Grim attempted to ward it off, and received so grievous a wound that his arm was nearly severed. The blow nevertheless fell upon the Saint, and wounded that part of his head where the sacred unction had been poured at his consecration, which was marked by his tonsure. It then glanced upon the left shoulder, and cut through the vestments to the flesh. We know that this stroke was inflicted by William de Tracy, for he afterwards boasted at Saltwood that he had cut off John of Salisbury's arm ; either the dim light or the excitement of the

[4] Grim, p. 436; Will. Cant. p. 133.

BB

moment having caused him to mistake the person
whom he had wounded. Grim·fled to the nearest
altar, our Lady's or St. Benedict's, where several
of the monks had also taken refuge. One of the
monks received a blow ·on the head from the
flat of a sword. William of Canterbury, fearing
a general slaughter when he heard the words
"Strike, strike," ran up the steps, clapping his
hands, and at the sound those·monks who had
remained in choir, at Vespers, dispersed.

The Saint wiped the blood that was flowing
from his head with his arm; and when he saw it,
he gave thanks to God, saying, "Into Thy hands,
O Lord, I commend my spirit." Bowing he
awaited the second blow, which struck him again
upon the head, but he did not move. When struck
a third time, probably by Fitzurse, the blow made
him fall[5] first on his knees, and then on his face.
His hands were still joined, and his cappa covering
him down to his feet, he looked as if he were
prostrate in prayer. He was lying towards the
north,[6] having fallen to the right hand, before the
altar of St. Benedict. He breathed his last words
in a low voice, but so as to be overheard by the
wounded Grim, who alone records them. They
were, "For the Name of JESUS, and the defence
of the Church, I am ready to die." The fourth
blow was dealt by Richard Le Breton, who, on

[5] Grim (p. 437) says that the fall was caused by the third
blow; Benedict (p. 13) and Fitzstephen (p. 141) by the second,
but the latter, though stating that the Saint received four blows
on the head, describes only three.

[6] Garnier, 74 b, 11.

being reproached for his backwardness, struck with such force that the sword was shivered on the pavement, saying, "Take that for the love of my lord William, the King's brother." This was an allusion to an unlawful marriage between William Plantagenet and the Countess of Warrenne, which St. Thomas had prevented.[7] Hugh of Horsea, the subdeacon, placed his foot on the Martyr's neck, and with the point of his sword drew the brains from the wound and scattered them on the pavement;[8] for Le Breton's blow had so separated the crown of the head from the skull, that it was attached only by the skin of the forehead. Hugh de Moreville contented himself with keeping back the people, and was the only one of the four who did not strike the Martyr. Hugh Mauclerc shouted out, "Let us go; the traitor is dead; he will rise no more." They all rushed from the church by the way by which they had entered, shouting the fatal watch-word to which the deed had been perpetrated, "The King's men, the King's men!"

[7] See Note J.

[8] Benedict (p. 13) attributes this to Le Breton, Herbert (p. 506) to Robert de Broc.

CHAPTER XXXII.

ABSOLUTION.

1170—1172.

The palace sacked—the Saint's body—devotion of the people—
threats of Randulf de Broc—the Saint's vestments—he is
buried in the crypt—the body removed for a short time—
miracles—the Cathedral reconciled—grief of the young King
—conduct of King Henry—his messengers to the Pope—
sentence of his Holiness—absolution of the Bishops—the
King goes to Ireland—his absolution at Avranches.

WILLIAM DE TRACY afterwards confessed to
Bartholomew, Bishop of Exeter,[1] that his heart
failed him when all was over, and he dreaded
lest the earth should open and swallow him up.
They allowed themselves no time for reflection

[1] So it is given in the MS. lessons for the Church of Exeter,
compiled by Bishop Grandisson, and kindly copied for me by
the Rev. Dr. Oliver from Grandisson's autograph copy in the
possession of the Dean and Chapter of Exon. Giraldus Cambrensis (*Angl. Sacr.* p. 426) affirms deliberately that William de
Tracy confessed to Bartholomew that the four knights had been
bound *by the King* by oath to put the Primate to death; and he
says that their reproach against Hugh de Moreville for not
having taking a more active part bears out this statement. He
adds, that this induced the Bishop of Exeter to change his
opinion respecting the King's complicity. It is singular that
Herbert should say (ii. p. 301), that when Tracy went to the
Pope, he gave an account of the whole matter that exculpated
the King as much as possible. That many of the guilty parties
came to Bartholomew for absolution is plain from instructions
the Pope sent him (Ep. Gilb. Fol. ii. p. 80), in answer to his
inquiries how he should distinguish between the degrees of
participation in the guilt.

or remorse. Robert de Broc had not come into
the church, but with some others had gone to
the Archbishop's room to guard his goods. As
the knights rushed away, they inflicted a severe
wound on a French servant of the Archdeacon
of Sens, for lamenting the Martyr. They then
joined Robert de Broc, and broke open the
Saint's chests and desks; the gold and silver
as well as the books which they found, they took
away. There was the gold chalice[2] with which
the Saint said Mass, and Garnier records, a
knife that was "worth a city," and his ring
with a sapphire in it of singular beauty. All
the documents, Bulls of Popes, charters and
privileges, and other papers, Randulf de Broc
took possession of, to send to the King in Normandy. The soldiers roamed all over the palace,
taking every thing of value, even precious stuffs
which were intended for vestments for the
church. They did not spare the rooms of the
clerics, and they took from the stables the Archbishop's horses. All this spoil, which Fitz-
stephens estimated at two thousand marks, they
divided amongst themselves. They found, to
their astonishment, amongst the Saint's things,
two hair-shirts, which they threw away.

As soon as the report of what had happened
got abroad, people flocked in. Their grief and
horror at the double sacrilege were general,—we
should have said universal, if Grim had not
heard one, an ecclesiastic like himself, say that
he was not a martyr, for he had died through

[2] Garnier, 74 b, 21.

his obstinacy. When the multitude of people had left the Cathedral, the monks locked the doors. The holy body lay for some time deserted, when Osbert,[3] his Chamberlain, came, and cutting off a portion of his surplice, placed it over the head. When it was known that the murderers were gone, the clerics and monks, with the servants and a number of the townspeople, surrounded the relics. The silence was broken, and the sobs and lamentations were the louder for the restraint that fear had hitherto placed upon them. They called him " St. Thomas ; " and there was not one among them who was not marked with his blood, for they dipped their fingers in it, and under his invocation signed with it their foreheads and their eyes. They raised the body and laid it on a bier, to carry to the high altar. Beneath it they placed a vessel to receive the blood, which was still running from the wound. All were struck with the beauty of the face ;[4] the eyes and mouth were closed, the colour was fresh, and it appeared as if he were asleep. The blood had formed a sort of crown round his head, but the face was clear, save only a light graceful line which passed from the right temple across the nose to the left cheek. They covered the wound with a white linen cloth, and the cap was fastened on. Beneath the body,

3 This Osbert (named also *Supra*, p. 413) is probably the same person as Osbern, who was with the Saint at Northampton (*Supra*, p. 185).

4 Ep. Gilb. Fol. ii. p. 304. This is a letter to the Pope from some one who arrived at Canterbury on the day of the murder and saw the Saint's dead body.

an iron hammer and the axe were found. The people, in the confusion, made the best use of their liberty by filling little vessels with the blood, and tearing off pieces of their clothing and dipping them in it. No one was content who had not secured a portion of it. After a short time, one of the monks who was a goldsmith, named Ernold, went to the spot of the martyrdom with some others, and collected into a vessel all the brain and blood which were on the pavement; and to prevent any one from treading on the place, they brought some movable benches and put them all round. Vigil was kept all night, the monks saying in silence the commendation of the soul. Robert, the Prior of Merton, who, as his confessor, knew his austerities, showed the monks, who had no suspicion of anything of the kind, how he was vested. He put his hand into the Martyr's bosom, and pointed out that his cappa, as a canon regular,[5] covered his cowl as a monk, and that under this was his hair-shirt. The sight turned their sorrow into spiritual joy; they knelt down, kissed his hands and feet, and called him, "St. Thomas, God's holy and glorious Martyr." Thus the morning found them, watching around the precious relics before the high altar. The night had set in dark and stormy, but later on a red light filled the sky.

The next morning, Robert de Broc was sent by Randulf with a message to the monks: "He

[5] "Sub habitu canonici regularis, eum in habitu et ordine monachorum tam secreto diu reperiunt exstitisse, ut etiam hoc suos lateret familiares" (Grim, p. 442).

died the death of a traitor, and the earth is rid
of him ; but he deserves no better treatment
dead than alive. Put his body somewhere where
it may not be known, or I will come and drag
him out by the feet, and fling him piecemeal to
the swine and dogs." The monks hurriedly
closed the doors, and carried the precious treasure into the crypt ; and both on account of the
haste which was necessary lest some further violence should be used, and out of reverence to
the Martyr's blood with which the body was
bathed, they refrained from washing it and
anointing it with balsams, as was usually done
to the Archbishops of Canterbury. Such was
also the counsel of the Abbot of Boxley and the
Prior of Dover. They prepared, however, to
bury him in his archiepiscopal vestments, and
for this purpose they took off his black cappa
with its white lambswool, and his fine linen surplice, which, enriched with the stains of his blood,
were given to the poor. They were sold for a
trifle, and came into the possession of William
of Bourne,[6] a worthy priest who lived in the
neighbourhood of Canterbury. Under these came
two other lambswool pelisses, which were also
parted with ; and Garnier speaks of them as
reverently preserved as relics. Then came the
Cistercian cowl that the Pope had blessed, with
its sleeves cut short, that it might not be observed. When the bystanders saw the habit,
they exclaimed, "See, see, he was a true monk,
and we did not know it."

They left on him the Benedictine woollen

[6] Bened. pp. 52, 54.

shirt and cowl,[7] as well as his hair-shirt,[8] which, to their astonishment, extended down to the knees. . This was covered with linen, and so made that it could be readily undone, to enable him to receive the discipline. This hair-shirt was alive with vermin, the torment of which must have made his life a martyrdom. In the breast of the hair-shirt, was the letter he had received on Sunday, warning him of his coming fate. He was vested in the vestments in which he had been consecrated; a simple superhumeral or amice, the alb, chrismatic,[9] mitre, stole, and maniple; all these he had preserved for this purpose: he had also the tunicle, dalmatic, chasuble, the pall with its pins, gloves, ring, sandals, and pastoral staff. The chalice as usual was placed with him, and he was laid in a new marble coffin in the crypt, behind the chapel of "Our Lady Undercroft," and before the two altars of St. John the Baptist and St. Augustine, the Apostle of England. The doors[10] were then securely fastened, and the vessel containing the blood and brain was placed outside. The crypt remained closed until the Easter following. If any one was admitted, it was secretly done; but

---

7 *Stamineam videlicet et cucullam* (Bened. p. 17).

8 The hair-shirt, which was afterwards hung up near the tomb, and the sacred vestments, were taken out later, probably at the Translation in 1220. See Note O.

9 The chrismatic was the linen band that was bound round the head, during the consecration, to prevent the holy oil, with which the tonsure is anointed, from running down upon the vestments. The amice was "simple," that is, without apparels: the alb on the seal (*Supra*, p. 88) has apparels on the sleeves only.

10 Bened. pp. 60, 77, 81; Gerv. p. 229.

the miracles becoming exceedingly frequent, as a subsequent chapter will show, and their fame very widely spread, so that the memorable places were much visited, the crypt was thrown open at the urgent petition of the people, on the 2nd of April, being the Friday in Easter week. Miracles followed in still greater numbers, and the report of them aroused anew all the hatred of the De Broc family. One day news was brought to the monks, that that night they were to be forcibly deprived of the treasure that they had learnt to prize so highly, the body of their great Martyr. They therefore moved it from the marble coffin into one of wood, which they hid behind the altar of the Blessed Virgin, and they watched all night in the church. Like the night after the martyrdom, there was a violent thunderstorm. The next day two more miracles took place, one of them at the altar of the Blessed Virgin, where the Saint's body had been placed during the night; so the monks, taking courage, restored the relics to the crypt, and built around the marble coffin walls, most solidly constructed of large wrought stones, united with iron clamps and lead. There was a space of about a foot between the top of the coffin and the roof of this structure, and they left two openings or windows, through which the devout pilgrim might touch and kiss the coffin itself.

In consequence of the violation of the church, no Mass was said; and the Cathedral remained in its widowhood and mourning for a year all but ten days, till the feast of St. Thomas the

Apostle, 1171. The Divine Office was recited
by the monks without chanting, in the chapter-
·house; the altars were stripped, and the cruci-
fixes veiled, as in Passion-tide. The power which
had been conferred by the Pope upon the Cardinals Theodwin and Albert, of reconciling the
Cathedral, was by them transferred to the Bishops
of Exeter and Lichfield, at the request of Odo,
the Prior.

When the account of the martyrdom reached
the young King at Winton, he threw up his
hands and his eyes to heaven, expressing his
thanks to God that he had known nothing of
it, and that none of his followers had been there.
Hugh de Gondreville and William Fitz John
were on their way to Canterbury, but they had
not arrived at the time of the martyrdom.
Doubtless his grief was sincere, for he had a
true affection for his old guardian; and whatever
there had lately been that seemed unkind in his
conduct, was probably done under the direction
of his father and his counsellors.

King Henry had gone from Bur, where the
words were spoken which caused the martyrdom,
to Argentan in Normandy. When he heard what
had happened, he remained there for forty days
in penance, on fasting diet, remaining solitary,
and saying again and again, "O that it should
have happened! O that it should have happened!" During this time he did not ride out,
nor hear causes, nor summon councils, nor conduct any of the affairs of Government. He sent
messengers to Canterbury as well as to the Pope.

The former were to say that he had given the knights no such commission, and that the body was to be properly buried; for though he had been opposed to the Archbishop when alive, he did not persecute him now that he was dead, and that he forgave his soul the injuries he had committed against him.   It is impossible to avoid one conclusion, that although it would probably be unjust to attribute the martyrdom to the will of King Henry II., or to consider as insincere his sorrow for it, as an act disgraceful to himself, and going further in severity than he would have gone, yet evidently he had no contrition whatever for the course he had pursued in the life of the Saint, nor any greater regard than before for the rights of the Church.   In this sense, with the sole exception of the verbal retractation of the Constitutions of Clarendon at his absolution, the blood of St. Thomas was shed in vain.

John Cumin[11] was at the Court of the Pope when the intelligence arrived.   He had come to try to obtain the absolution of the Bishops; and though, on his first arrival, it had cost him five hundred marks and hard entreaty to obtain an audience, yet he had nearly succeeded when the sad news came.   Alexander Llewellyn and Gunter, who had left the Saint so shortly before his death, were the bearers of his last letter.   The report of the martyrdom reached them on their journey; and to their despatches to the Pope were added the strongest denunciations from the

[11] The King's messengers give this account of themselves (Ep. Gilb. Fol. ii. pp. 198, 260).

Archbishop of Sens[12] against the guilty Bishops, and against the King as the virtual murderer. Similar letters were written by King Louis[13] and other personages. The Holy Father on receiving the news shut himself up in grief, not allowing even his own suite to see him for eight days, and a general order was issued, that no Englishman should be admitted into his presence.

It was fully expected that on Maundy Thursday the Pope would excommunicate the King, and lay the realm under an interdict. On the Saturday before Palm Sunday, King Henry's messengers reached Tusculum, now called Frascati, where the Pope then was. They consisted of the Abbot of Valacé, the Archdeacons of Salisbury and Lisieux, Richard Barre, Henry Pinchun, and a Templar. They were the bearers of letters[14] from the King, framed in very offensive terms: "On his first entrance he brought not the joy of peace, but fire and the sword, while he raised a question against me touching my realm and crown. Besides, he was the aggressor upon my servants, excommunicating them without a cause. Men not being able to bear such insolence, some of those who were excommunicated, with some others from England, attacked him, and, what I cannot say without sorrow, killed him." Henry must have had a very faint idea of the way in which the death of St. Thomas would be felt by

[12] Ep. S. Tho. ii. p. 160.
[13] Ep. Gilb. Fol. ii. p. 306.
[14] The letter is not in Dr. Giles's collection, but is given b Martene (*Thes. Nov. Anecd.* i. p. 559).

the Church, when he wrote that letter. It is simple effrontery to write to the Pope about "fire and sword," when the censures for the coronation were passed by the Pope himself. Henry must have known that the excommunications were not "without a cause," for he had himself consented to them; and he must have said "others from England," in order to conceal from the Pope that the murderers left his own Court in consequence of expressions used by himself.

The Holy Father would not admit the Embassy to kiss his foot, nor would the Cardinals receive them. At length, by the influence of some of the King's friends, the Abbot of Valacé, and the Archdeacon of Lisieux, as the least suspected parties, were admitted to the Consistory. When they named the King, and called him a devout son of the Roman Church, all the Court cried out, "Hold, hold!" Late in the evening they went from the Court to His Holiness, "to declare all the favours which the King had conferred upon St. Thomas, and the excesses he had committed against the Crown." Alexander Llewellyn and Gunter were there, and the King's messengers made no impression, though they repeated before the Pope and Cardinals what they had said to the Pope in private. Maundy Thursday was coming on, and as yet nothing effectual had been done to stop the sentence which had been so long deserved. At length, by the advice of those Cardinals who had always been partial to Henry, the messengers declared to the Pope, that the King had empowered them to swear in the presence of the Holy Father, that he would obey his command, and would renew the same oath in person. This oath, which, if the King had been really contrite, would have been offered at first, and which would not have required the tone of apology in which his messengers mention it in their report to him, was solemnly taken by them all, as well as by the representatives of the Archbishop of York and the Bishops of London and Salisbury, in the full Consistory on Maundy Thursday, at three in the afternoon. The Pope then, in general terms, excommunicated the murderers of St. Thomas, and all who had given them counsel, aid, or assent, or had knowingly harboured them.

The Archbishop of Sens had been added to the commission before the martyrdom was known, and had received the same powers as the Archbishop of Rouen. The latter prelate now protested [15] against any exercise of that legatine power, under pretext of an appeal to the Pope; but the Archbishop of Sens laid the King's continental dominions under an interdict, and notified what he had done to his Holiness. This sentence the King's messengers on their way to the Holy See had in vain attempted to avert. The Bishops of Worcester and Evreux, with Robert of Newburgh, reached Frascati a few days after Easter. After a fortnight they were summoned to hear the decision. The Pope confirmed the interdict published by the Archbishop of Sens, and forbade the King to enter the church, until Legates should

[15] Ep. S. Tho. ii. pp. 72, 165, 206.

arrive, whom he was about to send to judge of
his dispositions. With great difficulty, by the
intercession of some of the Cardinals, and, it
was reported, by the help of a large sum of
money, they succeeded in obtaining letters to
the Archbishop of Bourges, with powers to absolve the Bishops of London and Salisbury from
their excommunication, on the exaction of the
usual oath, if after a month from their receipt
he did not hear that the Legates had crossed
the Alps. These Bishops, however, as well as
the others, were to remain under their suspension.
About the beginning of August[16] the Bishop of
London was so far absolved, but by the Bishops
of Nevers and Beauvais, and the Abbot of Pontigny, at Gisors. On the 6th of December the
Archbishop of York was freed from his suspension
at Albemarle[17] by the Archbishop of Rouen and
the Bishop of Amiens, on his taking oath that
he had not received the Pope's letters prohibiting
the coronation before it was performed; that he
had not bound himself on that occasion to observe the Constitutions of Clarendon; and that he
had not wilfully caused the death of St. Thomas

16 Diceto, p. 557.

17 The letter in which he announces his absolution to his clergy
(Ep. Gilb. Fol. ii. p. 173; Ep. Jo. Sar. ii. p. 265), dated December 13, Monday in the third week in Advent, is petulant in the
extreme; and in it he calls St. Thomas *Pharao*, to the great
indignation of his followers (Ep. Jo. Sar. ii. p. 260). It is worthy
of remark, that, in the letter (Ep. Gilb. Fol. ii. p. 172) in which
he thanks the Pope for his absolution, he says that the King
heard " from many " what irritated him against the Saint; and
that then Gilbert Foliot did his utmost, even with tears, to pacify
him.

by word, by deed, or by writing. On the Bishop
of London taking an oath to the same effect, he
also was absolved at the same place, by the same
prelates, on the 1st of May following.

In the month of August, 1171, the King crossed
the Channel on his way to Ireland. During his
short stay in England he visited the venerable
Henry of Blois, Bishop of Winchester, who up-
braided him severely for his share in the death
of St. Thomas. The Bishop died on the 27th
of that month. The King gave orders,[18] after his
old fashion, that the ports on both sides of the
Channel were to be diligently kept, and any one
found bearing an interdict to be immediately
imprisoned. He ordered that no cleric was to
be permitted to leave the kingdom without an
oath not to be a party to any measure against
himself or the realm. He also added, that no
one bearing letters was to have access to him.
It was shrewdly conjectured, that one motive of
his invasion of Ireland, in addition to his other
schemes, was to be out of the way, lest any
ecclesiastical censures should be served upon
him.

Cardinal Albert, afterwards Pope Gregory VIII.
now Cardinal of St. Lorenzo in Lucina and Chancellor of the Holy Roman Church, and Theodwin, Cardinal of St. Vitalis, were sent as Legates;
but the reconciliation of Canterbury Cathedral
was the only work which they performed in 1171.
It was difficult, after all his precautions, to get
access to King Henry; but their letters of warn-

[18] Gerv. p. 234.

CC

ing being at length delivered, on Easter Tuesday the King returned to England, and, having sent messengers to the Legates to ask where they would meet him, they had an interview at the Abbey of Savigny. Its only result was, that Henry refused to do what the Legates required; and it was thought that he would return to England. The next day, however, Arnulf the Bishop of Lisieux, with the two Archdeacons, came to them to say the King had given way. The Legates accordingly entered Avranches, in company with him, on the Fifth Sunday after Easter.

"The great Norman Cathedral of that beautiful city," says a modern writer,[19] "stood on what was perhaps the finest situation of any Cathedral in Christendom,—on the brow of the high ridge which sustains the town of Avranches, and looking over the wide bay, in the centre of which stands the sanctuary of Norman chivalry, the majestic rock of St. Michael, crowned with its fortress and chapel. Of this vast Cathedral, one granite pillar alone has survived the storm of the French Revolution; and that pillar marks the spot where Henry performed his first penance. It bears an inscription with these words: ' Sur cette pierre, ici, à la porte de la cathédrale d'Avranches, après le meurtre de Thomas Becket, Archévêque de Cantorbéry, Henri II. Roi d'Angleterre et Duc de Normandie, reçut à genoux, des légats du Pape, l'absolution apostolique, le Dimanche, xxii Mai, MCLXXII.' "

[19] Stanley's *Canterbury*, p. 116.

The young King came that he might express his assent to all that his father should do. On the Sunday before the Ascension, with his hand on the Holy Gospels, King Henry swore that he had neither commanded nor wished the death of the Saint; and, he voluntarily added, that he had grieved more for it than for his father and mother. Still, as he feared that his angry expressions had been the occasion of the sin, he vowed to accept whatever penance the Legates might inflict upon him.

They first[20] made him swear that he would never leave the obedience of Pope Alexander and his successors, as long as they treated him like a Catholic and Christian king. His son Henry then took the same oath. The next clause was, that for a year, dating from Pentecost, he would pay for two hundred soldiers to be placed at the disposal of the Templars. He also vowed to take the Cross for three years, to date from the following Christmas; and in the summer to proceed in person to the Holy Land, unless the Pope gave him leave to remain. His joining the Crusade was to be delayed for any length of time he might spend in fighting against the Saracens in Spain. He then swore that he would not hinder appeals in ecclesiastical causes to the Church of Rome, nor would he suffer them to be hindered; and that in good faith, without fraud or evil design, in order that the causes might be judged by the Pope, and have their free course. He was at liberty, how-

[20] Ep. Gilb. Fol. ii. pp. 119, 122.

ever, in the case of those whom he suspected, to require bail that they would do no harm while abroad to himself and his kingdom. The possessions of the Church of Canterbury he swore to restore as they were the year before the exile of St. Thomas; and he finally promised his favour and restitution to all clerics or laymen who had been deprived of them on account of the Saint.

The customs which had been introduced against the Church in his time he renounced on oath, promising not to demand their observance from the Bishops. That he did not mean to pledge himself to much by this clause appears from his own comment upon it, in a letter written by him[21] to the Bishop of Exeter previous to the meeting at Caen on the subsequent Tuesday: "These customs, I think, are very few, if any." That the renunciation of the customs of Clarendon practically meant little is proved by that which Dr. Stubbs, in his Constitutional History of England,[22] calls "the fact that, notwithstanding the storm that followed, they formed the groundwork of the later customary practice in all such matters."

The young King made oath that he would observe all that his father had sworn; and that, if he survived him, and the penance were unfulfilled, he would himself fulfil it. There were added some private penances of fasting and alms, which were not published. The Archbishop of

21 Ep. Jo. Sar. ii. p. 268.
22 The Constitutional History of England. By William Stubbs, M.A., Regius Professor of History. Oxford, 1875, vol. i. p. 466.

Tours and his suffragans were present at Caen on the Tuesday after the Ascension, when the King repeated the oaths before a still larger audience than at Avranches; and he affixed his seal to the document[23] which the Cardinals had drawn up and sealed.

When the King had given a free assent to all that was required of him, he added, "See, my lords Legates, my body is in your hands. Know for certain, that if you order me to go to Jerusalem or Rome or St. James, or whatever else you may command, I am prepared to obey." The Legates then led him outside the church door, where, kneeling, he was readmitted into the church, from which he had been interdicted.

[23] Ep. Gilb. Fol. ii. p. 119; Gerv. p. 239.

CHAPTER XXXIII.

PENANCE.

1171—1174.

The four murderers—coronation of Margaret, wife of the young
King—elections to the vacant sees—rebellion of the young
King—King Henry's visit to Canterbury—his penance at the
Saint's tomb—St. Thomas's sisters and their children—
victory over the King of Scots—St. Thomas's dream—Her-
bert taxes the King with the Saint's death—pilgrimage of
King Louis of France—John of Salisbury elected Bishop of
Chartres—Herbert of Bosham—Alexander Llewellyn—other
friends of the Saint.

THE four knights went back to St. Augustine's,
and then to Saltwood, when they had done their
worst. The ancient tradition says, that they
were afraid to return to the King, for whose sake
they had committed one of the greatest crimes
on record. They went to Knaresborough,[1] which
belonged to Hugh de Moreville, one of their
number. No one would speak with them, eat
with them, or drink with them: and the very
dogs refused to eat of the fragments of their food.
They remained there a year; and then went to
the Pope, to receive from him their penance, by
whom they were sent to Jerusalem. It was said,
that they all died soon; and that there was good
reason to hope that, by the intercession of the
holy Martyr, they died penitent. Such was the

[1] Hoved. f. 299.

tradition : a recent writer[2] has, however, carefully traced the facts of their subsequent history ; and he has shown that "the murderers, within the first two years of the murder, were living at Court on familiar terms with the King, and constantly joined him in the pleasures of the chase." They were unpunished, and their social position unaffected. Tracy showed the most contrition, and went on a pilgrimage to Rome and the Holy Land. He also, "for the love of God, and of his soul, and of the souls of his predecessors, and for the love of blessed Thomas the Archbishop and Martyr of venerable memory," founded a chaplaincy for the maintenance of a religious, who should say Mass in the Cathedral, where he had committed the murder.

The King of France had complained, that his daughter Margaret had not been crowned as well as her husband. By the advice of the Cardinal Legates, and under the authority of the Holy See, that ceremony was performed at Winchester, on the 27th of August, 1172, the anniversary of the death of the last Bishop of that city, by Rotrou, Archbishop of Rouen, with the assistance of Giles, Bishop of Evreux, and Geoffrey, Provost of Chartres, as well as of a few of the suffragans of Canterbury. King Louis had especially petitioned the Pope, that the Archbishop of York and the Bishops of London and Salisbury might not be allowed to be present.

These coronations, however, which were intended as a weapon against the Church, recoiled

[2] See Note K.

heavily upon the head of the King, who had pro-
moted them. The young King began to assert
his right to interfere, and claimed a power independent of his father. One of his first acts against
him was to protest[3] to the Prior of Canterbury
against the election of the new Archbishop being
performed without his leave. It must be acknowledged, that it is impossible to feel any sympathy
with the old King, who had behaved in this
election just as he used to do, showing how un-
stable his amendment hád been. The archiepiscopal see was vacant for two years and five
months: at first, the Prior was put off with fair
words, when he begged for a free election; the
King then tried to persuade him to name the
Bishop of Bayeux, a man the very opposite in
character to St. Thomas. This failing, the Prior
and Convent submitted three names to the King,
through Richard de Luci; of these Roger, Abbot
of Bec was elected, who, however, absolutely
refused to accept the dignity. The elections for
the vacant suffragan sees now took place; and
the names of those chosen to them prove that it
was still easier to obtain promotion by having
taken the King's part than by having suffered
with the Martyr in the late struggle. Most of
the new Bishops were the worst enemies of
St. Thomas. Richard of Ilchester, and Geoffrey
Ridel, who have been almost equally prominent
as the King's partisans, so that they have been
called more than once in this narrative "the two
Archdeacons," were raised respectively to the

3 Gerv. p. 245.

sees of Winchester and Ely. John of Oxford, the not less notorious Dean of Salisbury, was made Bishop of Norwich. Reginald Fitz-Jocelin the Lombard, Archdeacon of Salisbury, who was originally in the service of the Saint, but who had deserted[4] him to take part with the King, and who had advised Prince Henry's coronation, became Bishop of Bath. The choice of Robert Foliot, Archdeacon of Oxford, for the Cathedral of Hereford, shows the power of the recommendation of his cousin, Gilbert of London, towards whom he had evinced[5] sympathy. The remaining nominations were, John, Dean of Chichester, for that see, and Geoffrey, the son of King Henry and Rosamond Clifford, who was raised from the archdeaconry to the episcopal throne of Lincoln. He never was consecrated, and was ultimately obliged by the Pope to resign. Finally Richard, the Prior of Dover, was elected Archbishop of Canterbury; and on the young King protesting against the election, he went to Rome, where he was consecrated by the Pope.

The young King took up arms against his father; and his example was followed by his brother, who was afterwards the famous Richard Cœur de Lion. These rebellions led King Henry to write his famous letter to the Pope, which furnished so striking a contrast to many of the actions of his own life, and showed how submissive he could be to the Holy See, when to

---

[4] Herb. p. 525. Reginald was made Archbishop of Canterbury in 1191, and died on Christmas day of that year.

Ep. Gilb. Fol. ii. p. 215.

be so furthered his interests, and did not interfere
with his passions. "The realm of England is in
your jurisdiction," he writes[6] to Pope Alexander;
"and I am bound to you alone by feudal obligation : let England now experience what the
Pope can do; and since he does not use the arm
of flesh, let him defend the patrimony of Blessed
Peter with the sword of the Spirit."

The young King threw himself into the arms of
Louis of France and Philip Count of Flanders,
so that his father had enough to do in defending
his Norman dominions. Whilst thus engaged,
William, the King of Scotland, invaded England,[7]
successfully besieged Carlisle, and devastated all
the North. Many of the powerful barons had
declared for the young Henry, who, with the
Earl of Flanders, was waiting only for a fair
wind to invade England in force. Richard[8] of
Ilchester, the new Bishop of Winchester, was
sent over to the King at Bonneville, on St. John's
day, 1174, to request his return; and so many
messengers had preceded him, that the Normans
said, when they saw him, "The next thing the
English will send, will be the Tower of London."

King Henry immediately embarked, with his
Queen, Eleanor his son's Queen, Margaret, and

6 Op. Petri Blesensis, Mogunt. 1600, p. 245, ep. 136.   In the
Vatican Library, MS. 5221, f. 79.   A copy of this valuable
letter, supposed to be in Father Parsons' handwriting, on the
fly-leaf of the copy of Fox's *Book of Martyrs*, used by that
venerable missionary, is preserved in the library of the English
College, Rome, of which that Father was once Rector.

7 Hoved. f. 308.

8 Diceto, p. 576.

his son John, and his daughter Jane. The wind
was very high; and the King openly prayed that,
if his arrival in England would promote peace,
both in the clergy and people, and only in that
case, his voyage might be prosperous. He landed
at Southampton on Monday, the 8th of July; and
neglecting public business altogether, though it
was in so critical a state, he began his pilgrimage
to St. Thomas. He fasted strictly upon bread
and water; and avoiding the towns, but visiting
chapels and hospitals, he made the best of his
way with all speed to Canterbury. On the
Friday following,[9] he came in sight of the city,
at St. Nicholas's Chapel, Harbledown, about two
miles from Canterbury. He then leapt off his
horse, and went the rest of the way on foot.
From St. Dunstan's Church, outside the city, to
the tomb of the holy Martyr, he walked barefoot,
and dressed in the common woollen garments of a
pilgrim. His footsteps along the streets were
marked with the blood which flowed freely from
his feet. He went to the church-porch;[10] and after
praying there, he visited the scene of the martyrdom, which he watered with his tears. Having
said his *Confiteor* before the Bishops who were
present, he went with much reverence to the tomb,
where he remained in prayer a very long time.
The Bishop of London, after a while, spoke to
all who were present in the King's name, saying,
that he knew that his angry expressions had been
made the occasion of the death of the Martyr,
though he never intended them to be so; and

9 Gerv. p. 248.　　10 Grim, p. 445.

that he also felt that he had been very wrong in his persecution of him during his life; and that he had therefore come to make full satisfaction. He begged their prayers, and trusted that his humble penance would be acceptable to God and St. Thomas. He that day restored in full all the dignities and rights of that church, and whatever, either in that or other lands, in past times the church had freely held. He made an offering of four marks of pure gold, and a silk frontal for the shrine, and he offered a revenue of forty pounds as a gift to the Martyr, for lights to be kept burning at the tomb. He also promised to build a monastery in honour of St. Thomas. When the Bishop had finished saying what it must have been a great humiliation for Gilbert Foliot to utter,[11] the King ratified and confirmed it all.

His shoulders were then bared, and having bent his head down to one of the openings of the tomb, he received five strokes from each of the Prelates present, and then three from each of the monks, who exceeded the number of eighty. When this was over, and he had been absolved,

[11] Gilbert Foliot granted an Indulgence of twenty days, and a participation in all the prayers and merits of his Church, to such as should assist in building "the Hospital at Southwark, in London, in honour of God and of the Blessed Martyr Thomas" (Ep. Gilb. Fol. i. p. 318). And he calls him "Saint Thomas" in a deed in favour of Lady Cecilia Talbot (Ep. Gilb. Fol. ii. p. 50). More curious still, when Foliot was in extreme sickness, his friend Jocelin Bishop of Salisbury gave him some of the blood of St. Thomas and vowed in his name a pilgrimage to Canterbury on his recovery, which vow Gilbert soon after fulfilled, in very penitent guise (Benedict, p. 251).

he remained there on the bare ground for the whole night in watching and prayer, not suffering a carpet to be brought for him, nor even water to wash his bleeding and muddy feet.

This night a sister of St. Thomas appears in our history, almost for the first time. During the days of his worldly greatness we never hear of his relations, nor, if it had not been for his troubles, should we have known that he had any so nearly akin to him. Among those who were exiled for his sake, were his sister and her children; for the Pope thanked the monastery of Clairmarais for the hospitality they had received:[12] and St. Thomas wrote to his friends, Fulk, Dean of Rheims, Richard, Archbishop-elect of Syracuse, and Stephen, the Chancellor of Sicily, in behalf of his sister's sons.[13] And the Pope wrote a letter dated October 23, 1168, to the Archbishop-elect of Sens, asking him to give to Gilbert, one of the Saint's nephews who was going to study at Bologna, the assistance he had already given to Geoffrey, another nephew.[14] And now Rohesia,[15] a sister of the Saint, probably still with the sentence of banishment unrevoked, certainly in poverty, comes to beg "mercy" of the King, who was praying to her brother. He made a grant to her of a mill, the rent of which was ten marks a year, and which was enjoyed by her son John after her. The Saint had another sister named Mary,[16] of whom all that we know is, that she

12 *Materials*, v. p. 242.   13 Ep. S. Tho. i. pp. 245, 321, 395.
14 *Materials*, vi. p. 485.   15 Garnier, 81, 3.
16 Matth. Paris, p. 126.

was a nun, and that after the martyrdom she was Abbess of Barking.

After Matins and Lauds, King Henry visited the altars of the upper church, and the relics of the saints there buried. He then returned to the crypt, to the tomb of St. Thomas. As soon as it was light on the Saturday, he asked for Mass; and having assisted at it, as well as having tasted some water in which a drop of the Martyr's blood had been diluted, he returned to London, with[17] one of the phials of the same, which had already become[18] the mark of the pilgrim to St. Thomas, as the palm was of the pilgrimage to Jerusalem, and the scallop to St. James at Compostella.

The news soon came, that his son Henry, with the Count of Flanders, had abandoned their intention of invading England, when they found that the King was returning. Freed from this danger,[19] he had sent his forces against Earl Hugh Bigod, who had joined the insurrection at Norwich. He himself was detained, after his arrival from Canterbury, for a few days in London by sickness; when one midnight there was heard a violent knocking at the gate of the King's palace. In spite of the refusal of the porter to admit him, the messenger insisted, saying that he was the bearer of good news, which the King must hear that very night. At length, by his importunity, he gained admission into the King's very chamber.

---

[17] "Signum peregrinationis asportans " (Will. Cant. p. 489).
[18] *Materials*, iv. p. 142; Bened. p. 42; Gerv. p. 249.
[19] Will. Neubrig. *Rer. Anglic.* Antverp. 1567, p. 196.

Going up to the bed, he aroused the royal sleeper, who demanded, "Who are you?" "I am the boy of your faithful Ranulf de Glanville," was the answer; "and he has sent me to your Highness with good news." "Is our Ranulf well?" asked the King. "My lord is well," he replied; "and he has taken prisoner your enemy the King of the Scots at Richmond." The King was stupefied by the news, and said, "Tell me again." After hearing the same report, he said, "Have you any letters?" On these being presented, the King glanced at them; and leaping from the bed, with his eyes wet with tears, gave thanks to God and St. Thomas. On the very Saturday[20] on which the King left Canterbury, and at the hour at which he was hearing Mass at the tomb of St. Thomas, Alnwick Castle had been taken, and the King of Scotland made prisoner. Within three weeks of the pilgrimage and penance of the King, all the rebellions were quelled, and peace was restored[21] throughout England.

The King had made his pilgrimage in consequence of a dream,[22] that he had no other way of obtaining peace but by a reconciliation with the holy Martyr. St. Thomas had himself had a vision on the subject, which he had thus related to Herbert of Bosham[23] during their exile. "I thought I stood," said the Saint, "on a very high mountain, and the King was in the plain beneath; when on a sudden I saw flying towards him all manner of birds of prey, which with their beaks

[20] So the King himself told Herbert of Bosham, p. 547.
[21] Gerv. p. 249.   [22] Grim, p. 445.   [23] Herb. p. 548.

and talons attacked him violently, and tore his
royal robes off him, leaving him half-stripped.
There was a dark precipice behind him which he
did not see, and towards which he was approaching as he was driven backwards by the onset of
the birds of prey. When he was in this strait,
one of the courtiers, whom the King had trusted,
and advanced to high places, turned his hand
against him, tried to tear from him the rags the
birds had spared, and to urge him over the precipice. The thought then came over me of all
our old friendship; and coming down from my
high mountain-top, as it seemed to me, in the
twinkling of an eye, his peril and my compassion
giving me wings, I was by his side. I had, I
know not how, a lance· in my hand, and I
scattered the birds of prey; and clad the King
in his royal robes once more, chiding the while
the courtier who had shown such ingratitude,
saying that of him, at least, the King had not
merited such treatment." St. Thomas told the
name of the courtier; but Herbert did not
publish it, as he was still alive when he wrote.
The Saint's brief commentary on his vision was,
that he yet should help Henry in some of his
troubles. When Herbert related this story to
the King in after years, he was very urgent to
know the name of the courtier; but Herbert
refused to tell him.

In another private conversation Herbert,[24] with
his characteristic boldness, told him that the
death of his sainted master was "for him and

[24] Herb. p. 542.

by him." The King quietly replied, without any signs of anger, "Your *for* I sorrowfully grant, but your *by* I boldly deny." We say, with Herbert, that on this matter "God, and God only, knows the truth." We now part from a King, whose passions were so ungovernable and produced such frightful effects, whose deliberate policy was the servitude of the Church, and whose penances were so striking and at the time probably sincere, though it is to be feared that his amendment was never of long duration.

A few years later, another royal pilgrim came to the tomb of St. Thomas; but without the feelings of remorse which had made the visit we have last related so penitential. In 1179, Philip,[25] the son of Louis VII. of France, then fifteen years old, fell ill, and a vision admonished the father that by the prayers of St. Thomas he should recover. He accordingly undertook this pilgrimage on his son's behalf, in spite of the danger of placing himself in the power of the King of England, with whom he was constantly at variance. On Wednesday, the 22nd of August, he landed at Dover, where he was met by Henry, who accompanied him to Canterbury. They travelled on horseback by night, in the course of which journey they witnessed an eclipse of the moon. They were received by the Archbishop of Canterbury, and a large assembly of prelates and clergy, with much honour; and the French monarch spent a night at the tomb of the Saint, where he made an offering of a magnificent chalice of gold, and

[25] Hoved. f. 338; Diceto, p. 605; Gerv. p. 1467.

DD

a hundred measures of wine, to be delivered annually cost free. Before leaving, he petitioned the Chapter to be admitted into their fraternity; and he carried away with him the patent which conferred upon him what he had asked. On his return to France, on the following Sunday, he found that his son Philip had perfectly recovered.

Before we return to the sacred relics of St. Thomas, we must relate in a few words the little that we know of what happened to his faithful companions. John of Salisbury, whom St. Thomas had found in the service of the church of Canterbury, having been recommended to Archbishop Theobald by the glorious St. Bernard,[26] and who had been the Saint's counsellor and friend in good report and evil report, at home and in exile, in life and in death, was elected Bishop in 1176 by the Chapter of Chartres, through their devotion to St. Thomas. On the 22nd of July,[27] the dean, precentor, and several of the clergy, came to Canterbury to announce their choice; and the Bishop-elect was conducted to the altar of the church in which he had seen his master die, for the *Te Deum* to be sung for joy. King Louis wrote[28] to beg his acquiescence, and to say that the Archbishop of Sens was as anxious as himself.

26. Ep. ccclxxxiii. ed. Horst.

27. He had written his very elegant Life of St. Thomas before this time; for Peter of Blois, Archdeacon of Bath, after congratulating him on being made Bishop, says, that by the Archbishop's orders he would certainly himself have written the Saint's life, if it had not been already so beautifully done by John of Salisbury (Pet. Bles. ep. 114, p. 204).

28. Ep. Jo. Sar. ii. p, 291.

The devotion of John of Salisbury to St. Thomas was shown by his prefixing to every act of his episcopate, and to every letter he wrote, his title as, " John, by the Divine condescension and the merits of St. Thomas, humble minister of the church of Chartres." He died on the 25th of October, 1180.

Herbert of Bosham had been sent by St. Thomas to King Louis and the Archbishop of Sens, and he had left him on the Sunday night before his martyrdom. He remained abroad, when he heard of what had happened, for some time. To his pen is attributed the letter[29] which the Archbishop of Sens wrote to the Pope, to pray that the King might be punished as the cause of the Martyr's death. He wrote to Pope Alexander himself some time afterwards, to complain that an oath was required of him, before he could return to England, to the effect that he would not leave the realm without the King's licence, nor send letters beyond the sea ; which oath, he said, John of Salisbury and Gunter had taken, but his conscience would not permit him to take. The Pope wrote him a very kind letter in reply, recommending him to the intercession of the Legates with the King, and calling him " a special and devout son of the Church." After his return to England, and after the interviews with the King which we have mentioned, in which it is plain that he was quite restored to favour, he lived a long time, occupying himself in writing the life of St. Thomas, which was not finished

[29] Ep. S. Tho. ii. p 160.

until the Pontificate of Pope Urban III., fifteen years after the Saint's martyrdom. He complains sadly of the neglect he suffered at the hands of the Bishops, who, he says, "worship the Saint's dead relics, but despise his living ones." He says, that the Saint once appeared to him, and told him that the verse of the Psalms which he must ever bear in mind was, "Redeem me from the calumnies of men, that I may keep Thy commandments." Though the year of his death is unknown, we know the day on which it occurred; for his *obit* was kept on the 22nd of November, by the Christ Church monks, who had given him the privilege of fraternity with their Order, and therefore a share in their prayers.[30] By a curious mistake, he has been confounded by many writers with Lombard of Piacenza, who was Cardinal Archbishop of Benevento, so that he appears in some of the catalogues of English Cardinals. The author of this mistake is Christian Wolf, commonly called Lupus, who published in 1682 the Life[31] and Correspondence of St. Thomas from the Vatican MS., which Cardinal Baronius had used.

There are very few others of those who were with St. Thomas of whom there is anything to tell. Those only received promotion who had not been remarkable for their zeal in the cause of the Saint. Excepting, indeed, his faithful crossbearer, Alexander Llewellyn, who was, with

30 10 *Kal. Dec. Obiit Magister Herebertus de Boscham, frater noster.* Necrology of Christ Church, Dart's *Canterbury*, App. p. xxxiii.

31 *Epistolæ et Vita S. Thomæ*, two vols. 4to, Brux. 1682; i. pp. 157, 162.

Herbert, the bearer of his last letter to the Pope.
He seems to have become Archdeacon of Bangor,
and this we learn from Giraldus Cambrensis, his
fellow-countryman, who would probably have had
better opportunities of knowing of this promotion
than Herbert, whose intercourse with Alexander
probably ended when the tie that bound them in
their master's service was broken.[32]

Gerard Pucelle, who, though a friend of St.
Thomas, had been dangerously near schism in
the beginning of the exile, and who accepted the
King's terms before its close, was made Bishop
of Coventry. Hugh de Nunant, Archdeacon of
Lisieux, who appeared in the Saint's train at
Northampton, but who was one of the King's
ambassadors to the Pope after the martyrdom,
was the successor of Gerard Pucelle in that see.
Gilbert de Glanville became Bishop of Rochester
after the death of Walter, Archbishop Theobald's
brother. He was sent by the holy Martyr to the
Pope with his last letter; but he had been a very
short time in his service. It is worthy of remark,
that John of Salisbury is the only one of the
Saint's prominent adherents who became a
Bishop, and that his see was in France, in the
very province of Sens in which they had spent
their exile.

[32] Giraldus, *De Instructione Principum.* Anglia Christiana
Society, 1846, ed. Brewer, p. 186.

CHAPTER XXXIV.

MIRACLES.

1170 – 1185.

The first miracle—Prior Odo's report: cures of William de Capella, William Belet, Huelina of London, Brithiva of Canterbury, William of London, an anchoret, a boy of fifteen —appearances of the Saint—Benedict's vision—story of the Patriarch of Jerusalem—Edward Grim's arm—John of Salisbury's account—St. Edmund and St. Thomas—Cure at Chartres.

THE rapidity with which miracles followed upon the martyrdom is as remarkable as their number. The first[1] was the case of a paralytic woman in Canterbury. Her husband was present at the martyrdom, and brought home, as all the faithful did that night, some linen dipped in the holy blood. When she had heard his account of the constancy of the martyr, and saw the stain of his blood, she was moved with so lively a faith, that she begged it might be washed, that water might be given her to drink in which it had been dipped. This was done; and she was immediately cured. The fame of this miraculous cure caused every one who came to set the highest value on the possession of some of the martyr's blood mingled with water. According to Fitzstephen, it was this that gave rise to the little leaden phials which

[1] Fitzstephen, p. 149. This miracle is not mentioned by William or Benedict.

have been already mentioned as the distinguishing
mark of a Canterbury pilgrim.

Odo the Prior sent Philip Count of Flanders a
report[2] of some of the miracles. The following
sentence occurs in his letter, which certainly
renders his testimony very trustworthy: "It is
said that some lepers also have been healed; but
I do not say so, because I have not seen them
since they left us; though some have told me
that they were much better as they were going
away." He says that, on the third day after the
martyrdom, that is, the Thursday in that week,
December 31, 1170, Emma, the wife of Robert
of St. Andrew, a soldier in Sussex, who was sick
and blind, when she heard the account of the
martyrdom, invoked the Saint; and before half
an hour had passed, she had received her sight,
and in a few days was perfectly well. This is
also told by Grim and Benedict.

On Friday night, a priest of London, named
William de Capella, who had lost his speech,
was warned that he should go to the tomb of
St. Thomas, and he should be there healed by a
drop of the martyr's blood. He did so, and was
cured accordingly. As speaking in favour of
St. Thomas had been publicly prohibited, even
by proclamation, probably by the De Brocs, this
priest was very cautious in mentioning his cure.

William Belet, a soldier, of Ainesburne in
Berkshire, was suffering from an arm and hand
which were enormously swelled. On the Sunday after the martyrdom, as soon as he heard

[2] Martene, *Vet. Scriptor.* Paris, 1724, i. p. 882 b.

what had happened, he immediately invoked the Saint, praying that he might be restored to health. The following night he slept soundly, which he had not done for some time before; and when he woke he was perfectly well, without any pain, the swelling having disappeared.

On the Saturday, Huelina the daughter of Aaliza of London, a child of sixteen, was cured of a disease in the head that she had had since she was five years old. This was at Gloucester, and the cure happened on the day on which the news of the martyrdom became known there, the mother of the child making a vow in her child's name to visit the tomb of the Saint.

On Monday, the 4th of January, a poor blind woman of Canterbury, named Brithiva, entered a neighbouring hospice and asked for some thing that had belonged to the martyr. A cloth was given her that was red with his blood. She applied it to her eyes and received her sight.

On the following day William, a priest of London, who had been rendered speechless by paralysis on St. Stephen's day, was warned to go to Canterbury, and that there he would be cured by a drop of the martyr's blood. On the octave day of the martyrdom he came, and obtained leave to spend the night in prayer at the tomb. A drop of the blood was given him, and some water to drink which was sanctified by a slight admixture of the martyr's blood. The priest was cured of his paralysis, and this is said by Benedict to be the beginning of the use of water thus hallowed.

A pious woman[3] who lived an anchoretical life, who had never learnt to read or write, and who knew no Latin, except some Psalms, the *Pater noster*, and the *Credo*, was very sorrowful day and night on account of the martyrdom which had just happened. Sometimes she was favoured with ecstasies; and one day she sent to the monks of Canterbury a paper on which were written these words, which, she said, a very beautiful lady had spoken to her: *Noli flere pro Archiepiscopo: caput ejus in gremio Filii mei requiescit.* "Weep not for the Archbishop; his head rests in the bosom of my Son."

A boy of fifteen years of age, who had been blind from his birth, received his sight at the tomb of the Saint. This is related by the Prior Odo, who thus concludes his letter: "There are others who were blind, deaf, dumb, lame, contracted, and suffering from other infirmities, who have been cured by the merits of St. Thomas, but which I cannot now touch upon, however briefly. The number of those who have been cured of fevers is without end."

The Saint appeared to some persons, with the faint graceful line of blood from his right temple across the nose to the left cheek; and those who thus saw him described this mark as accurately as if they had seen his body. To others he appeared showing them that he was alive, and that his wounds had left but scars. This must have happened very soon, for it is mentioned in the letter of the Archbishop of Sens to the Pope.

[3] Fitzstephen, p. 151.

On the night of the martyrdom, one of the Saint's household saw him in his pontifical vestments going up the altar-steps, as if to say Mass; seeing the same thing on the second and on the third night, he said to him, "My lord, art thou not dead?" The Saint answered, "I died; but I am alive." ·Then said he, "If thou art truly alive and among the martyrs, why dost thou not show thyself to the world?" The Saint replied, "I carry a light; but it is not seen for the cloud which is interposed."

The De Broc family made every effort in the beginning to check the honour which was paid to St. Thomas; so that these accounts were whispered in secret. But the fame of cures and other miracles increased so fast, and the concourse of people became so great, that they were obliged to give up the vain attempt of checking the devotion, and were forced to say, "All England is gone after him." When the doors of the crypt, which had been fastened when he was first buried, were opened at Easter, miracles increased so fast, that two volumes[4] containing the account of them were kept at Canterbury. One of these was compiled by Benedict, who was afterwards Prior of Christ Church, and ultimately Abbot of Peterborough, whose contribution to our knowledge of the martyrdom is particularly valuable. Benedict was succeeded, as Chronicler of the miracles, by William, like himself a monk of Canterbury. The collection made by him is an independent work, though in some instances he and Benedict

4 Gerv. p. 230.

both relate the same miracle. William's work, like Benedict's, grew as time went on, for Benedict's was at last divided into five books, and William's into six. William also wrote a life and passion of St. Thomas, much fuller than Benedict's, we may safely say, though of the latter we have only fragments remaining.

The King had entertained[5] a great indignation against Benedict before he was made Prior. When in that office, he was obliged to go to him on some of the affairs of the Church; but his threats made him fear to go into his presence. One night, after a day when Benedict had been insulted by the King and his officials, his Majesty had a dream, which produced such an effect upon him, that he declared that he would not for any sum of money suffer the agony of such a dream again. He dreamt that he was crossing a very high bridge over a deep and rapid stream, when the plank on which his foot was gave way, and he fell through the bridge, to which he clung with desperation. The place, he thought, was lonely, and his strength was fast failing him; when, thinking all human assistance hopeless, he invoked the sacred names of Jesus and Mary and his patron saints. Then he thought that he added, "Help me, O Martyr of Christ; St. Thomas, assist me. Do not remember the injuries of late; for in the beginning I loved you above every one." He had hardly ended the words, when he imagined that Benedict came to him, and said, "The holy Archbishop, whom you

5 Grim, p. 448.

have invoked in faith, has sent me to you;" and so saying, he rescued him. The King awoke; but he could sleep no more; and his dream had so shaken him, that it was past midday before he could rise. When the Prior came, Henry told him his dream; and he returned as hearty thanks to St. Thomas as if he had been really preserved from that death. The narrator says that, though it was but a dream, it had this reality about it, that the King received Benedict into favour, and gave him whatever he chose to ask.

On the 28th of January, 1185, Heraclius, the Patriarch of Jerusalem, visited Canterbury. While in England he told the following story to Herbert of Bosham, who has related it,[6] and who must have written it almost as soon as it was told him: A monk of a religious house in Palestine, who had lived a most holy life, was near his end on the day on which St. Thomas was martyred. His singular piety had endeared him to his Superior, who begged of him, with tears, that, if God permitted it, he would appear to him after death, and tell him of his state. The monk assented, and so died. A few days afterwards, in fulfilment of his promise, the Brother appeared to his Abbot, to tell him that he saw God, and that his soul was in Heaven. "And that you may be certain and have no doubt, know that, as soon as I left the body, I was borne up by angels and saw the Lord; when soon there came a great and eminent man with a procession, beyond expression wonderful, following him, surrounding

6 Herb. p. 514.

him, and leading him, such that no man could number it for the multitude of the Angels, the laudable number of Patriarchs and Prophets, the glorious choir of the Apostles, with the countless army of Martyrs in their purple, and Confessors in white. He stood before the Lord like a martyr, with his head all torn and the blood trickling, as it seemed, through the wounds. And the Lord said to him, ' Thomas, thus oughtest thou to enter the court of thy Lord. The glory that I have given to Peter, the same will I give to thee.' And the Lord took a golden crown, of wonderful size, and placed it on the torn and wounded head. Know, then, for certain, that Thomas, the great Bishop of Canterbury, has died in these days, and so is gone to God. Meanwhile note what I have told you, and mark the time; for before long the reports of those who come hither will prove these things to be true. And now, since I have told you of the death of this glorious Martyr which has taken place, henceforward you must not doubt of my salvation." The Abbot told every one what he had heard; and Heraclius affirmed to Herbert and to others, that he consequently knew of the martyrdom within a fortnight after it had happened, and that it was generally known throughout that country.

Edward Grim gives the following interesting account[7] of a miracle which the Saint wrought in

[7] From a MS. in the Bibliotheca Casanatense at the Dominican Convent of S. Maria sopra Minerva in Rome (lib. A. i. 21). It is a complete copy of the paper, of which a part has been published by Martene (*Thes. Nov. Anecd.* iii. p. 1737).

his behalf. It is the healing of the arm that was
broken by William de Tracy, when Grim held it
up to ward off the first blow from the head of
the Martyr, who did not lift a hand in his own
defence. The doctor had tried in vain for nearly
a year to set the broken bone; when one night
the venerable Martyr stood beside him, and,
taking hold of his arm, wrapped it in a wet linen
cloth, saying, "Go; you are healed." The cloth
was wetted with holy water and the Martyr's
blood, and, by the favour of God and St. Thomas,
the bones united and the arm healed. "A proof
of its healing," says Grim, "is the arm itself, the
hand of which has written these things for you
to read. And God has done many other things,"
he continues, "to prove His love for our blessed
Martyr: by cleansing the lepers, as we have ourselves seen; by putting devils to flight, by healing
the dropsical, the paralytic, the deaf, the dumb,
the blind, the lame, and those suffering from all
manner of sickness: in all of which things we are
awaiting the faithful testimony of the church of
Canterbury, in whose sight and knowledge all
these things are known to have been done."

John of Salisbury writes to the Bishop of
Poitiers to ask him whether he thought that they
could not, even before his canonization by the
Pope, treat him as a martyr in the Mass and
public prayers; or whether they ought to continue to pray for one whom God had honoured
by so many miracles: "For in the spot where
he suffered, and by the high altar where he was
placed before his burial, and at his tomb, para-

lytics are cured, the blind see, the deaf hear, the dumb speak, the lame walk, fevers are healed, men possessed by the devil are liberated, the sick of divers diseases are cured, those whom the devil makes to blaspheme are confounded." The monks of Canterbury could each day say, as one of them asserts, " We have seen wonderful things to-day."

From the vast number of accounts which might be here introduced, we have selected one or two others[8] on account of their connection with his successor St. Edmund. The Abbess of Lacoke was very ill of a fever. St. Edmund left her, after a visit, saying that he would send her a doctor who should cure her. He sent some relic of the blood of St. Thomas, and as soon as she had tasted it she recovered.

One day, before leaving England, St. Edmund saw St. Thomas in a vision; and, stooping down, he tried to kiss his feet. St. Thomas prevented him, drawing his foot away. When St. Edmund wept at this, St. Thomas said to him, " Why do you weep ? " He answered, " Because my lips are not worthy to touch your feet." Then said St. Thomas, " Weep not, for the time is coming when you shall kiss me on the face."

Another miracle, of which John of Salisbury when Bishop of Chartres was witness, must not be omitted. It is reported in a hitherto unpublished[9] letter by the Bishop, which is addressed

8 Martene, *Thes. Nov. Anecd.* iii. pp. 1798, 1812.

9 MS. Coll. Angl. Rom. fol. 40. This must have been between 1176, when John of Salisbury was made Bishop, and 1179, when, according to Gervase, Herlewin ceased to be Prior of Canterbury.

to Richard the Archbishop, Herlewin the Prior, Herbert the Archdeacon, and to the chapter, clergy, and people of Canterbury. Peter, a native of Chartres, and a servant of Count Theobald's, professed a disbelief in the sanctity and miracles of St. Thomas. One day he was at work cutting stones for St. Peter's monastery at Chartres, when, as he and his fellow-workmen were resting, the conversation turned upon St. Thomas. All spoke of the Saint with reverence but this man, who took a morsel of bread in his hand, and said, " Now, if St. Thomas can, let him choke me with this, or make it poison to me." The others beat their breasts, and made signs of the Cross in horror of the blasphemy. The poor man soon left them, and went home, stricken dumb. The neighbours flocked in when they heard of what had happened ; and, as he got rapidly worse and worse, they carried him, now half dead, into the Church of the Blessed Virgin, and laid him on the tomb of St. Leobin.[10] The report soon spread ; and from nine o'clock till Vespers the church was crowded. The Bishop, who tells the story, happened to be out of town ; but coming in in the evening, the poor man's mother and friends ran and, kneeling before him, begged his help and counsel. He went straight to the church, and there found the dumb man beating his breast and lifting up his hands and eyes to Heaven. The Bishop had taken some of the blood of St. Thomas with him to Chartres. He

[10] St. Leobin, Bishop of Chartres, whose feast, in the Roman Martyrology, is September 15.

now sent for it and some water. After praying before the relics, the Bishop gave him the reliquary to kiss, on which the man burst forth in a loud voice with the words, " St. Thomas, St. Thomas, have mercy on me ! " He then drank some water in which the reliquary and a knife of the Saint had been washed by the Bishop, when, on being quite restored, he vowed a pilgrimage to St. Thomas in penance for his blasphemy, and in thanksgiving for his cure. He was himself the bearer of John of Salisbury's letter relating these facts.

Not a single one of the stories in this chapter has been taken from either Benedict's book or William's, and there the matter is sufficient, not for another chapter merely, but for a volume. The narratives are interesting for the insight they give us into the manner of life and the spirit of devotion of the English people of those times. In this place we will refer but to one detail, as it shows us a common practice in the manner in which those who stood in need of St. Thomas's help, had recourse to him. There is frequent mention of the body or the affected part being measured, sometimes to offer an effigy or a silver thread of the length at the shrine, more commonly for the measure of a candle to be burnt there. The practice was so well understood, that a girl in danger is described as calling out, " Measure me to St. Thomas, measure me to St. Thomas," [11] meaning that a candle of that size was to be offered for her.

[11] Benedict, p. 265.

EE

CHAPTER XXXV.

HONOUR AND DISHONOUR.

1173, 1220, 1538.

Canonization of St. Thomas—the Bull—Council of Bishops—
Choir of Canterbury burnt and rebuilt—Translation of
St. Thomas—Cardinal Langton's sermon—the *Quadrilogue*—
the altar at the sword's point—the tomb—the Crown of
St. Thomas—the shrine—its description—its destruction—
St. Thomas tried by Henry VIII.—Bull of Paul III.—
Patronage of St. Thomas.

THE Pope deputed the Cardinals Albert and
Theodwin to examine the miracles, and to make
a report to him with a view to the Saint's canonization. They could not have been very long in
accumulating materials; for in their letter[1] to the
chapter authorising the reconciliation of the
Church before the first year was past, they say
that "God has shown how precious the Saint's
death was in His sight, and has illustrated his
venerable memory with so many miracles, that
the odour of his unguents is now spread through
the whole body of the Church, and his virtue is
commonly preached both in the East and West."
Accordingly, at Segni, on the 21st of February,
being Ash Wednesday, 1173, having taken counsel with the Cardinals and Bishops, the Pope
himself solemnly singing Mass, Alexander III.

[1] Ep. Gilb. Fol. ii. p. 121,

canonized St. Thomas of Canterbury as a martyr
for the cause of the Church of God.

The Bull[2] is remarkable for its praises of his
life as well as of his martyrdom. " He who is
glorious in His saints has glorified, after his
death, this His Saint, whose laudable life, shining
with great glory of merits, was at length con-
summated by the martyrdom of a glorious contest.
And although no one can doubt of his sanctity,
who attends to his praiseworthy conduct, and
considers his glorious passion ; yet our Saviour
and Redeemer wished to give brilliant proofs of
it by magnificent miracles, that so he, who has
borne want and perils for Christ with the constancy of insuperable virtue, may now be known
by all to have received the triumph of his labour
and of his contest in eternal blessedness." It
then relates how the Cardinal Legates had taken
accurate information, and had sent the report of
" numberless and great miracles." After an-
nouncing the canonization, the Bull orders the
festival of St. Thomas to be observed throughout
the world. This was sent to the Legates,[3] together with apostolic letters[4] to the chapter of

---

[2] *Redolet Anglia*, dated Segni, March 12, 1173. The Bull is in
the Roman Bullarium. A copy was addressed to the clergy and
people of England (Ep. St. Tho. ii. p. 75). St. Thomas was thus
canonized two years and three months after his death. We have
amongst the English Saints examples of canonizations performed
in the shortest and in the longest time after death. St. Edmund
of Canterbury was canonized within a year, and St. Osmund of
Salisbury was canonized after four hundred and seven years
(Bened. XIV. *De Canon. SS.* lib. ii. cap. liv. n. 7).

[3] Ep. Gilb. Fol. ii. p. 58.

[4] Ep. S. Tho. ii. p. 39.

Canterbury, which thus begin : " The whole body
of the faithful must rejoice at the wonders of that
holy and reverend man, Thomas your Archbishop;
but you must be filled with a fuller joy and exul-
tation, since you often with your own eyes look
upon his miracles, and your church has deserved
to be rendered illustrious by the possession of
his most holy body." The Pope also bids them,
on some fitting day, with a solemn procession
and concourse of clergy and people, place his
relics on the altar or in some fitting shrine, " and
try to gain by pious prayers his patronage with
God for the salvation of the faithful, and the
peace of the Universal Church." There is also
extant a letter[5] from Pope Alexander to the Bishop
of Aversa, in the kingdom of Naples, informing
him of the canonization, which the Pope says
had been done "after counsel taken with our
brethren, and after many petitions from Archbishops and Bishops;" and he bids him inform
the Bishops of the province, that they were to
observe the feast of the holy Martyr.

St. Thomas was canonized before his see was
filled; and Bartholomew, Bishop of Exeter, writes[6]
at once to thank the Pope for the canonization,
and to recommend to him Richard, the Archbishop-elect. On the 7th of July,[7] in the council
that was held at Westminster, in the chapel of
St. Catherine, for the election, the Bull of Canonization was read, and then a solemn *Te Deum*

5 Ep. S. Tho. ii. p. 88.
6 Ep. Jo. Sar. ii. p. 281.
7 Matth. Paris, p. 88.

was sung. The Bishops who had opposed him confessed their fault, and, in the name of them all, one Bishop sung the prayer, *Adesto, Domine*: "Hear, O Lord, our petitions; that we, who of our iniquity acknowledge ourselves to be guilty, may be freed by the intercession of blessed Thomas, Thy Bishop and Martyr."

On the 5th of September, 1174, the choir of Canterbury Cathedral was burnt, which had been built forty-four years previously by Prior Conrad in the time of St. Anselm. It was immediately rebuilt, and we are fortunate in having a minute description of the old choir as well as of the new from the pen of Gervase the chronicler, who was himself a monk of Christ Church. The architect first employed was William of Sens, and on his being disabled when he had built as far as the eastern transepts inclusively, he was succeeded by another William, an Englishman. To him we owe all that is east of the choir, that is to say, the chapel of the Blessed Trinity, with the beautiful apse that was called "the Crown of St. Thomas," and is still known as "Becket's Crown." The crypts beneath them he also built, the tomb where the body of St. Thomas lay being protected by woodwork. The new building extended considerably further eastward than the old. The site chosen for the shrine was the Saint's favourite chapel of the Blessed Trinity, so that it was immediately over the tomb in the crypt, or perhaps a few feet further to the east.

The Priors of Christ Church, Benedict who

recorded the martyrdom and miracles, and Alan[8] who collected the correspondence, were very anxious to fulfil the Pope's injunction respecting the translation of the relics. Indeed, a letter of Alan's, written probably in 1185, on the completion of the chapel and crown, proposes the following May for the solemnity. Several years however elapsed before it took place.

By the year 1220 every preparation had been made. Cardinal Stephen Langton was Archbishop of Canterbury, and he celebrated the translation with a worthy magnificence.[9] The new shrine was a gorgeous work of gold and silver, set with precious stones, supported on stonework. Such a multitude of persons attended, that it was supposed that so many had never been collected in one place in England before. Two years previously the Cardinal Archbishop had published an edict, declaring his intention, and he had collected from all his manors and possessions all that was possible for the entertainment of such vast numbers of persons. The youthful Henry III. was present, with Pandulf

8 According to Gervase, Alan became Abbot of Tewkesbury in June, 1186. He had been a Canon of Benevento, though his novitiate was passed at Canterbury.

9 "The expenses arising from this ceremony were so great to Stephen Langton, then Archbishop of Canterbury, that it left a debt upon this archbishopric which Boniface, his fourth successor, could hardly discharge. Besides other vast expenses of the sumptuous entertainment made in his palace, he provided at his own cost hay and oats, on the road between Canterbury and London, for the horses of all who came to the solemnity; and he caused several pipes and conduits to run with wine in several parts of the city" (Hasted, *Hist. of Canterbury*, 1801, ii. p. 337).

the Legate, the Archbishop of Rheims, nearly all the Bishops of the realm, and some of France, in number twenty-three, as well as the abbots, priors, earls, and barons, besides the clergy and people.[10] The summer time was doubtless chosen for the convenience of pilgrims, who would always wish to attend one of his festivals, and that of his martyrdom was in mid-winter. The 7th of July became thus the feast of his translation.

In the sermon[11] made by Cardinal Langton, probably on a recurrence of this solemnity, he says, that they purposely selected a Tuesday,[12] as the day of the week on which the Saint had been martyred: they had not, however, adverted to the fact that it was the fiftieth year since that event; and they were much struck by the coincidence that the translation of St. Thomas happened on the anniversary of the day on which Henry II. was buried. A life of the Saint was compiled from his various biographers, which is now well known under the name of the *Quadrilogue*, probably for this occasion, and by the direction

[10] Matth. Paris, p. 214; Martene, *Thes. Nov. Anecd.* iii. p. 703.

[11] *Ep. et Vita S. Thomæ*, ed. Lupus, p. 901.

[12] The Saint was born and baptized on a Tuesday; on a Tuesday he left Northampton; on a Tuesday he returned from Flanders for England, and on that day four weeks he was martyred (*Materials*, iii. p. 326; iv. p. 78). Herbert further says that it was on a Tuesday that he fled from England, but in this, as we have seen (*Supra*, p. 194), he was mistaken. In consequence of the number of memorable Tuesdays in the Saint's life, that day of the week was chosen as the fitting day for a Votive Mass in his honour. This is noted in the Rubrics of the Sarum Missal, and it is often mentioned; for instance, by the Black Prince in the foundation of his chantries (Stanley's *Canterbury*, 7th edit. p. 165).

of Cardinal Langton. William, who was then Prior of Canterbury, published the letters[13] of Pope Honorius III. by which he granted an Indulgence of forty days to all who should be present at the Translation or within the Octave, and subsequently another Indulgence, to be perpetually in force, of one year and forty days, to all who should come to visit the church on the feast or within a fortnight after it. The same Pope had previously invited[14] all the faithful to attend, in proper dispositions, on the solemn occasion. He then said, " The heavenly King, the Lord of Angels, has honoured in our time the realm of England more highly than others, and He has adorned the English nation with an especial prerogative; for while the world is in wickedness and the malice of men increasing, He has chosen from thence for Himself a man without spot, who priestlike, not only in a time of wrath was made a reconciliation,[15] but when invited to the heavenly banquet, merited to taste that chalice of passion which the Lord drank. Let, then, the happy church of Canterbury sing to the Lord a new song, the church whose altar the martyr Thomas has purpled with his precious blood."

The shrine, to which the relics of St. Thomas were now translated, became a place of pilgrimage, second only to the great sanctuaries of Rome, of Jerusalem, and perhaps of Compostella.

13 Rymer, *Fœdera*, i. p. 154, dated Jan. 26, 1219; Ep. Gilb. Fol. ii. pp. 118, 171, dated Dec. 18, 1221.

14 Gilb. Fol. ii. p. 116, dated Jan. 25, 1219.

15 Ecclus. xliv. 17.

Multitudes of pilgrims all the year round thronged to Canterbury, and that more especially on the two festivals of the Saint, on the 29th of December, the anniversary of his martyrdom, and, most of all, on the 7th of July, that of his translation. The jubilees of his death and of his translation were observed with the greatest solemnity for three centuries, 1520 being the last.

There were four places in the church that were visited by pilgrims out of devotion to St. Thomas, and there was, besides, the chapel of Our Lady Undercroft, which was one of the richest sanctuaries of the Blessed Virgin in England. The first of the altars of St. Thomas was the little wooden altar erected on the spot where he was martyred, called *ad punctum ensis*—"at the sword's point." It was placed against the wall between the steps leading to the crypt and the altar of St. Benedict; and space was provided in the transept, and pilgrims were enabled to see the little altar by the removal of the column that hid St. Thomas from the four knights as they first entered the church. This column had supported a chapel of St. Blaise over that of St. Benedict. To reach this altar and the Martyrdom conveniently, and to prevent crowds of pilgrims from being in one another's way, a passage which still exists was made under the steps leading from the nave to the choir, providing thus direct access to the northern transept from the southern. The altar "at the sword's point" was left untouched for centuries, and we can form a good idea to ourselves of the appearance of this simple little altar, as a panel representing it still exists in the middle of the south porch, over the doorway. The fragments [16] of Le Breton's sword are there represented as lying at the foot of the altar.

Secondly, there was the tomb in the crypt, in which the body of the Saint had rested for fifty years, where so many of the early miracles were wrought, and where Henry II. did his penance.   To reach this the pilgrims had to pass the splendid chapel of Our Lady Undercroft, the existing reredos and screens of which were erected about the year 1370.   In the crypt of the Trinity chapel, immediately under the Saint's shrine, was the marble sarcophagus, remaining just as it was when the Saint's bones were transferred from it to the iron coffer, which in 1220 was placed in the shrine above. This sarcophagus stood on solid masonry between the two slender columns that support the vaulting of the crypt, which alone now remain to mark the place. Over the tomb hung the shirt and drawers of haircloth, worn by the Saint at his death.   A part of the skull was kept here, showing the fatal wound, the

[16] Dean Stanley remarks that there is a similar representation of a broken sword in the seal of the Abbey of Aberbrothock.

silver reliquary that held it having an open part where the skull might be kissed.[17]

The other part of the head of the Saint was enclosed in a gold and silver bust adorned with jewels, which was exposed for veneration in the chapel east of the shrine, and this was the third place in the church were St. Thomas was venerated. Whether the chapel was called the Crown of St. Thomas because of its architectural position as the head and crown of the church, or whether it took its name from the head or crown of the Saint, is uncertain. But, though it has been questioned, there can be little doubt that there was an altar in Becket's Crown, and it is highly improbable that there was one in the crypt at the empty tomb. Both relics may well have been called the head, but the crown only was kept at an altar; and the Black Prince, by his will in 1376, left hangings "for the altar where my lord Saint Thomas lies, for the altar where the head is, and for the altar where the point of the sword is."[18] There is an entry in the Registers of Prior Henry of Eastry in 1314, "For ornamenting the crown of St. Thomas with gold, silver, and precious stones 115*l.* 12*s.*"[19] This would seem distinctly to indicate the reliquary made to receive the portion

[17] The skull of Charlemagne at Aix-la-Chapelle is enclosed in a reliquary answering to this description.

[18] *A servir devant l'autier ou monseignour Saint Thomas gist, et à l'autier la ou la teste est, et à l'autier la ou la poynte de l'espie est* (Stanley's *Canterbury*, 7th edit. p. 171).

[19] *Pro corona sancti Thome auro et argento et lapidibus preciosis ornanda cxv. li. xij.s. (Ibid.* p. 283).

of the head of the Saint that was cut off by
Le Breton's blow. The greatness of the sum
expended on the reliquary for the crown is shown
by another entry made at the same time. "For
a new cresting of gold for the shrine of St.
Thomas, 7*l.* 10*s.*"[20] The contrast clearly proves
the magnificence of the reliquary, for the cresting
that was placed on the shrine in the fourteenth
century must certainly have been sumptuous,
and yet it cost but a twentieth part of the sum
expended on the reliquary.

The altar on the western side of the shrine
in the chapel of the Blessed Trinity was that
which the Black Prince described as "the altar
where Monseignour Saint Thomas lies," and this
was the fourth and the most important of all
the places in the church that devotion to St.
Thomas induced the pilgrims to visit.

Each of the four places where the Saint was
venerated had its *Custos* or Guardian among the
officials of the monastery, to whom offerings
were consigned by the pilgrims. An entry still
exists in a Book of Accounts, showing the different offerings made at one time in these various
places :

"From the Guardian of the Crown of St.
    Thomas 40s.

From the Guardians of the Shrine of St.
    Thomas 30s.

Also from the Guardian of the Crown of St.
    Thomas 20s.

[20] *Item, pro nova crista auri feretrum S. Thomæ faciendum* [sic]
vii.li. x.s. (Dart's *Canterbury*, in the Appendix).

Also from the Guardian of the Tomb of Blessed
    Thomas 3s. 4d.

Also from the Guardian of the Martyrdom of
    St. Thomas 3s. 4d."[21]

This was in the thirtieth year of Henry VI.,
i.e. 1451. The relative greatness of the offerings
at the Crown seems to show that the Crown
that was second only to the Shrine must have
been the relic of "the part in which the martyr
suffered,"[22] which the Church has always regarded
as deserving of especial reverence.

Behind the high altar was a flight of steps,
now removed, that led up to the Trinity chapel,
where the Shrine was. Similar flights of steps
in the choir aisles still remain, furrowed by the
feet of many generations of pilgrims. Considerable portions of the well worn mosaic pavement
of the chapel also remain, as well as a Crescent
in the roof, brought probably as a trophy from
some Eastern fight. But of the Shrine there is
not now a vestige, though fortunately three
beautiful stained glass windows in the aisle that
once surrounded the Shrine, have escaped des-

----

[21] *Oblaciones cum obvencionibus.*
    De Custode Corone beati Thome xl.s.
    Denarii recepti pro vino conventus—
    Item, de Custodibus Feretri Sancti Thome xxx.s.
    Item, de Custode Corone Sancti Thome, xx.s.
    Item, de Custode Tumbe beati Thome, iij.s. iiij.d.
    Item, de Custode Martyrii Sancti Thome, iij.s. iiij.d. (*Ibid.*
        p. 283).
[22] *Insignes autem Reliquias S. R. C. declaravit esse caput, brachium,*
*crus, aut illam partem corporis in qua passus est Martyr modo sit
integra, et non parva, et legitime ab Ordinariis approbata* (Decree
prefixed to the Roman Breviary).

truction.   The Shrine was covered by a wooden
case or canopy, that, from time to time, was
drawn up with ropes.   Of the appearance of the
Shrine itself we can form some idea, partly from
the descriptions we have of it, and partly from
two representations that have happily come
down to us.

Of these the plainest, little more indeed than
an outline, is a pen-and-ink sketch among the
Cottonian Manuscripts[23] in the British Museum;
which, as it was drawn after the spoliation, seems
to represent, except as far as the finials are con-

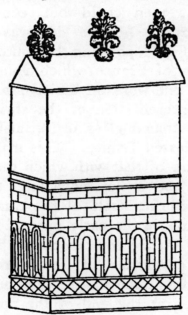

[23] Tib. E, viii. fol. 269.   Mr. George Austin says that "there
can be little doubt that it does not attempt to represent the
Shrine, but only the outside covering or case" (Stanley, p. 299).
But the finials are enough to show that this is not the covering.
These three finials, which are marked on the sketch as "silver
gilt, 60 and 80 ounces" respectively, were on the shrine itself.

cerned, its denuded state. The portion destroyed
by the fire that injured the Cottonian library in
1731 is made good in the woodcut. The sketch
is accompanied by the following description,
which shows how the sides were ornamented.

"Tem. Henr. VIII. All above the stone-work
was first of wood, jewels of gold set with stone,
covered with plates of gold, wrought upon with
gold wire, then again with jewels, gold as
brooches, images, angels, rings, ten or twelve
together, cramped with gold into the ground of
gold, the spoils of which filled two chests, such
as six or eight men could but convey one
out of the church. At one side was a stone
with an angel of gold pointing thereunto, offered
there by a King of France, which King Henry
put into a ring, and wore on his thumb."[24]

The other representation of the shrine is to
be seen in the stained glass in the aisle of the
chapel of the Blessed Trinity. This magnificent
glass is a portion of that with which the Shrine
was surrounded, and is not much later than the
erection of the Shrine itself, at the time of the
Saint's translation, in the early part of the thirteenth century. At the top of one of the lights,
Benedict, the chronicler of the miracles, is
represented asleep at the foot of the Shrine, and
from the opening at the end of the upper part
of the shrine, St. Thomas is leaning forward to
speak to him. When the figures are removed,
as well as the lines of the architecture of the

[24] The burnt parts of this description are supplied by Dean
Stanley from Dugdale and Stowe (Stanley, p. 232).

church behind the Shrine, the stained glass would represent the Shrine itself as in the accompanying woodcut.

In this the substructure differs from that of the Cottonian sketch, made three centuries afterwards, as here the slab on which the shrine rests is borne on six columns with lofty arches, while in the other representation the solid masonry has five little openings or windows at the sides and three at the ends. The stained glass gives purely fanciful architecture for the church in which the shrine stands; so that perhaps the artist may not have cared to give a faithful picture of the shrine which stood close by.

Whatever may have been the construction of the lower portion, the sketches and descriptions combine to show us that the shrine was of unrivalled magnificenee. Albert Archbishop of

Livonia, when writing the account[25] of the translation of St. Edmund at Pontigny, says that he
believes that there was not in the whole world
another shrine for value or beauty like that of
St. Thomas at Canterbury.   It is similarly described by all the writers who mention it, until
the time of Henry VIII.   A single instance will
be sufficient.   It is a description written by a
Venetian,[26] who visited it about the year 1500,
which was probably the time of its greatest
splendour.   "The tomb of St. Thomas the
Martyr, Archbishop of Canterbury, exceeds all
belief.   Notwithstanding its great size, it is all
covered with plates of pure gold; yet the gold
is scarcely seen, because it is covered with
various precious stones, as sapphires, balasses,
diamonds, rubies, and emeralds; and wherever the eye turns, something more beautiful
than the rest is observed.   Nor, in addition to
these natural beauties, is the skill of art wanting;
for in the midst of the gold are the most beautiful sculptured gems, both small and large, as
well as such as are in relief, as agates, onyxes,
cornelians, and cameos; and some cameos are
of such a size, that I am afraid to name it; but
every thing is far surpassed by a ruby, not larger
than a thumb nail,[27] which is fixed at the right of

[25] Martene, *Thes. Nov. Anecd.* iii. p. 1868.

[26] *A relation of England under Henry VII.*, published by the
Camden Society.

[27] "A carbuncle that shines at night, half the size of a hen's
egg," is the Bohemian Ambassador's description in 1446
(Stanley, p. 266).   This gem, which was called the "Regall of
France," is last mentioned as set in a collar, among the other

FF

the altar. The church is somewhat dark, and
particularly in the spot where the shrine is
placed; and when we went to see it, the sun
was near setting, and the weather was cloudy:
nevertheless, I saw that ruby as if I had it in
my hand. They say it was given by a King of
France."

The history of the Church has been a series
of undulations. Kings and nobles throw riches
into her bosom, and then these very riches allure
the covetous, and she is despoiled and becomes
poor; and then offerings are made to her again,
to become again in their turn the sacrilegious
booty of the rapacious. The shrine of St. Thomas
was not spared when the property of the Church
in England fell into lay hands; and St. Thomas
was himself so clearly her protector, that the
despoiler waged war against his very name. The
following is the account given by a lawyer[28] of
this parody of the forms of law:

" Henry VIII., when he wished to throw off
the authority of the Pope, thinking that as long
as the name of St. Thomas should remain in the
calendar men would be stimulated by his example to brave the ecclesiastical authority of the
Sovereign, instructed his Attorney-General to
file a *quo-warranto* information against him for
usurping the office of a saint, aud he was formally

jewels delivered to Queen Mary, March 10, 1554 (Nichols'
Erasmus, p. 224). If indeed this be the same "Regall of
France," for Mary's seems to have been a diamond, and it is
hard to imagine how a diamond could have been taken for a
ruby or carbuncle.

[28] Lord Campbell's *Lives of the Chancellors*, vol. i. p. 95.

cited to appear in court to answer the charge.
Judgment of *ouster* would have passed against
him by default, had not the King, to show his
impartiality and great regard for the due administration of justice, assigned him counsel at the
public expense. The cause being called, and the
Attorney-General and the advocate for the accused being fully heard, with such proofs as were
offered on both sides, sentence was pronounced,
that 'Thomas, some time Archbishop of Canterbury, had been guilty of contumacy, treason, and
rebellion; that his bones should be publicly burnt,
to admonish the living of their duty by the
punishment of the dead; and that the offerings
made at his shrine should be forfeited to the
Crown.'[29]   A proclamation followed, stating that,
'forasmuch as it now clearly appeared that
Thomas Becket had been killed in a riot excited
by his own obstinacy and intemperate language,
and had been afterwards canonized by the Bishop
of Rome as the champion of his usurped authority, the King's Majesty thought it expedient to
declare to his loving subjects that he was no
saint, but rather a rebel and traitor to his prince,
and therefore strictly charged and commanded

[29] Doubt has been thrown on this narrative by Mr. Gough
Nichols, in his *Erasmus*, p. 232, but though there is some
confusion in the dates, there does not seem to be sufficient
reason for denying the positive statements of Sanders and
Pollini, and the contemporary Bull of Pope Paul III. The
arguments for and against are given by Dean Stanley, p. 251,
note 2. Stowe asserts that not only the head but all the bones
of the Saint were burnt, and this is strong evidence in favour of
the mock trial, for those who deny the trial, deny the burning
of the relics.

that he should not be esteemed or called a saint ;
that all images and pictures of him should be
destroyed, the festivals in his honour be abolished,
and his name and remembrance be erased out of
all books, under pain of his Majesty's indignation,
and imprisonment at his Grace's pleasure.'"

This did not pass unnoticed in the Rome for
which St. Thomas lived and died. Pope Paul III.
in a Bull[30] against Henry VIII. recounting his
crimes, said : "After he had, for the greater
contempt of religion, summoned St. Thomas,
the Archbishop of Canterbury into court, and
caused him to be condemned as contumacious,
and to be declared a traitor, he has ordered
his bones, which in the realm of England, for
the numberless miracles there wrought by Almighty God, were kept in a golden shrine at
Canterbury, to be disinterred and burnt, and
the ashes to be scattered to the winds: thus far
surpassing the cruelty of all nations; for even
in war conquerors do not rage against the bodies
of the dead. And in addition to this, he has
usurped possession of all the offerings given by
the liberality of different kings, some of them of
England, and of other princes, which were attached to the shrine, and were of immense value;
and with all this, he thinks he has done religion
no injury."

Such events as these have placed St. Thomas
in a peculiar position among the saints, as the
protector of every effort to resist the spirit of
King Henry VIII. and his successors in all their

30 Bulla *Cum Redemptor*, Dec. 17, 1538.

attempts to exercise an ecclesiastical jurisdiction over the Church.

The English Hospital in Rome was under his invocation, and the College which has succeeded to it is under the same august patronage; and its members, in common with their brethren of the English clergy secular and regular, have so far trodden in his footsteps, that Cardinal Baronius is naturally led, when speaking of the Saint, to praise the martyrs who have followed him in England.

The following fact shows the devotion towards this great Saint which was entertained in the Colleges, whence the "Seminary priests," as Missionaries Apostolic were called, proceeded. In 1599, the Cardinals Borghese and Farnese received from Pope Clement VIII. power over all the English Seminaries, and amongst other matters, to grant two festivals to each of them with the privileges of the feasts of the Blessed Trinity and St. Thomas, as celebrated in the English College at Rome. It is remarkable that the five Seminaries in different parts of Europe, choosing in the second place various great English saints, unanimously named in the first instance St. Thomas of Canterbury.

Northampton, where St. Thomas fought a good fight, has in our time been made a Bishop's see by the Apostolic authority in whose behalf he fought, and the new diocese[31] has been very

---

[31] In the diocese of Northampton St. Thomas is commemorated by a proper antiphon and versicle, approved Jan. 26, 1852.
Ant. Ego sum Pastor bonus, et cognosco oves meas, et

fitly placed under his patronage. Our Saint is usually called the Protector of the English secular clergy; and though no document of the Holy See is extant expressly ordaining this, he has been mentioned as such in recent rescripts. But the most venerable body of whom St. Thomas is the patron is the Sacred Congregation of Ecclesiastical Immunities, which assembles every year on his festival and at his altar, and at whose petition Pope Gregory XVI. made his feast of double rite for the States of the Church. At the instance of the Cardinal Duke of York, Pope Benedict XIV. (Jan. 8, 1749) gave leave for all ecclesiastics of the English nation, wherever they might be living, to keep his festival as a double of the second class with an octave; and previously to these Decrees Pope Urban VIII. (March 23, 1641) had granted to all English people the power of celebrating the octave, notwithstanding its occurrence at a season when, by the ordinary rubrics, it would be forbidden. Finally, Pope Pius IX. (June 3, 1857), confirmed the celebration of the festival as a double of the first class with an octave, the rite with which it has been observed in England from time immemorial.

cognoscunt me meæ, et animam meam pono pro ovibus meis.

V. In patientia vestra.

R. Possidebitis animas vestras.

Deus pro cujus Ecclesia, as on the feast of the Saint.

CHAPTER XXXVI.

LEGENDS.

The Saracen Princess—St. Mark's day at Sens—the water made wine—the chasuble turning red—the Mass of a Martyr—the eagle and the oil-cruet—the tails of the people of Stroud—St. Thomas's well—the nightingales at Oxford—our Lady's little chasuble—the Seven Joys of our Lady.

AN account of St. Thomas of Canterbury which should make no mention of the legends respecting him would be very incomplete. The first that would naturally deserve a place in this chapter is the account of the Saracen princess, who was said to have been the mother of the Saint. As this, however, has been already given, we may pass on; adding merely that it naturally became a favourite subject for ballads, in the hands of whose writers the story slightly changed its shape. Gilbert is there said to have been urged to marry after his return to England; and he having at length consented, though grievously against his will, the Saracen lady, who had procured his freedom when a captive in the East, arrived in her wanderings at his house on the very morning of the wedding.

The following extracts are taken from an exceedingly rare old *Lyfe of Saynt Thomas of Caunturbury*, printed by Rycharde Pynson. The spelling alone has been changed. It begins by saying that St. Thomas was born in the place where now standeth the church called St. Thomas of Akers. When forty-four, "he was sacred and stalled, and became an holy man, suddenly changed into a new man, doing great penance, as in wearing hair with knots, and a breech of the same down to the knees. Under his habit he wore the habit of a monk, and outward a clerk; and did great abstinence, making his body lean and his soul fat."

We now make a leap to Sens. "And anon, after St. Thomas came to come on St. Mark's day at afternoon. And when his caterer should have brought fish for his dinner, because it was a fasting day, he could get none for no money, and came and told his lord St. Thomas so; and he bade him buy such as he could get. And then he bought flesh, and made it ready for their dinner, and St. Thomas was served with a capon roasted, and his man with boiled meat. And so it was that the Pope heard that he was come, and sent a Cardinal to welcome him; and he found him at his dinner eating flesh, which anon returned and told to the Pope how he was not so perfect a man as he had supposed; for, contrary to the rule of the Church, he eateth this day flesh. The Pope would not believe him, but sent another Cardinal, which, for more evidence, took the leg of the capon in his kerchief, and affirmed the same, and opened his kerchief before the Pope; and he found the leg turned into a fish called a carp. And when the Pope saw it, he said they were not true men to say such things of this good Bishop; they said faithfully that it was flesh that he eat. And after this, St. Thomas came to the Pope, and did his reverence and obedience; whom the Pope welcomed, and after certain communications, he demanded him what meat that he had eaten, and said, Flesh, as ye have heard before, because he could find no fish, and very need compelled him thereto. Then the Pope understood of the miracle that the capon's leg was turned into a carp, of his goodness granted to him and to all them of the diocese of Canterbury license to eat flesh ever after on St. Mark's day when it falleth on a fish-day, and pardon withal; which is kept and accustomed."

If this was "kept and accustomed," it is singular that our Catholic ancestors should have lost the tradition, for amongst English Catholics St. Mark has been a day of abstinence until lately. By a Rescript of July 8, 1781, Pope Pius VI. abrogated the fast which, in consequence of an immemorial tradition, was kept in England on all the Fridays of the year, with the exception of the Paschal season. The Pope then refused to dispense with the abstinence on St. Mark's day and the three Rogation days, which the Vicars Apostolic had asked at the same time, but this was granted by Pope Pius VIII. by a Rescript dated May 29, 1830.

Another legend, that deserves to be classed with that of the carp, is narrated by Roger Hoveden the chronicler. "One day the Archbishop was sitting at the table of Pope Alexander, when his domestic placed before him a bowl of water. The Pope tasted it, and found it to be an excellent wine, and saying, 'I thought you drank water,' put it back before the Archbishop, when straightway the wine returned to its former taste of water." It is a pretty story, but it must be confessed that St. Thomas was not a water-drinker. "Being of a very chilly temperament," says ·Herbert of Bosham,[1] "water did not agree with him, so that he never drank it, and but seldom beer, but he always took wine, though in great moderation and with all sobriety." The testimony of Garnier de Pont St. Maxence is to the same effect.[2]

> Le meillur vin useit que il poeit trover ;
> Mès pur le freit ventreil, eschaffé le beveit ;
> Kar le ventreil aveit et le cors forment freit.
> Gimgibre et mult girofre, pur eschalfer, mangeit,
> Ne pur quant tut adès l'eve od le vin mesleit.

Another version of the story is given by a German chronicler[3] early in the thirteenth century. "One day the Apostolic [*i.e.*, the Pope] was sitting with the Bishop, he chanced to be thirsty, and he said to the boy who was waiting on him, 'Bring me water from the fountain to drink.' When it was brought, the Apostolic said to the Bishop, 'Bless it and drink.' He blessed it and it was changed into wine, and when he had tasted, he gave it to the Apostolic. When the Apostolic perceived that it was wine, he called the boy aside and said, 'What did you

[1] Herbert, p. 235.   [2] Edit. Hippeau, p. 136.
[3] Arnold of Lubeck, *Materials*, ii. p. 291.

bring me ?' The boy answered, 'Water.' Then said he, 'Bring me some more of the same.' And when he had done so a second time, the Apostolic again said to the Bishop, 'Brother, bless it and drink.' And he, not being aware that virtue had gone out of him, and thinking that wine had been purposely brought, simply blessed it and it was again changed into wine, which he drank and gave to the Apostolic. And he not yet believing, and thinking that a mistake had been made, a third time secretly asked for water, and the third time it was changed into wine. Then the Apostolic was afraid, perceiving that the man was a saint and that the virtue of God was manifested in him."

We have not, however, yet finished with Richard Pynson's *Lyfe*, so to it we return.

"And after, St. Thomas said Mass before the Pope in a white chasuble; and after Mass he said to the Pope, that he knew by revelation that he should die for the right of Holy Church, and when it should fall, the chasuble should be turned from white to red."

We now pass to Canterbury. "On Christmas Day, St. Thomas made a sermon at Canterbury in his own church, and weeping, prayed the people to pray for him; for he knew well his time was nigh, and there executed the sentence on them that were against the right of Holy Church. And that same day, as the King sat at meat, all the bread that they handled waxed anon mouldy and hoar, that no man might eat of it, and the bread that they touched not was fair and good for to eat.   And these four knights aforesaid came to Canterbury on the Wednesday in Christmas week, about evensong time."

"Then said Sir Reynold, 'But if thou assoil the King and us under standing the curse, it shall cost thee thy life.'   And St. Thomas said, 'Thou knowest well enough that the King and I were accorded on Mary Magdalen's day, and that this curse should go forth on them that had offended the Church.'   Then one of the knights smote him as he kneeled before the altar, on the head; and one Sir Edward Grim, that was his crozier, put forth his arm with the cross to bear off the stroke, and the stroke smote the cross in sunder, and his arm almost off, wherefore he fled for fear, and so did all the monks that were that time at Compline.   And they smote each at him, that they smote off a great piece of the skull of his head, that his brain fell on the pavement. And so they slew him and martyred him, and there cruelly that one of them brake the point of his sword against the pavement; and thus this holy Archbishop St. Thomas suffered death in his own church for the right of Holy Church.   And when he was dead, they stirred his brain; and after went into his chamber and took away his goods, and his horse out of his stable, and took away his bulls and writing, and delivered them to Sir Robert Broke to bear into France to the King.   And as they searched his chamber, they found in a chest ij shirts of hair, made full of great knots; and they said, Certainly he was a good man.   And coming down into the church-

yard, they began to dread and fear the ground
would not have borne them, and were sore
aghast; for they supposed that the earth would
have swallowed them all quick[alive]; then they
knew that they had done amiss. And anon it
was known all about how that he was martyred,
and anon after took this holy body and unclothed
him, and found bishop's clothing above, and the
habit of a monk under, and next his flesh a hard
hair full of knots, which was his shirt; and his
breech was of the same, and the knots stuck fast
within the skin, and all his body full of worms.
He suffered great pain, and was thus martyred
the year of our Lord XI.C.LXXI., and was liij
years old. And soon after tidings came to the
King how he was slain; wherefore the King took
great sorrow, and sent to Rome for his absolution. And after that St. Thomas departed from
the Pope, the Pope would daily look upon the
white chasuble that St. Thomas had said Mass in,
and that same day that he was martyred he saw
it turn into red; whereby he knew well that that
same day he suffered martyrdom for the right of
Holy Church, and commanded a Mass of *Requiem*
solemnly to be sung for his soul. And when that
the quire began for to sing *Requiem,* an angel on
high above began the Office of a martyr, *Lætabitur
justus;* and then anon after, all the whole quire
followed singing forth the Mass of the Office of a
martyr. And then the Pope thanked God that it
pleased Him to show such miracles for His holy
Martyr, at whose tomb, by the merit and prayers
of this holy Martyr, our Blessed Lord there hath

showed many miracles; the blind have recovered
there their sight, the dumb their speech, the deaf
their hearing, the lame their limbs, and the dead
their life.   Therefore let us pray to this glorious
Martyr to be our advocate, that by his petition
we may come unto everlasting bliss.   Amen."

There is another very curious legend connected
with St. Thomas of Canterbury which runs thus
in the first person, as if it were related by the
Saint himself: "When I Thomas Archbishop of
Canterbury fled from England into France, I
went to Pope Alexander, who was then at Sens,
where I showed him the evil customs and abuses
which the King of England had introduced.   One
night, when I was in prayer in the Church of
St. Columba, I prayed to the Queen of Virgins
to give the King of England and his heirs purpose and will of amendment towards the Church,
and that Christ of His mercy would make him
love the Church with a fuller love.   Straightway
the Blessed Virgin appeared to me, having in
her bosom this golden eagle, and holding in her
hand a little stone cruet.   Taking the eagle from
her bosom, she shut the cruet in it, and placed
the cruet with the eagle in my hand; and spoke
to me these words in order: 'This is the unction
wherewith the Kings of England should be anointed, not these who now reign and will reign,
who are and will be wicked, and for their sins
have lost and will lose much; but there are
Kings of England to come, who shall be anointed
with this unction, who shall be kind and cham-
pions of the Church; for they will recover in

peace the land which their fathers have lost,
when they shall have the eagle with the cruet.
For there shall be a King of England who shall
first be anointed with this unction; he shall
recover without force the land lost by his fathers,
to wit, Normandy and Aquitaine. The King shall
be the greatest among Kings; and he shall build
many churches in the Holy Land; and he shall
put to flight all pagans from Babylon; and shall
build therein many churches. As often as the
King shall carry the eagle in his bosom, he shall
have victory over his enemies; and his kingdom
in like manner shall be increased. And thou shalt
be a martyr.' Then I asked the Blessed Virgin to
show me who should keep so precious a treasure;
and she said to me, 'There is in this city a monk
of St. Cyprian of Poitiers named William, who
has been unjustly expelled by his Abbot from his
abbey, and who is petitioning the Pope to compel
his Abbot to restore him to his abbey. Give him
the eagle with the cruet, for him to take it to the
city of Poitiers; and let him hide it in the Church
of St. Gregory, near the Church of St. Hilary, at
the head of the church, towards the west, under a
great stone. There it shall be found at a fitting
time, and shall be the unction of the Kings of
England.' The cause of the finding of this eagle
shall be among the pagans. And all these things
I gave him shut up in a vessel of lead." The old
MS. goes on to say, that "the above-written was
accidentally found by my lord the King of
England, on the vigil of St. Gregory, in the year
of our Lord 1337, in an old chest." Walsingham

says, that King Richard II. found it in the Tower of London in 1399; and that Henry IV. was the first King who was anointed with this oil.

Lambarde, an historian of the county of Kent in the seventeenth century, recounts various traditional legends of St. Thomas, of which the following are specimens. It is curious to see how the old affectionate feeling for St. Thomas had died out, while nothing remained in the mind of the Kentishmen respecting him, but a sense of his power.

"Polydore Virgil (handling that hot contention between King Henry II. and Thomas Becket) saith that Becket (being at the length reputed for the King's enemy) began to be so commonly neglected, contemned, and hated, that when as it happened him upon a time to come to Stroud, the inhabitants thereabouts (being desirous to despite that good Father) sticked not to cut the tail from the horse on which he rode, binding themselves thereby with a perpetual reproach: for afterwards (by the will of God) it so happened that every one which came of that kindred of men which had played that naughty prank, were born with tails, even as brute beasts be." [4]

"It was long since fancied, and is yet of too many believed, that while Thomas Becket lay at the old house at Otford (which of long time, as you see, belonged to the Archbishops, and whereof the old hall and chapel only do now remain) and saw that it wanted a fit spring to water it, that he stuck his staff into the dry

[4] *Perambulations of Kent*, Chatham, 1826, p. 356.

ground (in a place thereof now called St. Thomas's Well), and that immediately the same water appeared, which running plentifully, serveth the offices of the new house till this present day. They say also, that as he walked on a time in the old Park (busy at his prayers) that he was much hindered in devotion by the sweet note and melody of a nightingale that sang in a bush beside him: and that therefore (in the might of his holiness) he enjoined that from thenceforth no bird of that kind should be so bold as to sing thereabout. Some men report likewise, that forasmuch as a smith (then dwelling in the town) had cloyed his horse, he enacted by like authority, that after that time no smith should thrive within the parish."[5]

A story of a very different kind comes to us from the Icelandic *Thomas Saga*, a fourteenth century compilation. The same story was known in the south of Europe in the last century, necessarily from an entirely independent source, for it is inserted by St. Alphonsus Liguori in his *Glories of Mary*. The quaintness of the wording is due to the literalness of the translation from the Icelandic.[6]

" The school of Paris is a large congregation wherein there be many sons of well-born fathers, . . . Out of all their number scarce one might be found who had not one woman-friend with

5 *Ibid.* p. 460.
6 *Thomas Saga Erkibyskups.* By Eirikr Magnusson, Sub-Librarian of the University of Cambridge. Rolls Series, vol. i. p. 21.

GG

whom he kept fellowship; and none do we know
outtaken therefrom but Thomas the English; he
alone hath no sweetheart of earth, nay but rather
is she his only beloved who is the Queen of the
maidens; her he serveth even now to the utmost
of his power, in purity of life, both as to spirit
and body, in beauty of mind and fair prayers.
Unto this he addeth what has since become
widely renowned, in that he compoundeth praises
of our Lady, both for private reading and for
proses in the church. He was of all men the
first to find, as far as has become known here
in the north, how to draw meditation out of
every psalm in the Psalter, out of which medi-
tations he afterwards made verses of praise to
our Lady. Following his example, Stephen
Langton did the same in England, and later
still the same was done by three masters west
in Scotland, at the request of Queen Isabell,
whom Eric Magnusson had for wife.[7] It is also
averred by all folk that the blessed Thomas
composed the prose *Imperatrix gloriosa*, and
another, a lesser one, *Hodiernæ lux diei*. Now
for such things, and other good works which
he wrought, he got such love from our Lady,
that it may well be said she took him unto
her bosom, thus saying unto him: *Dilectus meus
mihi et ego illi.*

"Next to these things let us see what the

7 "The marriage of King Eric Magnusson of Norway and
Isabella Bruce took place in 1293. The King died six years
afterwards, July 13, 1299, and the dowager Queen in 1358"
(*Mr. Magnusson's note*).

clerks busy them about, since now time passeth
on and weareth towards Lent. . . , They now
hold a great parliament whereat in a brawly
wise each one praiseth his own beloved, saying
that she is goodly of look, and wise of speech,
and dealeth with all things with a deft hand.
This is a meeting whereat Thomas the English
sitteth and sayeth nought at all. They now
cast glances at him with some rude jeering or
mockery. . . . At the playmote, which was to
be the next morning, . . . there was to be
brought forth for show the cleverest trifle in
needlework which each one's mistress had
wrought. And when as the blessed Thomas is
threatened with hard dealing, he betaketh him
to his well-beloved, and kneeling down prayeth
unto our Lady that she might deign to spare
him of her needlework something fit to be shown
among his companions, no matter if it were not
a thing of great worth. Thus he prayeth, and
the night passeth away and the parliament
taketh place. And he, as well as each and all
of them, beareth forth unto the show-stand the
glitter which each one hath got for himself.
Now again they look askance to Thomas, asking
what he might be about. He answered even
thus: ' I shall go forthwith and show you what
mine own beloved brought to me last night;'
whereupon he went to his private study, where
he found that a certain casket had come, snow-
white, of shining ivory, locked and fashioned .
with images in a manner to surpass all polish
that might be wrought by the hand of man.

This little thing he now taketh with him and showeth to his companions. The casket being unlocked, it appeareth what it containeth, which in short was this, there here was found, folded down, a full set of bishop's robes, so heedfully gathered together that even the staff was there-among also. At this the noise of the clerks abateth somewhat, since by this wonder they understand that an election hath already fallen to the lot of this very Thomas, and that his path lieth somewhat higher than the ways of such folk, who sink into the sins and the filth of this miserable life. But that which was told of these robes is by right understanding to be taken to mean as much as that they were of such smallness of size, that they could be kept within a small space before the eyes of man."

This extract has mentioned the belief in Iceland in the fourteenth century that St. Thomas was the author of hymns to the Blessed Virgin. One such hymn, believed to be his, may here be given from a paper[8] taken from a very different source, that is to say, from a manuscript in one of the great libraries at Rome.

" These are the Seven Temporal Joys of the Blessed Virgin Mary.

> Gaude Virgo, Mater Christi,
> Quem per aurem concepisti,
>   Gabriele nuntio :
>
> Gaude, quia Deo plena
> Peperisti sine pœna
>   Cum pudoris lilio :

[8] Miscell. MSS. in 4to, Bibl. Casanatense, D. v. 26, f. 108.

Gaude, quia Magi dona
Tuo Nato ferunt bona,
  Quem tenes in gremio :

Gaude, quia reperisti
Tuum natum quem quæsisti
  In doctorum medio :

Gaude, quia tui Nati
Quem dolebas morte pati
  Fulget resurrectio :

Gaude, Christo ascendente
Et in cœlum te tuente
  Cum Sanctorum nubilo :

Gaude, quæ post Christum scandis,
Et est tibi.honor grandis
  In cœli palatio.

"We read that Blessed Thomas, the Archbishop of Canterbury, was wont to repeat with great devotion the Seven Temporal Joys of the Blessed Virgin Mary. Once when he was saying these joys in his oratory, as he was accustomed, the Blessed Virgin appeared to him and said, 'Why are you glad only for my joys which were temporal, and do not rather rejoice over the present joys which I now enjoy in Heaven, which are eternal? Rejoice, therefore, and exult with me for the future. First, because my glory surpasses the happiness of all the saints. Secondly, because as the sun gives light to the day, so my brightness gives light to the whole court of Heaven. Thirdly, because all the hosts of Heaven obey me, and ever honour me. Fourthly, because my Son and I have but one will. Fifthly, because God rewards, at my pleasure, all my servants, both now and hereafter. Sixthly, because I sit next to the Holy Trinity, and my body is glorified. Seventhly, because I am certainly sure that these joys will last for ever, and never end. And whoever shall honour me by rejoicing in these my joys, shall receive the consolation of my presence at the departure of his soul from the body, and I will free his soul from evil enemies, and I will present him in the sight of my Son, that he may possess with me the everlasting joys of Paradise.' Blessed Thomas the Martyr aforesaid composed these seven joys, as they here follow.

" These are the Seven Heavenly Joys of the Blessed Virgin Mary.

> Gaude flore virginali
> Quæ honore speciali
>   Transcendis splendiferum
> Angelorum principatum,
> Et sanctorum decoratum
>   Dignitate munerum.
>
> Gaude Sponsa cara Dei,
> Nam ut lux clara diei
>   Solis datur lumine,
> Sic tu facis orbem vere
> Tuæ pacis resplendere
>   Lucis plenitudine.
>
> Gaude, splendens vas virtutum,
> Tuæ sedis est ad nutum
>   Tota cœli curia :
> Te benignam et felicem
> Jesu dignam Genitricem
>   Veneratur gloria.
>
> Gaude, nexu voluntatis
> Et amplexu charitatis
>   Juncta sic altissimo

Ut ad nutum consequaris
Quicquid, Virgo, postularis
   A Jesu dilectissimo.

Gaude, mater miserorum,
Quia Pater præmiorum
   Dabit te colentibus
Congruentem hic mercedem,
Et felicem poli sedem
   Sursum in cœlestibus.

Gaude, humilis beata,
Corpore glorificata,
   Meruisti maxima
Flore tantæ dignitatis
Ut sis Sanctæ Trinitatis
   Sessione proxima.

Gaude Virgo, Mater pura,
Certa manens et secura
   Quod hæc tua gaudia
Non cessabunt, non durescent,
Sed durabunt et florescent
   In perenni gloria. Amen.

V. Exaltata es Sancta Dei Genitrix.
R. Super choros Angelorum ad cœlestia regna.

Oratio.

O dulcissime Jesu Christe, qui beatissimam Genitricem Tuam, gloriosam Virginem Mariam perpetuis gaudiis in cœlo lætificasti, concede propitius ut ejus meritis et precibus continuis, salutem et prosperitatem mentis et corporis consequamur, et ad gaudia Tuæ Beatitudinis ac ejusdem Virginis feliciter perveniamus æternam. Per Te, Jesu Christe, Salvator mundi, qui vivis et regnas cum Deo Patre in unitate Spiritus Sancti Deus per omnia sæcula sæculorum. Amen."

Dr. Smith, the Bishop of Chalcedon, quotes, from Parker's *History of St. Thomas*, that there was a hymn composed in his praise by St. Thomas of Aquin, which was sung daily. It is

much to be regretted that it has not come down
to us, for it would indeed have been pleasing to
have connected the name of our Saint with that
of his holy Dominican namesake, as we have had
occasion in different ways to associate him with
the memory of Saints Bernard and William, and
Gilbert, as well as Saints Anselm and Edmund.

CHAPTER XXXVII.

KINDRED AND MEMORIALS.

The Butlers, Earls of Ormond—the Saint's sisters—two nephews buried at Verona—Blessed John and Peter Becket, Augustinian Hermits at Fabriano—Minerbetti —Becchetti—Morselli—St. Catherine of Bologna—Mosaics at Monreale—vestments at Anagni—chapels at Fourvières and St. Lo—mitre at Namur—altars at Liège and Rome—relics at Veroli and Marsala—relics now existing and many more that have perished.

SPEAKING of the Butlers, Earls of Ormond, Father Campion[1] says, "The Latin History calleth him *Dominum de Pincerna*, the English *Le Bottiller*, whereby it appeareth that he had some such honour about the Prince. His very surname is Becket, who was advanced by H. le 2 in recompense of the injury done to Thomas of Canterbury their kinsman."

Of the family of the Saint, we have already seen something[2] on the occasion when Rohesia his sister presented herself at Canterbury before the King in his penitential mood. There are some few further points of history to note respecting St. Thomas's sisters. The community of Christ Church continued to keep up some relation with

[1] *History of Ireland*, cap. 2, Dublin, 1633, reprinted 1809, p. 8.
[2] *Supra*, p. 445.

them, as in a Necrology[3] of the monks and their friends and benefactors, the *obits* of two of them occur. On the 21st of January Mary the Abbess of Barking died; and the same day was the anniversary of William the priest, the martyr's chaplain—perhaps the William whom he had made chaplain of Penshurst,[4] who might well have been called, as by a special sort of title, "the martyr's chaplain." On the 2nd of February there is the entry of the death of another sister of St. Thomas, Agnes, the widow of Thomas,[5] son of Theobald of Helles in Tipperary, foundress in conjunction with her husband of the Hospital of St. Thomas of Acre, on the site where Gilbert Becket's house had stood, where St. Thomas was born, and where the Mercers' Chapel now stands. She gave ten shillings rent to St. Saviour's Hospital, Bermondsey, and the deed of gift was witnessed by Sir Theobald, "the nephew of Blessed Thomas the Martyr," who may have been her son. It is supposed that the Butlers of Ormond were descended from Agnes, and this relationship is mentioned in a petition to Parliament in 1454.

Of the other members of the family who were scattered over Europe in exile for his sake, we are told that two of his nephews were buried at Verona, which will probably account for the pos-

3 12 *Kal. Feb. Obiit Maria Abbatissa de Berkin, soror beati Thomæ Martyris, et Wilhelmus sacerdos, ejusdem Martyris capellanus. 4 Idus Feb. Obiit Agnes, soror beati Thomæ Martyris* (Cott. MSS. Nero, C. ix, 2, fol. 1, printed by Dart, *History of the Church of Canterbury*, App. p. xxxiii.).

4 *Supra*, pp. 389, 397.

5 Robertson's *Becket, a Biography*, p. 353.

session of a relic of him by the parish church of
S. Tommaso Cantuariense, which was built in
his honour in 1316.

Some other relatives were at Rome, who under
Innocent III., finally settled at Fabriano, where,
in the fourteenth century, two were born of the
family,[6] who imitated his sanctity and were raised
to the dignity of the altar. Blessed John and
Peter Becket were of the Augustinian Eremitical
Order at Fabriano. The first went to Oxford
about the year 1385, being then a Bachelor in
Theology, to give lectures in that University,
where he had assigned to him, by the general
chapter of his Order, held at Strigonia, or Gran,
in Hungary on the 24th of May, 1385, " the first
place given to foreigners by the University of
Oxford in the Lectureship of the Sentences."
Various favours are recorded in the registry of
the order, as conferred upon him by the General;
amongst others that of going to London with one
companion when he thought proper, of remaining
in the convent at Oxford during the vacations,
and of having a scribe. He returned with his
master's degree, about 1392, to the convent where
he had been professed, in which, on the 7th of
May, 1420, he had the full powers of the General
delegated to him.

Blessed Peter Becket was chosen, in 1388,
joint visitor of the convent of his Order at Rimini,
as a substitute for the famous Gregory de Ari-
mino. In the following year he received leave

6 This account is entirely taken from the documents presented
to the Sacred Congregation of Rites in 1835.

to preach; but this occupation was not allowed to distract him from his studies, for in 1391 he was made second lecturer at Venice. Two years later he was permitted to visit the Holy Sepulchre; and his name reappears in the chronicles of the order, in 1421, as being allowed an attendant, probably because of his advanced age. It is said, that on his return from the Holy Sepulchre, he awakened in his saintly relative a desire to visit those holy places also, and that they made their pilgrimage together. On their return, they built in their native town a church in honour of the Holy Sepulchre, with two chapels and five altars, on one of which the relics of the two holy religious ultimately rested. Their translation from the burial-place of the convent was owing to a miracle; for a bundle of dry thorns left between their graves budded and blossomed with numerous and beautiful flowers. They were moved to the convent church; and afterwards, in 1565, they were solemnly translated to the Church of the Holy Sepulchre at Fabriano, where their festival is kept on the 1st of January, the anniversary of their translation. The little church in which they are is now called by their name; and the wooden shrine in which their bodies rest is covered with paintings representing miracles wrought by their intercession, considered to be of about the date of 1450. In 1591 the community of Fabriano made a vow to observe their festival as a day of obligation for twelve years, to obtain their deliverance from pestilence and famine. Their claim to the title of Blessed, and the confirmation of the honour hitherto shown to them, were allowed by Pope Gregory XVI. on the 28th of August, 1835.

In a Life of St. Thomas published at Lucca in 1696, by John Baptist Cola, of the Congregation of the Mother of God, various Italian families are named as claiming descent from the banished relations of the Saint. Of these the author gives the first place to F. Andrea Minerbetti, a Knight Commander of the Order of St. John at Florence, and then he enumerates the Signori Becchetti of Piacenza, Fabriano, Verona, of Sacca in Sicily, and of Berceto in the territory of Parma, to which latter place he attributes the possession of a precious relic of our Saint. He then speaks of the Signori Morselli of Vigerano and Piacenza. In the former place this family rejoiced in the possession of a fountain which St. Thomas had caused to spring up miraculously on one of his journeys to Rome, which favour was recorded in verses engraved on the city standard, which it was their privilege to carry in procession on St. Mark's day.

The same book contains an interesting account of a vision of St. Catherine of Bologna. In order to devote herself to prayer, this Saint had deprived herself of her natural rest to such an extent that her spiritual daughters, fearing both for her mind and body, implored her to devote less time to this holy exercise. St. Catherine, after asking fervently for God's guidance, fell asleep and saw St. Thomas of Canterbury, to whom she was particularly devoted, appear to her in his pontifical vestments, and make a sign to her to observe what he should do. She noticed that he prayed for some time and then devoted a while to rest, and then returned again to prayer; and then, drawing near to St. Catherine, he gave his hand to her to kiss, on which she awoke and saw him and kissed his hand before he disappeared. The account of this the Saint wrote in her breviary, " which is still amongst her relics at Bologna," with these words: " Oratio pro Sancto Thomâ meo gloriosissimo Martyre, tam benignissimo, qui manus suas sanctissimas concessit mihi, et osculata sum illas in corde et corpore meo; ad laudem Dei et illius scripsi, et narravi hoc cum omni veritate." In both the lives of St. Catherine given by the Bollandists (March 9), this is narrated, with a slight variation in the words written by the Saint in her breviary. " S. Thomas meus gloriosissimus et clementissimus Patronus," one says are the words used respecting our great English martyr by the wonderful virgin who now for four hundred years has dwelt incorrupt amongst her Poor Clares at Bologna.

The devotion to St. Thomas spread very rapidly. The earliest known representation of the Saint is executed in mosaic, in the church of Monreale, near Palermo, built by William the Good, King of Sicily, who began its erection in the very year St. Thomas was canonized. This King married Princess Jane of England, daughter of our Henry II., who arrived in Sicily in the year 1177.

In the Cathedral at Anagni are preserved a full set of very beautiful vestments, given in the year 1200 by Pope Innocent III.; and on one of the dalmatics,[7] amongst some representations of other English saints, is the martyrdom of St. Thomas. In the history of Anagni by De Magistris, it is said that in 1169, while Alexander III. was living in the canonica of that Cathedral, St. Thomas himself arrived not long after the ambassadors of King Henry; and that during his stay there he always celebrated Mass in the basilica. Such a journey, however, would surely have been betrayed at least in the voluminous correspondence, if not in the biographies of the Saint. The local tradition is very strong that the Saint came thither in person during his exile; and an altar in the crypt, which has been removed to form a burial-place for the canons, is stated to be that on which he used to celebrate. In the choir-chapel an inscription[8] on a picture, which may once have formed the door of a treasury, tells us that in 1325 they possessed a relic of him.

It is said that when the Saint was at Lyons, he was asked to consecrate the church on the hill to our Blessed Lady, which has since become so famous as Notre Dame de Fourvières. When the function was over, there

7 Mrs. Jameson is wrong in calling it the cope (*Legends of Monastic Orders*. London, 1850, p. 115).

8 *Hoc opus fieri fecit Dominus Raynaldus Presbyter et Clericus istius Ecclesiæ sub anno Domini* 1325, *mense Maii. Ibi sunt de Reliquiis Sanctorum Thomæ Archiepiscopi Cant., Thomæ de Aquino, et Petri Episcopi Anagnini.*

was a little chapel close by, which he was asked
to dedicate also. He inquired in whose honour
it was to be consecrated. They told him that
a titular Saint had not been chosen, but that he
himself must select one. He thought for a few
moments, and then said that he would not consecrate it; but that they must reserve it to be
dedicated to the first martyr who should give his
blood for Christ. The chapel was accordingly,
a few years after, dedicated to God in honour of
St. Thomas of Canterbury.

A precisely similar story is told of St. Lo. " In
another part of the town is a building, now La
Halle au Bled, which before the Revolution was
a church dedicated to St. Thomas of Canterbury.
The original church was finished in 1174. It
was in progress when Thomas à Becket, having
incurred the resentment of Henry, went abroad
and passed through St. Lo. There was a dispute
at the time to whom the new church should be
dedicated. The illustrious stranger was consulted; and his reply was, ' Let it be dedicated
to the first saint who shall shed his blood for
the Catholic faith.' Providence allowed it to be
dedicated to himself. He was murdered in 1171,
and canonized in 1173. The original church,
however, was pulled down in 1571, to make room
for improvement in the fortifications, and rebuilt
in its present situation in 1630."[9]

In the convent of the Sisters of Notre Dame at
Namur, his martyrdom is represented on a mitre

9 *Architectural Tour in Normandy.* By H. Gally Knight, Esq.,
M.P. London, 1836, p. 123.

which formerly belonged to the celebrated Cardinal James de Vitry, the director and biographer of Blessed Mary of Oignies, which he left in 1244 to the Abbey of Oignies, whence at the death of the last prior it, with the abbey relics, passed to Namur.

The first altar erected to him in Belgium[10] was in the Monastery of St. Laurence at Liège, by Abbot Everlin, "for the love which he bore him, as he studied with him at Paris." In Rome, the earliest altar known to have been raised in his honour[11] is that in the chapel dedicated to him in the crypt or Confession of the Church of St. Alexius on the Aventine, which was consecrated, in 1218, by Pelagius, Cardinal Bishop of Albano, who placed therein some of his relics, together with those of several other saints. There is a fine relic at Veroli, preserved in a very handsome bust decorated by a canon of the church two centuries ago. And at Marsala, where the feast of St. Thomas is a day of obligation, there is also a large relic in a silver bust, given to the church in that place by Antonio Lombardo, a native of Marsala, who became Archbishop of Messina in 1572.

[10] Martene, *Vet. Scriptor.* Paris, 1724, vol. iv. p. 1090. In 1196 Adalbert III., Archbishop of Saltzburg, ordered the monastery of Admont to celebrate the feast as a double of the second class, "et ut meliori pane et vino et etiam piscibus ob honorem ejusdem Martyris nostrique memoriam illa die congregationi ministretur."

[11] "Ex pervetusto membran. cod. qui Lectionarium dicebatur, ad Alexianorum usum monachorum" (Felix Nerinius, Abbas Hieronymianus, *De templo et coenob. SS. Bonifacii et Alexis.* Romæ, 1752, p. 220).

HH

A chasuble of the Saint is at Courtrai, a chasuble and chalice are preserved at Dixmude, and a set of vestments at Sens; his Eminence Cardinal Wiseman obtained a mitre, and the apparel of an amice is at Erdington, both from the same treasury. The late Bishop Gillis obtained permission to take from the Cathedral of Sens one half of the altar stone, on which, according to the local tradition, St. Thomas said Mass. With this he made an altar for his domestic chapel in Edinburgh, and at the altar's foot he placed the heart of King Henry II.

Perhaps the most interesting relics which remain are those at St. Mary Major's at Rome. Baronius says[12] that the Cardinal Legates, Albert and Theodwin, brought back with them a portion of his brain which had been scattered on the pavement, and his tunic stained with blood, and that they were then placed in that church.

Vast numbers of other relics have been honoured in different churches, but no longer survive the various storms which have assailed religion. Prior Benedict, when he was made Abbot of Peterborough in 1176, made two altars in that Minster of stones taken from the floor of the martyrdom. He also enriched his new abbey with two vases of the blood of St. Thomas and parts of his clothing.[13] Roger, who had become

12 *Annales*, vol. xii. p. 655.

13 It is difficult to see why Dean Stanley should call this "an act of plunder." Nothing could have been more natural than that the monks of Canterbury should help their own Prior on his promotion, himself the historian of the martyrdom and miracles, to spread the devotion to St. Thomas.

keeper of the shrine when Benedict was made Prior, was elected Abbot of St. Augustine's in the place of Clarembald, in the hope that he might take with him some relic of St. Thomas; and Thorn, a monk of that abbey, who records it, says that they were enriched by him with some portion of the Martyr's blood, brain, and skull. Prior Geoffrey took some relics with him to Rouen, and he was accustomed to wear a reliquary containing a small piece of the crown of the Saint. In the books of miracles written by William of Canterbury[14] and Benedict very frequent mention is made of relics, usually small pieces of the Saint's clothing, as at Hythe, Whitchurch, Bapaume, Châtillon near Laon, and in the house of the Bishop of Moray at Spynie.

From more recent records we learn that a hair-shirt[15] was shown in a reliquary in the English College at Douay, a small part of one in the Abbey of Liesse, another[16] in St. Victor's at Paris; a bone of his arm in the great Church of St. Waldetrude at Mons; his chalice in the great nunnery of Bourbourg;[17] his mitre and linen dipped in his blood at St. Bertin's at St. Omer; the rochet[18] that he wore at his martyrdom was in the Abbey of St. Josse-au-Bois or St. Judoc's, commonly called Dammartin;

14 Will. Cant. pp. 188, 244, 250, 305, 384.

15 Alban Butler, *Lives of the Saints*, Dec. 29.

16 *La Vie de S. Thomas.* Par De Beaulieu, Paris, 1674, p. 388.

17 Destombes, *Vies des Saints*, Cambrai, 1852, tome iv. p. 167. For various other memorials in the Low Countries mentioned by this author, see Note F.

18 Stapleton, *Tres Thomæ*, Colon. Agr. 1612, p. 108.

vestments in many other monasteries in the Low Countries.

The ring[19] which he wore when he was martyred was among the relics at Glastonbury: at Windsor was a portion of his blood, and also a shirt: at Warwick a portion of a hair-shirt: at St. Alban's a portion also of a hair-shirt, of his cowl, his chasuble, his dalmatic and pallium: in the nunnery of St. Mary at Derby a piece of a shirt: at St. Mary's, Chester, a girdle:[20] and the Commissioners for the Suppression of Monasteries[21] say that they found at Bury St. Edmund's his penknife and boots. With a little pains this list of relics in England could be largely increased.[22]

In conclusion we turn to the church from whose stores most other churches derived their treasured relics of St. Thomas, Christ Church, at Canterbury. There, besides the body of St. Thomas in its shrine, the head in one reliquary and the crown in another, we have the following, which are here selected as the more interesting,[23] from a list made in 1315 by Prior Henry of Eastry.

"In a wooden lectern at the altar of the Holy Cross in the nave of the church, covered in part with silver gilt and jewelled, with a cross in the middle, are contained a silver gilt cross with

19 *Mon. Angl.* Lond. 1682, vol. i. p. 6.
20 All these are mentioned by Gough Nichols, p. 228.
21 Wright, *Letters on the Dissolution*, Camden Society, p. 85.
22 See Note O.
23 Cotton. MSS.; Galba E iv. f. 122; Dart's *History of the Church of Canterbury*, App. p. xlii.

gems, with the wood of our Lord in the middle, and relics of St. Thomas the Martyr, part of a finger of St. Andrew, a bone of St. Stephen, and some of the body of St. Wulstan." This wooden lectern cannot be a bookstand on the altar, as until recent times the missal was placed on a cushion.

"In a little silver gilt cup is contained the pallium of St. Thomas the Martyr." This pallium the engraving of the Saint's seal has shown us[24] was covered with embroidery, which is very unusual; for generally the pallium is of pure white wool, with black crosses. Erasmus says: "A pall was shown, which, though wholly of silk, was of a coarse texture, and unadorned with gold or jewels." If Erasmus is speaking of the pallium, he can only mean that it was embroidered in silk.

"In a great round ivory coffer, oblong at its head, with a lock[25] of copper—The white mitre with an orfrey of St. Thomas the Martyr, in which he was buried; another white mitre of the same, which he used on simple feasts; gloves of the same, adorned with three orfreys; shoes of the same, of Inde, embroidered with gold roses, besants and crescents, with stockings[26] of black samit [silk], embroidered; his hair-shirt; part of his bed and girdle.

[24] *Supra*, p. 88.

[25] *Serura* (MS.), which Mr. Nichols translates "rimmed with copper."

[26] *Subtalaribus* (MS.), which Mr. Nichols translates "strings." *Subtalares* and *sotulares* (*sub talis*, under the ankles) usually mean shoes, but here they are in conjunction with *sandalia*.

"In the same coffer, folded up in a white diapered[27] cloth—Some of the dust of the body of Blessed Thomas the Martyr; part of his cappa and his other clothing; part of his coverlet; of his cowl; of the fastening of his hair-shirt; some of his flesh and blood dried up; part of his girdle, and of his pillow; some of his hair.

"In the same coffer, folded up in another cloth, of silk— Part of the chasuble of St. Thomas; part of his dalmatic; of his tunic; of his monastic woollen shirt; of his cope; some cloth dipped in his blood; part of his cowl, and of his cap; his discipline made of thongs."

Most of the relics here mentioned must have been buried with the Saint—of the white mitre it is expressly said—and disinterred at his translation just a century before this list of relics was made.   At that time, among the chasubles in the sacristy, one is noted as "St. Thomas's red chasuble, with gold crescents and stars;" among the amices, "St. Thomas's amice adorned with gems;" and among the croziers, "the pastoral staff of St. Thomas, of pear wood, with the head of black horn."   Some time during the next two hundred years this simple crozier was covered with silver, and probably it was shortened by portions being given away as relics.   Erasmus mentions it thus: "After this we were led into the sacristy.   What a display was there of silken vestments, what an array of golden candlesticks! There we saw the pastoral staff of St. Thomas.

27 *Diasperato* (MS.), "from O.F. diaspre, later diapre, a jasper, a stone much used for ornamental jewellery" (Skeat).

It appeared to be a cane covered with silver plate; it was of very little weight, and no workmanship, nor stood higher than to the waist." The saint's seal, to which attention has already been drawn, shows that the pastoral staff there depicted was not originally as short as it is described by Erasmus. The extreme simplicity of the crozier used by St. Thomas is remarkable. His Archiepiscopal Cross does not seem to have been preserved.

We have lingered with affectionate interest among the memorials and relics of our Saint, as a Catholic might linger in the aisles of the old Cathedral Church of Canterbury, itself our best relic of him. The footprints left in the hard stone by the multitudes who once thronged that Church vividly recall the past, and fill our minds with memories of the days that were so like and so unlike our own. They were like to our times, because the strife between the Church and the world ever continues, but the aspect of the strife differs widely. The battle is always substantially the same. The world is, and ever will be, the Church's foe, and however the appearance of the battle may change, the Church always needs the loyal devotion and self-sacrifice of her sons. In her contest of every age she looks for generous souls, to whom the will of God shall be dearer than wealth, dearer than position and influence and power, dearer than home and country, dearer than family and friends, dearer than life itself. Such a one, and a prince among such, was St. Thomas of Canterbury. The Church's battles are not fought and won, as the world supposes. In them the wounded and the slain are the conquerors, and to die is to live. The Prince of Peace Himself has said, "Do not think that I came to send peace upon earth; I came not to send peace, but a sword. He that findeth his life shall lose it; and he that shall lose his life for Me, shall find it."[28]

28 St. Matt. x. 34, 39.

NOTE A (page 5).

THE SARACEN PRINCESS.

Writers so various as Godwin, Cave, Thierry and Sharon Turner, Froude and Giles, the author of the Cologne Life of 1639, Cola, Beaulieu, and our own accurate Alban Butler, all admit the story of Gilbert's escape from a Saracen prison, and his marriage with a Saracen princess. Mr. Berington was the first to reject it.

About the time of the Translation of the relics of St. Thomas by Cardinal Langton, in 1220, a compilation was made from the several biographers, which has since gone by the name of the *Quadrilogue*. A large number of copies of this book exist, and, if one may say so, it has passed through several editions, as it has many different prefaces or prologues. The best-known *Quadrilogue* is that published by Christian Lupus, or Wolf, at Brussels in 1682. It had been previously printed at Paris in black letter, in 1495, under the title of "Vita et Processus S. Thomæ." This latter book is sometimes called the first *Quadrilogue;* though it has no claim to the distinction except in having been the first in print. It differs from the second *Quadrilogue* not only in the opening chapters, in which the story of the Saracen princess is related, but also by quotations from Fitzstephen and Grim, so that in its case, at least, the title of *Quadrilogue* is a misnomer. This greater fulness shows that it is the later compilation.

John of Brompton is generally quoted as the authority for this legend; but he has simply copied the first seven chapters of the first *Quadrilogue*, altering only the beginnings and endings of the chapters, and omitting the names of the various authors; and, when the history begins to be rather intricate, he refers his readers to the Life "quam iiij viri famosi scripserunt" (Ed. Twysden, pp. 1051, 1058).

John Grandisson, Bishop of Exeter (from 18th October 1327, until his death, 15th July 1369), informed his old Professor of Divinity at Paris (Doctor James Fournier), who was elected Pope on 20th December 1334, and crowned by the name of Benedict XII. on the following 8th January, in his complimentary letter on his promotion, that he himself had compiled a Life of St. Thomas the Martyr, which he intended to submit to his Holiness. "Vitam beati Thomæ Martyris, ex multis scriptoribus per me noviter redactam, Sanctitatis vestræ oculis destino intuendam" (Registr. Grandissoni, vol. i. fol. 40). The book has not been printed, but copies exist in the British Museum, the Library of Corpus Christi College, Cambridge, in the Students' Library of the English College, Rome, and in the Vatican (Chr. 623). This compilation also contains the story of the Saracen princess, written rather more concisely than the first *Quadrilogue*.

The anonymous author of the Lambeth MS. (*Materials*, iv. p. 81) says, "Habuit uxorem nomine Roesam,[1] natione Cadomensem, genere burgensium non disparem:" giving a Christian name and nationality to St. Thomas's mother different from any other writer, but agreeing with all the biographers in the rank of life assigned to her. St. Thomas himself says, "Non sum revera atavis editus regi-

---

[1] It will have been noticed that St. Thomas had a sister named Rohesia (*Supra*, p. 445).

bus " (*Materials*, v. p. 499) ; and again, " Quod si ad generis mei radicem et progenitores meos intenderis, cives quidem fuerunt Londonienses, in medio concivium suorum habitantes sine querela, nec omnino infimi " (*Ibid.* p. 515). At least Garnier, who took such pains with his " bons romanz," would have introduced a tale so well adapted to his " rime en cinc clauses cuplez," if he had but heard of it. He thus disposes of the parentage of our Saint:

> Saint Thomas l'arceueske, dunt precher m'oez,
> en Lundres la cité fu pur ueir engendrez,
> des barons de la cit estraiz e aleuez.
> e Gilebert Beket fu sis pere apelez,
> e sa mere Mahalt.   de neite gent fu nez.

(fol. *4, 1. 21.)

NOTE B (page 19).

THE SAXON SCHOOL IN ROME.

" The Cardinal-Deacon Peter to the Archbishop of Canterbury.—We believe that your lordship is aware that the Church of Blessed Mary of the Saxons (*quæ Sassonorum dicitur*) in Rome is appointed by the considerate provision of the Roman Pontiffs for the reception of the English who visit the threshold of the Apostles, that they may here find and receive consolation and charitable assistance after their various labours, as in a house of their own. Through our sins, it has come to such poverty, that but a few clerics and hardly any lay person can be found to serve the church and attend upon the pilgrims. Our Holy Father, Pope Alexander, out of compassion for its poverty and misery, has given in its favour exhortatory letters for England, which you will see. Since we know how ready and willing your goodness is in everything relating to piety and religion, we much trust in your brotherliness, and we pray you in the Lord to receive kindly the bearer of these presents, Nicholas, a canon of the aforesaid church, and, according to the tenor of the letters of our lord the Pope, to vouchsafe at our prayer to grant him your letters for reverence of the Mother of God.   Farewell in the Lord " (*Materials*, v. p. 64.)

This is the latest notice of the church of the Saxon school with which the writer is acquainted.   The Bull of Innocent III., which erected the hospital of S. Spirito, gives to that new foundation " the Church of Blessed Mary in Sassia, *formerly* attached to the Saxon school ; " and in the hall of the hospital is an inscription commemorating the good deeds of that Pope, amongst which is recorded, *Angeli monitu, expositis infantibus excipiendis educandisque, hospitium in veteri Saxonum schola designat.*

Ven. Bede (*Hist. Eccl.* v. 8) relates, that in 727, Ina, King of the West Saxons, visited Rome in the pontificate of Gregory II., and that at that time many English of all ranks and states of life were accustomed to perform the same pilgrimage.   Matthew of Westminster (ad ann. 727, ed. Francof. 1601, p. 135) adds, that he founded in Rome " the English school, to which the kings and royal family of England, with the bishops, priests, and clerics, might come to be instructed in doctrine and the Catholic faith.   And near this house he built a church in honour of the Blessed Virgin Mary, in which the English might say Mass, and where they might be buried, if they happened to die in Rome. For the support of this foundation, he enacted that the penny called Romescot should be paid from every family to Blessed Peter and the Church of Rome."

Matthew Paris (Ed. 1644, p. 19) tells us, that Offa II., King of the Mercians, in 794, in thanksgiving for the canonization of St. Alban by Pope Adrian, extended the contribution of Peter's pence in behalf of the English school, *quæ tunc Romæ floruit*, to his province. According to Anastasius Bibliothe-carius, this school and church were burnt down in 817, and Pope Paschal I. rebuilt them; and they were again destroyed by fire in the conflagration of the Borgo, that the pencil of Raffaelle has rendered so famous; after which they were rebuilt from the foundations by Pope St. Leo IV. One of the gates of the Leonine city, from which Leo IV. gave his blessing to the burning suburb, was called, from the neighbourhood of the school, "the Saxon postern," *Saxonum posterula;* and the same writer assures us that the name of the "Borgo" was derived from our countrymen:. *Per quorumdam gentis Anglorum desidiam omnis Anglorum habitatio, quæ in eorum lingua* Burgus *dicitur, flamma ignis combusta est.*

Passing over the visits of several Saxon kings to Rome, by which new privileges were conferred upon the national establishment, we find the following interesting mention of it in the letter of Pope Alexander II. to William the Conqueror, in 1068 (Baron. ad ann.): *Nam ut bene nosti, donec Angli fideles erant, piæ devotionis respectu ad cognitionem religionis annuam pensionem Apostolicæ Sedi exhibebant, ex qua pars Romano Pontifici, pars Ecclesiæ S. Mariæ quæ vocatur Schola Anglorum in usum fratrum deferebatur.*

NOTE C (page 43).

GILBERT FOLIOT'S PAMPHLET.

Lord Campbell, in his *Lives of the Chancellors* (i. p. 68) says, "The Chancellor overruled their scruples, and compelled them to pay up their arrears" of the tax substituted for personal service. "Upon this, the heads of the Church uttered the most violent invectives against him. Foliot, Bishop of London, publicly accused him of plunging a sword into the bosom of his mother, the Church; and Archbishop Theobald, his former patron, threatened to excommunicate him. Becket still showed an entire indifference to ecclesiastical censures, and established Henry's right to personal service and scutage for all the lands held by the Church." Then follows an exaggerated account of the Battle Abbey controversy. Archbishop Theobald's sole threat of censures the reader will find mentioned in the text, a sportive threat that if the Chancellor did not return to England, he would lay him under anathema, and confiscate all the revenue he derived from Canterbury; and Foliot (who was not Bishop of London until St. Thomas ceased to be Chancellor), if he wrote the letter which contains the passage Lord Campbell refers to, did so long afterwards, when St. Thomas was in exile for opposing the King. This is not the only instance in which Lord Campbell has made a most unjustifiable use of this letter. Any one reading this passage would conclude that the violent invectives were uttered by "the heads of the Church" at the time; whereas it is years afterwards, when every conceivable accusation was heaped together against St. Thomas, that they are met for the first time, and then only in a doubtful letter of a single Bishop.

The letter in question evidently never reached St. Thomas's hands, or he would have answered it, as he did all the others. It is a very specious *ex parte* pamphlet, and so unscrupulous, that Mr. Berington (*Henry II.* p. 657) considers that it is unjustly attributed to Gilbert Foliot. "Who in the world is so stupid," it says, "as not to know that you bought the dignity of Chancellor for several thousand marks? . . . Our father Theobald died; and you, who had ever been on the watch for this event, immediately returned from Normandy to England." Theobald died on the 18th of April, 1161, and the election was in May, 1162. "When we saw that the Church of God was overpowered, we spoke out in defence of her liberty; we had straightway a sentence of proscription passed against us, and we were cruelly doomed to exile; and not our own person merely, but our father's house and all our relations and connections." In answer to an assertion made by Gilbert in another letter (*Materials*, v. p. 412) of the opposition made to the election, John of Salisbury wrote (*Ibid.* v. p. 161; Froude, p. 591): "I do not mind the lies which he has dared to insert concerning your election, for I was present, and both heard and saw. He alone was not pleased when you were elected; for, above every one else, as then appeared and still appears, he aspired to be placed in your see. Yet he did not dare to speak against it for long, while the others found fault with his ambition and insolence. Whatever, therefore, might be his inmost thoughts, of which God is the judge, he was amongst the first who voted for you; and when your election was made, he applauded it, almost more than they all."

I I

Mr. Berington (*Henry II.* p. 663) considers that
Foliot, if he was the writer of the pamphlet,
has confused together the Councils of Clarendon
and Northampton, attributing to the former the
violence of the latter; but there was quite violence enough at Clarendon to justify so far the
account given by him. The most singular part
of the letter is the tone in which it speaks of the
King's proceedings. It condemns St. Thomas, not
for resisting them, but for not resisting them suffi-
ciently. Not merely does it blame him for being the
cause of the submission of all the Bishops at Clarendon, but it attacks him for giving up the immunity
of the clergy by giving sureties at Northampton for
the payment of the fines. As might be imagined,
the letter is not consistent, and at once brings every
accusation, even though one answers the other. Lord
Campbell has chosen to attribute to St. Thomas the
exclamation at Clarendon: "It is my master's
pleasure that I should forswear myself, which I
resolve to do, and to repent afterwards as I may"
(*Chancellors*, i. p. 75). Surely he should have told
his readers, that his sole authority for his assertion
was this production of a bitter enemy, and that even
of this, doubts of the genuineness have been entertained. It is certainly not contained in Alan's collection of the correspondence, nor in the Vatican MS.
from which Wolf's edition of Alan's collection was
taken, though, singularly enough, it is twice named
in the index of that MS.; but it is given by Dr.
Giles from two MSS., both in the Bodleian (Douce,
287, part 2, n. 18, and Cave, 249, n. 447). Canon
Robertson, in the fifth volume of the *Materials*, p.
521, gives the further authority for it of the Cottonian, Claud. B. II. in the British Museum.

It is greatly to be regretted that Canon Robertson,
who has generally been quick to correct Lord Camp-

bell's unfairnesses, should, in his *Becket, a Biography*, which was published in 1859, have put the same exclamation into the mouth of the saint that Lord Campbell had adopted: and, to make the matter worse, he has subjoined this note. " Dr. Lingard attempts to throw discredit on this statement [that St. Thomas confessed himself to be guilty of wilful perjury] on account of the source from which it comes—the letter or pamphlet of Foliot. But even if that letter were a forgery, the accounts of the biographers bear it out in all essential points as to the occurrences at Clarendon, except that the letter named Jocelin of Salisbury as having stood firm with the other bishops, whom it accuses Becket of deserting " (p. 101, note b). This can be met only by repeating that Foliot's letter is the *sole* authority for this speech. Canon Robertson gives in his text these words. " At length the Archbishop was moved, he withdrew for a short time for consideration, and on returning said to his brethren, ' It is the Lord's will that I should forswear myself; for the present I submit, and incur the guilt of perjury, to repent hereafter as I may.' " These words he has not found, nor anything like them, in *any one* of the biographers.

In order to complete all that need be said of Lord Campbell's blunders, it may be well to add here a letter by John of Salisbury to St. Thomas with Lord Campbell's comment on it.

This letter (*Materials*, v. p. 161) begins with an account of the dispositions in which John of Salisbury found King Louis, which were not encouraging. It then proceeds thus: " Wherefore my counsel and the height of my wishes is, that you should turn to the Lord with all your mind, and to the help of prayer. Put off meanwhile, as much as you can, all other occupations; for though they may seem very necessary, what I now recommend is to be preferred as more necessary. Laws and canons are very good; but, believe me, there is no need of them now, for they rather promote curiosity than devotion. Do you not remember how it is written, that in the trouble of the people the priests and ministers of the Lord shall weep between the porch and the altar, saying, 'Spare, O Lord, spare Thy people?' 'I was exercised,' says the Prophet, 'and I swept my spirit, searching with my hands for God, in the day of tribulation.' Who ever rose with a feeling of compunction from the study of law or the canons? I say more than this: the exercises of the schools sometimes increase knowledge till a man is puffed up, but seldom, if ever, inflame devotion. I would rather that you meditated on the Psalms, or read the moral books of St. Gregory, than that you philosophized in scholastic fashion. It is good to confer on moral matters with some spiritual man, by whose example you may be inflamed, rather than to study and discuss the disputatious articles of secular learning. God knows in what sense, with what devotion I propose these things. *Take them as you please*. But if you do them, God will be your helper, that you need not fear what man may scheme. He knows that we have no mortal to trust to, as I think, in our present trouble. But I have heard that the King of France has spoken to the Pope for you, and has thanked the monks of Pontigny." He then refers to a rumour he had heard of earthquakes at Canterbury, London, and Winchester; mentions how some English Bishops were taking advantage of the Archbishop's absence to usurp some of his peculiars in their dioceses; and he concludes with an offer of the Bishop of Chalons to give a refuge to one of the Saint's clerics, who "must behave himself modestly, like the people of this country."

Lord Campbell refers to this letter in the following wonderful note (*Chancellors*, i. p. 79, note *q*): "John of Salisbury wrote him a private letter in a still severer strain, concluding with the words, 'Take it as you please'—'Vos accipiatis ut placet;' and was excommunicated for his pains." His lordship has confused the faithful John of Salisbury, who wrote the letter, with the notorious John of Oxford, Archdeacon of Salisbury, who *was* excommunicated—though not, certainly, for writing a letter like this.

———

NOTE D (page 47).

BATTLE ABBEY.

Though the story of the lawsuit between the Bishop of Chichester and the Abbot of Battle is far too long for insertion in the text, it is but right, as St. Thomas was so much concerned in it through his official position as Chancellor, that we should put it in our readers' power to acquaint themselves with its details. For this purpose we have recourse to the Chronicle of Battle Abbey, excellently edited for the *Anglia Christiana Society* in 1846, and translated into English by Mr. Lower in 1851. The Chronicle embraces 110 years from the foundation of the abbey, that is, from 1066 to 1176.

The Abbey of Battle was founded in honour of St. Martin, by King William the Conqueror, on the spot where the Battle of Hastings was fought, in suffrage for the souls of those who died there, and in thanksgiving for the victory there gained. Its royal founder conferred upon it many privileges, especially of exemptions from burdens, and amongst other grants in the act of its foundation occur the words:

"Let it be free and quit for ever from all subjection to bishops, and from the rule of all persons whatever, as is Christ Church at Canterbury."

Hilary had not long succeeded to Seffrid in the See of Chichester, when he began to try to extend his jurisdiction over the éxempt Abbey of St. Martin at Battle. His claims were that the Abbot should be blessed in the Church of Chichester, having first made his profession of canonical obedience to it; next, that the Abbot was bound to attend the Diocesan Synod; and further, that the Bishop had the right of lodging in the Abbey and its manors, by which latter claim he hoped in time to subject it altogether to himself. The Abbot, on his side, with all patience and humility, pleaded the exemption in the Act of Foundation, which bore the signatures of Lanfranc the Primate, and Stigand, the Bishop of Chichester. The Bishop, however, hoped to be successful through the favour of Pope Eugenius and of Archbishop Theobald.

In the time of King Stephen, the Bishop began the strife by summoning the Abbot to his Synod, and on his non-appearance he punished him with suspension, unless he should make satisfaction within forty days. When this came to the Abbot's ears, he immediately complained to the King, whose Court was at St. Albans, who sent Robert de Corneville, one of his clerics, to the Bishop, warning him to leave the Abbey as free as the chapel royal itself. The contending parties were cited to appear before the King in London, in the presence of the Bishops and Barons, but on the appointed day the Bishop was not present. The charters and grants were produced and read, and in the Bishop's absence the King decreed the exemption of the Abbey.

Thus matters remained during the life of King Stephen. Immediately on the King's death, which

occurred October 28, 1154, Hilary summoned the
Abbot to his Synod once more, and on his non-
appearance he excommunicated him in solemn
council.   One of the Brothers of the Temple hastened with the news to London, where, by Archbishop Theobald's advice, the Abbot was waiting for
the new King's arrival, with his brother Richard de
Luci, a nobleman whose name often appears in the
history of St. Thomas.   On this Theobald sent a
message to the Bishop by Salamon, one of his
clerics, to the effect that the Abbot was absent at his
bidding, and that the Bishop should withdraw the
sentence until they could meet.   This Hilary accordingly did.

In 1155, the first year of King Henry's reign, in
the Council which was held in London, in Lent,
some Bishops and Abbots brought forward their
charters to have them confirmed by the King; and
amongst the others was the Abbot of Battle.   The
Bishop of Chichester hastened to Archbishop Theobald, and warning him that the liberties and dignities of Canterbury and Chichester were in danger,
requested him to interfere.   The King, "yielding to
the wishes of so eminent a personage, by whom he
had so recently been invested with his sovereignty,"
ordered the Chancellor not to put the Great Seal to
the charter of Battle Abbey.   The day following the
Abbot went to Court, but as the King was going
out to hunt, he returned to his dwelling-house at
Battlebridge, in Southwark.   On the third day he
went to Westminster, where he found the King
before the altar, about to hear Mass.   After the
Introit, he went up to the King, and said: "My
lord, your Excellency ordered that the charter of our
Church was to be confirmed with the royal seal:
why it is now refused, I do not know: let your
clemency command that the royal word be kept, and

not overthrown by any one's envy." The Chancellor[a] was then summoned, and the King ordered him to place the seal to the charter; but while he was yet speaking, the Bishop, guessing what was going forward, hurried up, and said: "My lord, your clemency must remember that the day before yesterday the venerable Archbishop of Canterbury and myself laid a complaint before you of the Abbot of Battle, who is seeking for charters against the dignities of our Churches, so that if his subtlety prevails, they will lament the loss of those rights which they have canonically possessed hitherto. Let your royal dignity therefore prohibit its having any confirmation, lest through his example others should rise against their Bishops." The King, however, ordered the charter to be sealed, and bade the Bishop and Abbot, together with the Chancellor, to appear before the Archbishop, when, if the matter could not be arranged, the charter was to be left in the chapel royal in the keeping of the Chancellor, until the King's pleasure should be known. When the Mass had been sung as far as the *Pax Domini*, the Bishop took the *Pax* as usual to the King, and afterwards, to the astonishment of many, to the Abbot also.

The Chancellor accordingly accompanied the Bishop and the Abbot to the Archbishop at Lambeth, before whom the charter of King William the Conqueror was read. At the clause declaring the Abbey to be as free from all jurisdiction of Bishops as Christ Church, Canterbury, there was a great outcry, some declaring it to be against the canons, others against the dignities of Canterbury, while others said that the words were "frivolous." Hilary

---

· [a] We thus learn from the Chronicle that St. Thomas was appointed to the chancellorship within the first few months of Henry's reign.

not finding the names of any of his predecessors to attest the grant, and holding the clause to be un-canonical, declared that it ought to be erased by the authority of the judges there present. The Arch-bishop was of the same opinion. Although the opposition of the Abbot was but reasonable, they would not rest quiet. When the Chancellor per-ceived the difference of opinion amongst them, he carried off the Abbot's charter to the chapel royal. The Abbot returned home, and the Bishop rejoiced as if he had won the day.

The Abbot, however, took the opportunity of a Parliament which was held in the summer of the same year, in order to receive the submission of a noble rebel, called Hugh de Mortimer, to renew his petition for his charter, and owing to the interest of Reginald, Earl of Cornwall, and Richard de Humet, " the King's Tribune," who were members of his council, and friends of Richard de Luci and of his brother the Abbot Walter, the petition was suc-cessful.

[³ The Abbot took leave of the King with thanks, retired from the Court with his charter, and in due time arrived at Battle, to the great joy of the brethren.

In the following Lent the Bishop renewed hostili-ties by summoning the Abbot to Chichester, and there, in the Chapter-house, on Mid-Lent Sunday, a long debate ensued between the Dean on the one side and the Abbot on the other; the text being a mandate from Adrian IV., the English Pope then reigning, to the Abbot to give due obedience to Hilary " to whom he had made profession thereof." The Dean demanded a written and sealed profession of obedience : the Abbot asked for a respite that he

³ The meaning of these brackets will be subsequently ex-plained.

might visit and consult the King, "whose chapel royal and a pledge of whose royal crown Battle Abbey is acknowledged to be." By quiet pertinacity, the Abbot carried his point ; and, "having made his prayers before the altar of the Holy Trinity there, and fortified himself with the sign of the holy Cross, he returned home with his friends."

King Henry had celebrated the anniversary of his accession at Westminster, and at the beginning of 1156, he passed over to Normandy. It was Easter 1157 before he returned to England, and, for the last six months Hilary, the Bishop of Chichester, had been in attendance on the King's Court. On the complaint of the Abbot, made through his powerful brother Richard de Luci, the King commanded the Bishop " that he should permit the Abbot of Battle, as his own chaplain, to rest in peace from all com- plaints, till he should return to England."

After landing at Southampton, Henry proceeded to Ongar in Essex, which belonged to Richard de Luci, and when the Abbot came to meet him there, the King summoned him " to attend on the coming Whit Sunday at St. Edmund's (where he was then to be ensigned with the royal crown)," when, he promised him, the cause between him and the Bishop should be tried. The Abbot awaited the appointed day at his manor of Hou, not far from Ongar.]

In the year 1157, the King was solemnly crowned anew in the third year of his reign at Bury St. Edmund's, in the presence of the prelates, nobles, and a multitude of people, on the feast of Pentecost, which fell that year upon St. Dunstan's day (May 19).[4] Hilary, Bishop of Chichester, and Walter, Abbot of Battle, were present, having been summoned, that their long dispute might be brought

[4] This coronation, Mr. Brewer tells us, is unmentioned by any other writer.

to a conclusion. The cause was adjourned for a few
days to be heard at Colchester, where the parties
arrived on Thursday in Whitsun week. On the
Friday, the Abbot, with Richard de Luci, went to
the King, who bade them wait in the Chapter-house
of the monks for him. When the King had heard
Mass, [he entered the Chapter-house, strictly ordering
that no one but those whom he should summon by
name should follow. He then called Thomas the
Chancellor, Robert Earl of Leicester, Richard de
Humet the Tribune, Richard de Luci, Warine Fitz-
Gerald, and Nicholas de Sigillo. There was also
present a certain physician named Ralph; and likewise Henry of Essex, the King's Tribune, who had
been previously sent to the Chapter-house to the
Abbot by the King. In addition to these, William,
the King's younger brother came, and took his seat
with the rest, near the King.

All having taken their places, and the Abbot sitting by with three of his monks, Richard de Luci
opened the proceedings: stating that the Abbot was
prepared to produce his charters. This the King
directed should be done, and] Thomas the Chancellor read the charter of the great King William ✓
before them. [The King thereupon took the charter
into his own hands, and having closely examined it,
deigned to commend it in high terms, blessing the
soul of that noble King, who had regarded the
Abbey he had erected with so strong affection as to
bestow upon it such great liberties and dignities.]
The Chancellor next read another charter of King
William upon the personal affairs of the Abbot, and
[this, in the same manner, the King took and examined, and commanded to be put up with the rest,
and carefully kept. He also declared that if ever he
himself, under Divine inspiration, should found an
Abbey, he would prescribe for it similar liberties and

dignities to those of Battle Abbey. He also ex-
amined] the charters of the other Kings, namely,
those of King William the younger, and of King
Henry [and at the same time, the charter confirmed
by his own seal, and commanded that they should be
carefully preserved. Then] the Chancellor looking to
the Abbot, said, " My Lord Abbot, the Bishop of
Chichester has, what seems to many, a strong argument against you, when he says that you made your
profession in the Church at Chichester." The Abbot
protested that he had done nothing against the
dignity and liberty of his Church. The King, looking
towards the Chancellor, said, " Profession is not
against the dignities of Churches; for they who
make profession promise only what they owe."
Richard de Luci, hearing this, again spoke:

My lord, your Highness has heard the privileges granted
by the noble King William to his Abbey, which he styled
Battle, because God had there given him victory over his
enemies, and which that Abbey—which is your own royal
chapel, and the pledge of your royal crown—has preserved
inviolate until now. Wherefore I avow that that Abbey
ought to be held in high account by you and by all of us
Normans, inasmuch as at that place the most noble King
William, by God's grace, and the aid of our ancestors,
acquired that whereby you, my lord King, at this time
hold the crown of England by hereditary right, and
whereby we have all been enriched with great wealth. We
therefore pray your clemency to protect with the right
hand of your authority that Abbey, with its dignities and
liberties, in order that it, with all its possessions, may
remain as free as it has ever been known to be in the
times of your ancestors. But if this please you not, I
humbly beg that you will remove my brother the Abbot
from his place, that the Abbey may not mourn the loss, in
his time, of the liberties which it had preserved inviolate
in that of his predecessors.

And Robert, Earl of Leicester [and others, cried
out that the King would take equal care to preserve
this Abbey as he would his crown, or the acquisitions
of their ancestors] and the King declared that he

never could bring his mind to permit the Church in question to lose its dignities and liberties in his time, and that he would speak to the Bishop, and arrange all the matter peaceably.

On the Tuesday after the Octave of Pentecost May 28), the King entered the monks' chapter-house in the company of the two Archbishops, Theobald of Canterbury, and Roger of York, the Bishops Richard of London, Robert of Exeter, and Robert of Lincoln, Silvester, Abbot of St. Augustine's, Canterbury, and Geoffrey, Abbot of . Holme, Thomas the King's Chancellor, Robert Earl of Leicester, and Patrick Earl of Salisbury, and amongst the Barons, Henry of Essex, Reginald de Warenne, Richard de Luci, and Warine FitzGerald, together with a great number of commoners. Hilary and Walter were also present. When a dispute between Archbishop Theobald and Abbot Silvester, of much the same character, had been decided, Richard de ·Luci rose and made a speech to the King in his brother's behalf, in much the same words as before.

[The Abbot then expressed himself as ready to answer all objections that might be alleged against the privileges of Battle, "which is your own free chapel, and the pledge of your crown;" but he prayed that the charter of the Conqueror, granted at the foundation of the Abbey, might be first read.] When this had been done by one of the clerics present, Thomas, the King's Chancellor, said to .the Bishop of Chichester:

My lord Bishop, your charity has heard what has been here done before our lord the King, in the hearing of all present. And now if it pleases your prudence to make answer against these things, it is lawful for you to do so: for to you, as it seems to us, this parable appertaineth.

The Bishop then rose, and thus began:

With no desire of wandering, as many have, but from our love and honour towards you, my lord the King, and knowing nought of this opposition, have we come with others here present into these parts of the kingdom. Wherefore if it should please you and the Abbot and the others who are before you that a peaceful arrangement should be made by your mediation, between myself and the Abbot, saving the right of our Church of Chichester, it might be done. For, therefore, am I come hither.

But when some refused a compromise, saying that the matter had been so long pending, that it ought to be definitely settled, the Bishop, in a loud voice, amidst a strict silence, resumed:

Since you have rendered a peaceful compromise impossible, I will expound before the King and all here assembled the rights of the Church of Chichester, and the previous state of the question.
Jesus Christ, my lord King (and then repeating himself) our Lord Jesus (and saying the same a third time) hear all of you and understand, Jesus Christ our Lord appointed two mansions and two powers in the constitution of this world, the one spiritual and the other temporal. The spiritual is that of which our Lord Jesus Christ spoke to our first Pastor, Peter the Apostle, and his successors, saying, "Thou art Peter, and on this rock I will build my Church." So your charity knows that from the earliest times the custom has prevailed in the Church of God, that the Pastors of the Church being the Vicars of the same Peter, the Prince of the Apostles, shall preside in due rule over Holy Church. Hence in those blessed Apostles to us who preside over the Church of God, was it said by our Lord Jesus Christ, *He who hears you, hears Me.* So also the Roman Church, adorned with the Apostolate of the same Prince of the Apostles, hath held through the breadth of all the world so great and magnificent a princely dignity that no Bishop and no ecclesiastical person can, without its judgment and permission, be deposed.

To this the King said, holding out his hands:

It is most true that a Bishop cannot be deposed, but he can be driven out by hands held thus.

Everybody laughed, and the Bishop went on again:

What I said before, I now repeat. The Roman Law proves that this state of the Church has been so appointed

from ancient times, and that no lay person, not even a
King, can give to Churches ecclesiastical dignities or
liberties, or confirm the same, except by the permission of
the same Father.

Then the King got angry, and said:

Dost thou think with thy subtle cunning to strive *for the
Pope's authority which was given him by man*, against the authority of royal dignity which was given me by God? I bid
thee by thy fealty and oath of allegiance to submit to right
reason thy presumptuous words, which are contrary to my
crown and royal dignity. I beseech the Archbishops and
Bishops who are present, saving the right of my royal
crown given me by the Supreme Majesty, to do me right
justice on thee; for thou actest, it is plain, against my
royal dignities, and thou art working to take away from
the King's majesty the liberties of old rightfully granted to
me.

A murmur arose amongst the people against the
Bishop, which could hardly be suppressed. Then
the Chancellor:

[It is not worthy that it should] have dropped from the
memory of your heart, venerated Bishop [whose excel-
lency]......for you......against our lord the King, to whom,
beyond doubt, [you made] the oath of allegiance. Wherefore your prudence must provide.

The Bishop, seeing that the King was offended,
and that all were against him, as soon as the murmur was quieted, continued his speech thus:

My lord, if anything has been uttered by my mouth
offensive to your royal majesty, I call the Lord of Heaven
and your royal dignity to witness, that I have not said,
with studied cunning, anything against you or the excel-
lence of your dignity. For I have by all means had the
highest regard for your paternity, extolled your excellency,
magnified your dignity, and ever loved you with the most
hearty affection as my dearest lord. May your Royal Highness then, I pray, suspect no evil in me, nor easily believe
any one who suggests it. I wish to diminish nothing of
your power, which I have always loved and magnified with
all my might. All that I have said has been to the honour
and glory of your Highness.

To this the King answered:

Far be such honour and glory from us and ours, and away with all by which, as all can see, you try in your soft and deceitful speech to annul what has been granted to me, by the help of God's grace, by the authority of the Kings, my predecessors, and by hereditary right.

Then said the Bishop:

All things, my lord, which in your hearing have been pronounced by me, by your leave, and that of all here present, I now bring to an end. And since my preface does not please, omitting these things, we will despatch the business in a few words.

Hitherto we have given our account of this controversy, almost in the words of the chronicler. It has been of importance to give our report in full up to this point, but it will not be necessary to do more than give a summary of the conclusion of the discussion, which runs to a length worthy of a modern Chancery suit.

Hilary's speech stated that the Abbot had been present at his consecration and installation, that he had attended at a Synod, and had received him as his Diocesan at a Visitation. Henry of Essex interrupted him with, "And now you repay evil for the good services he showed you!" The Bishop resumed with an account of how the controversy had arisen by the Abbot's refusal to attend a subsequent Synod, and that when the see of London had fallen vacant, the Abbot thought that he had interfered to prevent his advancement. Henry of Essex and Richard de Luci both protested that the Abbot's desire for the bishopric had been in no way unworthy or simoniacal. The Bishop continued his statement of the case by recounting how he had been summoned before King Stephen on this question, but that the Abbot had not appeared, and how, finally, at the expiration of the year, he had excommunicated the

Abbot for his contumacy. This sentence he had relaxed at the Archbishop's request. " If so," said Henry of Essex, " you did that after King Stephen's death which you would not have done in his lifetime. What the King is now about to do belongs to *his* prerogative." The Bishop concluded his speech by referring to all that had happened since the King's accession, complaining in every respect of the Abbot's conduct, and praying the King " to order the ancient and rightful institutions of the canons to be confirmed between us in all things, and to decide these matters in accordance with the customs of the Church."

To this the King replied, " We have heard a statement which has much surprised us, that you, my lord Bishop, esteem as frivolous, the charters of the Kings, my predecessors, confirmed by the lawful authority of the Crown of England, with eminent men as witnesses." This word " frivolous "—*peremptorias* [5]—was used when the matter was argued before the Archbishop at Lambeth, and St. Thomas seems to have reported it to the King.

The Abbot then handed in King William's charter, and pointed out that it was confirmed by the attestation of Archbishop Lanfranc and of Stigand, then Bishop of Chichester. In it, it was specified that the Abbot should not be bound to attend the Synod, though he might do so voluntarily. The Bishop said that he had never seen this charter, and on the Abbot commencing a reply, the King interrupted him: " From henceforth it is not for your prudence to make good your claim; but it becomes *me* to defend it, as my own royal prerogative." After much

[5] In giving this singular meaning to the word, Mr. Lower (pp. 83, 111) is borne out by a passage given by Ducange from the Statutes of Liège of 1287. *Cum judex viderit aliquam partium per exceptiones frivolas, dilatorias et peremptorias litem protrahere.*

JJ

further talking, at the suggestion of Richard de
Luci, and with the King's permission, the Abbot
retired to another part of the chapter-house to con-
sult with his friends, who are enumerated, and prove
to be nearly all the influential persons present: Roger
Archbishop of York, Thomas the King's Chancellor,
John Treasurer of York, Robert Earl of Leicester,
Patrick Earl of Salisbury, Henry of Essex, Reginald
de Warenne, Warine FitzGerald, and some other
barons, and a considerable number of knights. The
King, in the meantime, went into the church to hear
Mass, and this being over, returned to his seat, and
Thomas, the Chancellor, was called upon to deliver
judgment—as, from its effect, we suppose we must
style what certainly reads more like the speech of
an advocate.

He began with a little sarcasm of the Abbot's
thankfulness for the account the Bishop had given
of the hospitality he had received at the Abbey. He
admitted the fact of the Abbot's presence at the
consecration, installation, and Synod, but he said it
was from no ecclesiastical obligation, as the charter
proved: it had been at the command of the Archbishop of Canterbury. Theobald hereupon acknowledged that he had given such a mandate. As to the
sermon in the chapter-house at Battle, a Bishop
from Ireland, or from Seville, might have done the
same. In the matter of the see of London, the
Bishop's conscience must have suggested suspicions
that the Abbot never entertained. The Abbot averred
that he attended before King Stephen in the King's
chapel at the Tower of London, and that the
Bishops of Winchester and Ely were present, and
heard the King's confirmation of the charters. He
could not have been excommunicated by the Bishop,
the Chancellor argued, for when hearing Mass with
the King at Westminster Abbey, he had given the

Pax to the Abbot after the King had received it. " For this, if I have done wrong," apologized Hilary, " I will confess my fault to the Archbishop, and do penance."

The Chancellor then spoke of letters of Pope Adrian IV., commanding the Abbot to attend at Chichester. The King, on hearing of this, demanded with evident signs of anger, whether the Bishop had procured them. The Bishop declared that he had not, and that they were sent by the Pope, who was our countryman, Nicholas Breakspeare — as the Abbot had defamed him in Rome, and thus had procured them against himself. The Archbishop, hearing this denial, made the sign of the Cross in token of astonishment. The Chancellor demanded whether there were any other letters that could affect the Abbey of Battle, and the Bishop solemnly affirmed that there were none.

Archbishop Theobald now addressed the King : " Will your Excellency command us to retire and determine these matters according to the legal method of ecclesiastical custom ? " " Nay," said the King, " I will order you to determine them in my presence, and after due deliberation *I* will decide." So saying he arose and retired to the cemetery of the monks, the rest, except the Bishop and the Abbot, accompanying him. After some consultation, the King sent for the Bishop, and after much discussion, the King commanded Henry of Essex to bring in the Abbot and the monks. The Bishop then solemnly liberated and " quit-claimed " the Abbey of Battle, as a chapel royal, of all the rights he had hitherto maintained—that he had not, nor ought to have any authority over it—and that he absolved the Abbot as having been unjustly excommunicated by him, and finally, he declared him, from that day for ever, free from all episcopal exactions and customs.

" Is this done of your own free will, and not by compulsion ? " demanded the King. The Bishop replied : " I have done this of my own accord, induced by considerations of justice." After this, on Theobald's proposal, the kiss of peace was given by the Bishop to the King, the Abbot, and Richard de Luci. And now, with the rejoicings of the Abbot, and the list of the witnesses to the final arrangement, the chronicler brings to a close his account of this memorable suit,

The reader will have seen, with the liveliest surprise, the speech put by the chronicler into the mouth of the angry King, to the effect that the Pope's authority was of human origin, while his own royal power was Divine,—a phrase absolutely without parallel in the records of that age,—and he will ask whether the sentence is genuine, or at least on what evidence it rests. We now proceed to examine the MSS. of the Chronicle, and in so doing we will direct our attention to the speech of King Henry to which we have just referred, and to the short speech in which St. Thomas reminds Hilary of his oath of allegiance, the fragmentary state of which is most tantalizing.

The MS. from which Mr. Brewer has printed his edition of the Battle Abbey Chronicle is a beautiful parchment MS. of the latter part of the twelfth century, or, in other words, dating from the very time when its record closes. It is in the Cottonian Library in the British Museum—Domitian II. It is remarkable for two erasures—one in each of the two speeches we have now under consideration. In the King's speech, the words attributing a Divine origin to his own authority are given, but not those which in the narrative above speak of the Pope's power as human, and are given in italics. Consequently, in Mr. Brewer's edition and in Mr. Lower's translation those words do not appear, and the former gentleman supposed that the gap had once been filled with some profane Norman oath, erased by some puritanical hand.

We were not quite without knowledge of this portion of the history of Battle Abbey, even before the whole of it was printed by the Anglia Christiana Society. Spelman, and after him, Wilkins,[6] had published long ago the greater part of this portion of the narrative; but singularly enough, the extract given by them has not been collated by Mr. Brewer, and seems to have been entirely overlooked by him. The manuscript from which Spelman printed is also in the Cottonian Library (Vitellius D. vii. fol. 152). It suffered much in the fire, but it is perfectly legible. It was written by Joscelyn, whom Hearne[7] calls "Archbishop Parker's Domestic Antiquary," and the true author of the lives of the Archbishops of Canterbury that appeared under Parker's name. That Spelman printed from it, is clearly seen by a comparison, the last sentence in Joscelyn being scored out, and printed by Spelman with the note *Sequentia tenui linea cancellantur.*

The twelfth century MS. is very much more full than Joscelyn, as the reader will at once see by observing what large portions of the narrative we have given between brackets. All these portions are omitted by Joscelyn, but in the King's speech is found the phrase given by us in italics, in the place of the erasure in the old MS. Joscelyn has underlined it, perhaps because it was marked for omission in the MS. he copied. The other gap exists exactly as *it once did* in the old MS., ending even with the same part of a word—*tis.*

[6] Spelman, *Concil. Orbis Britan.* (Lond. 1644), vol. ii. p. 53; Wilkins, *Conc. Magn. Britan.* (Lond. 1737), vol. i. p. 427.

[7] Rob. de Avesbury (Oxon, 1720), p. xxiii.

At first sight it would seem from this that the
erasures in Domitian II. had been made at two
different periods, the one before and the other after
the transcript was taken, and that the copyist had
omitted some of the speeches for the sake of short-
ness. This is, however, very improbable. The
clause respecting the Pope's authority is not likely
to have been erased since Parker's time; and as to
the other gap, though Joscelyn has exactly the gap
that Domitian II. once had, as we have said, even
to the half word, it is not a copy of the present state
of this speech. We believe that Joscelyn did not
copy from Domitian II. at all: and that the erasures
in the latter were made by the hand that wrote it.
Of the latter point a careful examination of the
MS. leaves us in little doubt.

The speech of St. Thomas, the appearance of
which in the MS. has convinced us that the erasure
is as old as the MS. itself, ran originally thus:

......deme
re elaboras.   Murmure itaq in poplo contra
epm ccitato vix sedari potuit.   Tunc cancell
A cord vri excidisse memoria psul venande
a line erased
tis eni in dnm nrm regē, cui fidem sacramtū
erasure   Unde prudentie vre pvidendū

The scribe then erased the " A " in the third of
these lines, and the " m " of " fidem " in the fifth;
and he wrote partly in the margin and partly over
the erasure of the fourth line, as well as over the
erasure of the sixth, so that the MS. now stands
thus:

......deme
re elaboras.   Murmure itaq in poplo contra
epm ccitato vix sedari potuit.   Tunc cancell
Haut dignū e a cord vri excidisse memoria psul venande
cui' excellentiā
tis eni in dnm nrm regē. cui fidei   sacramtū
vos fecisse nulli dubiū e.   Unde prudentie vre pvidendū

These amendments are in the same hand as the rest of the MS., but the colour of ink shows clearly where the writing is over an erasure. The word "excell-entiam" is half on the margin and half over the erasure.

From this examination we have come to the con-clusion that the original which Joscelyn copied was not Domitian II., but a transcript taken from it, while it was in the state of transition which we have here first given, and before it received the partial amendments which we now find in the MS. The gap ending with the part of the word "*pecca*tis" (if that was the word) renders it very difficult to doubt that it was from this MS. Joscelyn's original was derived: and the erasures in this speech having been made by the scribe himself render it exceedingly probable that the erasure in the King's speech was made by the same hand. This seems to us to prove that we have but one report, and that the reporter in these two instances doubted the accuracy of his narrative. We should certainly not place much confidence in the genuineness of a sentence in a judgment, if the shorthand writer himself were to erase it from his notes. In all probability the itali-cized words in the speech of Henry II. once stood in the MS., but it is exceedingly improbable that even that irascible monarch ever spoke them, blasphemous as his speeches sometimes were in his anger. This the compiler of the Chronicle felt, and he has erased it. This being the case, it would be futile for us to attempt to complete by conjecture the fragmentary speech attributed to St. Thomas. If a sentence once correct has been corrupted in transcription or erased in part since it left its author's hands, some-thing may be done in the way of restoration by plausible conjecture: but what can be done when the writer himself does not know how to complete his sentence? There is, however, no reason in the world that we should assume that the missing line here was of a similar character with the erased line in the King's speech; in fact, the words *cujus excellentiam* require something complimentary to the Bishop.

In estimating the value of the Chronicle as an historical record, we must bear in mind that it is a thoroughly *ex parte* statement. It was written by a religious of the Abbey, the privileges of which were at stake: and it is the account we might expect from one of the three monks who accompanied the Abbot to Colchester, and who sat by his side and shared his anxiety in that Chapter House. As a partisan, the writer was consequently anxious to make the Chancellor, St. Thomas, speak as much in favour of the Abbot, and against the Bishop, as possible.

Before we leave this point of the trustworthiness of the Chronicle as evidence, one further consideration must be duly weighed. St. Thomas himself, when in exile, mentions this very controversy in a way which Mr. Hurrell Froude considered[8] to be fatal to the authority of the Battle Chronicle. In a letter to the Pope,[9] the Saint meets the accusation that the troubles of England were to be imputed to himself by citing the proofs of tyranny and oppression of the Church which had taken place before his own promotion to the archbishopric. After several instances he says: "And how did the Bishop of Chichester succeed against the Abbot of Battle, when, in virtue of apostolic privileges, having named and denounced the Abbot in Court as excommunicate, he was straightway compelled to communicate with him before them all, without any absolution,

8 Froude's *Remains*, pt. ii. vol. ii. p. 576.

9 Lupus, bk. 4, ep. 14. vol. ii. p. 648; Giles, ep. S. Thomæ, i. p. 54; Froude, p. 348; *Supra*, p. 292.

and to receive him to the kiss of peace? For so it pleased the King and the Court, whom he did not dare to contradict in anything. And this, Most Holy Father, happened in the time of your predecessor and of ours." This does not read like the statement of the man who had taken the part ascribed to him by the Chronicler of the Abbey.

We will not only leave it to the reader to say how far these considerations affect the credibility of the narrative we have placed before him, but we will ask him also to judge what view should be taken of the conduct of St. Thomas. We will content ourselves with summing up what it seems to us may be said for and against him, if the correctness of the report of the Colchester trial be assumed.

Against him, it may be and has been said, that his principles respecting ecclesiastical independence of the royal authority were very different during his chancellorship to what they were when he previously held a purely clerical office under Theobald, or subsequently, after his own elevation to the primacy. In this instance, the Bishop of Chichester had the authority of a letter from Pope Adrian IV., which enjoined the Abbot of Battle to submit and obey; he had Archbishop Theobald on his side, who, when the matter was referred to him by the King, declined to give judgment in the Abbot's favour, and who is evidently anxious all through the controversy, that the King should permit a purely ecclesiastical cause to be tried "according to the legal method of ecclesiastical custom:" while the sole argument against the Bishop was a Charter of William the Conqueror, no Papal confirmation of which was alleged: and yet the Chancellor delivered judgment against the Bishop.

For the line of conduct followed by St. Thomas as Chancellor in this affair there is more to be said than at first sight appears. Pope Adrian had said to the Abbot, " It has come to our knowledge that you refuse due obedience to our venerable Brother Hilary, Bishop of Chichester, to whom you have made profession thereof." The very foundation therefore of the Pope's judgment rested on a misrepresentation, which was that the Abbey was not exempt, and that the profession of obedience was therefore absolute. The exemption of the Abbey was expressly assented to by Lanfranc, Archbishop of Canterbury, and Stigand, the Bishop of Chichester, at the time of its erection, and in the original Charter of the Conqueror, which is confirmed by the anathema against its violators, not only of these prelates, but also of one of no less venerable a name than St. Wulstan, then Bishop of Worcester. The canon law was not as express in its enactments then as it was after its codification into the *Corpus Juris* a century later by St. Raymund of Pennafort. The reservations to the Holy See were by no means as explicit. An archbishop received his pallium from Rome, and then his powers were very little short of what, in our time, we should consider patriarchal. The Holy See exercised its higher jurisdiction by Legates, and on every point appeals were carried to Rome in the last instance; but subject to these limitations the power of an archbishop was hardly restricted, and his acts, unless overruled, were held to be canonical if they did not go counter to the decrees of Synods or to ecclesiastical tradition. It is not to be wondered at that he who could confirm the election of a bishop and consecrate him to his see without reference to Rome, could also, especially when in conjunction with the bishop of the diocese, give exemption to an abbey from episcopal control.

There are, besides, viewing this transaction by the light of modern canon law, two points well worthy of consideration. The privileges of royal chapels are well known, and it is to be remarked that the argument most frequently brought forward in the controversy was that Battle Abbey was a *Dominica Capella*. And next, all canonists acknowledge in a founder the power even of derogating from the canon law in the act of his foundation. Conditions that he might ask for in vain when the act was completed, a founder might impose of his own authority before the transfer to the Church was carried into effect. It was for the Church to choose whether she would accept the foundation so hampered; and in the case of Battle Abbey, the Church was a party to the conditions imposed in the Conqueror's Charter. We are therefore inclined to regard the opposition of the Bishop of Chichester and the manifest tendencies of Archbishop Theobald, not so much as zeal for ecclesiastical liberty as jealousy of monastic exemption. When St. Thomas afterwards in his exile came to refer to this matter, it was to blame the King for having compelled a bishop to give the kiss of peace to an abbot whom he had excommunicated, and not for having, by an encroachment on a Papal privilege, exempted an abbey from episcopal jurisdiction. The conclusion now arrived at was never afterwards disputed, but received all manner of subsequent ecclesiastical sanction, for not only is Archbishop Theobald's confirmation of the exemption of the Abbey extant, but we have similar confirmation by Popes Honorius and Gregory, which recite the recognition of the rights of the Abbey by Bishop Hilary, in the presence of Henry King of England, of illustrious memory, and of Theobald the Archbishop, his Metropolitan and Legate of the Apostolic See; which recognition the Archbishop confirmed by apostolic and metropolitical authority.[10]

[10] *Chron. de Bello; Appendix ex Registro de Bello*, p. 187.

We have said nothing of the temper King Henry displayed on this occasion, a temper worthy of the Norman monarchs and of Henry Plantagenet. It was cunningly fostered by Richard de Luci, the most powerful nobleman of the Court, and the brother of the abbot whose cause was at stake. Nothing could have been suggested more certain to move the King's irascibility than the insinuations that the attack on the Abbey was to be attributed to English jealousy of this great monument of the Norman Conquest, and that it was therefore a proof of disloyalty to the King himself. Little wonder when the King had silenced the Abbot by saying that he would be spokesman for him, that Roger de Pont l'Eveque, the Archbishop of York, should be found in consultation with the Chancellor, whom, years before, he had nicknamed "Clerk Baillehache," and on the side of the regular against the secular, though he so hated religious himself that he used to say that his predecessor Thurstan had never done a worse thing than when he built Fountains.[11] Considering the circumstances, the Chancellor, who was by his office the mouthpiece of the King, spoke most temperately in his concluding speech, even according to an *ex parte* report. He answers in detail the various arguments adduced by the Bishop, but he in no way claims the right to decide the matter by secular authority. After he had concluded, the King having been irritated anew by mention of the letter of Pope Adrian which the Bishop had obtained without his consent, declares that *he*, and not the Archbishop of Canterbury, shall decide the cause; and it is brought to an end by the *quiet-clamatio*, or quit-claim, of the Bishop himself. We cannot, however, wonder that the remembrance of scenes such as this, in which the Chancellor found himself powerless in the presence of his jealous and

11 *Chron. Walteri de Hemingburgh* (Histor. Soc.) vol. i. p. 119.

violent master, should have led him to the well-known conclusion, that if he were, by virtue of his office, bound to defend the liberties of the Church, the love between them would speedily be turned to hatred. "I knew," he said, when the King offered him the archbishopric, "that you would require many things, as even now you do require them, in Church matters, which I could never bear quietly; and so the envious would take occasion to provoke an endless strife between us."

————

NOTE E (page 49).

THE CHANCELLOR'S POLICY.

Two contemporary documents express an opposite view to that given in the text, and it is but right that the reader should have the opportunity of forming his own judgment. Of these two passages, one has been often quoted, but it does not seem to furnish much ground for an unfavourable view of the conduct of St. Thomas while Chancellor towards the Church; the other, which has not been referred to by modern writers, is very much more to the point, and if it stood alone, would go far to settle the matter unfavourably. The first is the passage in which John of Salisbury rhetorically contrasts the treatment St. Thomas received when he was Chancellor and a man of the world, and that which he met with when Archbishop and thoroughly ecclesiastical. In it the writer may have been led by his rhetoric to strengthen his antithesis. The letter (*Materials*, vi. p. 101) was written by John of Salisbury to his friend Baldwin, Archdeacon of Exeter, and in it this passage occurs: "What do they now persecute in the Archbishop of Canterbury, except that in the sight of kings he has dared to uphold God's justice, defend the law, and protect the liberty of the Church?   Certainly when he was a splendid trifler in the Court, when he seemed to despise the law and the clergy, when with the powerful he followed the follies of the world, he was held to be a great and famous man, pleasing to everybody, and he was proclaimed by one and all as the only one quite fit for the archbishopric. But from the moment when he was made a Bishop, and, mindful of his condition and profession, he chose to show that he was a priest, and preferred to take the Word of God for his master rather than the world, he has become their enemy, telling them the truth and correcting his life: and thus they fill up the measure of their fathers, who for like reason persecuted the Prophets and Apostles, persecuting yet the martyrs of Christ, that is, the witnesses of truth and justice."

A much stronger expression is to be found in one of the miracles recorded by Benedict (*Materials*, ii. p. 163).   Henry of Houghton, one of St. Thomas's clerics, reports a conversation that took place after the martyrdom between himself and a nobleman, who during the Saint's life had been one of his opponents.   It would appear from the context, in which Newington, where miracles were wrought, is spoken of as his manor, that the nobleman in question was Richard de Luci, Justiciar of England. He said that he should have had difficulty in believing the miracles attributed to St. Thomas, unless he had seen one of them with his own eyes.   A priest with whom he was well acquainted, had long been paralyzed in his right arm, so as not to be able to raise his hand to his mouth.   He had thus for some years been unable to say Mass, but after a visit to Canterbury, he not only could

perform his priestly duties freely and quickly, but when the esquires and servants were throwing weights, he beat them all by throwing the weight the furthest. "Now, Henry," the nobleman continued, "how do you account for this? None of us was harder on the Church of God than he was, when he was Chancellor, and now he excels all the saints in the calendar in the number and greatness of his miracles." Henry of Houghton might have pleaded, Benedict says, the holy Martyr's hard and most holy life, but he preferred to take a lower ground.[1] "Which is worst," he asked, "to deny Christ or to be hard on the Church, as you accuse yourself or the Saint of being? And if tears washed away Peter's crime; if confession of guilt and short penance took the thief to Paradise before the other saints; what will not seven years of exile, violent despoiling of his goods, banishment of his relations, imprisonment of his friends, his hair-shirt, and most of all, this cruel death, its cause, its time, and its place, have done for the anointed of the Lord and the champion of the Church?" The nobleman acknowledged that the answer was satisfactory, and thanked him for it, saying that "he would not have had that tumour rooted in his heart for twenty pounds." The story is not remarkable precisely because Richard de Luci, if it were he, took that view of St. Thomas's life, but because Prior Benedict and Henry of Houghton do not deny the wrong done of old to the Church, regarding it as atoned for by his subsequent life. Such testimony should be taken at its full worth, but it must be remembered that no facts are quoted to counterbalance the plain and convincing facts given in the text, chiefly from Fitzstephen, who certainly had

[1] It is not easy to see how Benedict's proposed answer differs from that given by Henry.

no interest in making out the Saint to have been consistent all through his life in his allegiance to the Church.

Undoubtedly the King thought that St. Thomas would not oppose him in his oppression of the Church, in spite of the Saint's outspoken declaration to the contrary, or he would not have urged his appointment to the Archbishopric. And this belief of Henry's must have been due to St. Thomas's conduct as Chancellor, where his duty was simply to do his best under difficult circumstances. Indeed Roger of Pontigny (*Materials* iv. p. 14) says expressly that "Thomas of set purpose showed himself as if he were very severe on ecclesiastical persons and things so to avert from himself any mark of suspicion and to be able better under this cloak to meet [and counteract] the King's intention, which he thoroughly understood. The King then, believing that he could best fulfil his purpose against the Church through him, whom he had found to be most faithful to him in all things, and very prone to his intentions, firmly resolved that he should be made Archbishop of Canterbury." Our question is not, What did the King expect of St. Thomas? The answer to that is plain enough. Our question is, In what sense did St. Thomas, when Chancellor, justify Roger of Pontigny's statement that he showed himself "as if he were very severe"—*quasi severissimum*—on ecclesiastics? Roger himself gives the answer (*Ibid.* p. 12) when he speaks of the Saint's chancellorship. "And though the King had already conceived the idea [of the oppression of the Church] that he afterwards carried out, yet meanwhile under Thomas's protection the state of the Church remained safe and quiet, for he frustrated in all things the evil intentions of the King and the covert plots of the courtiers, but cautiously and as it were secretly, lest he might be open to suspicion." This means that he did not put forward his churchmanship, but substantially, and in all important matters, prevented any harm being done to the Church; and this is the very opposite to the statement that, when Chancellor, St. Thomas was an open persecutor of the Church, that on the strength of this severity, he was made Archbishop, and that he then suddenly changed his policy. We may safely say that St. Thomas did what Theobald expected and hoped of him when he recommended him to the King. That Theobald should have recommended one who would, with great prudence and moderation, avert evil that he feared, surely does not deserve the hard title of "confessedly an ecclesiastical plot," given to it by Mr. Magnusson in his Preface (p. xcix) to the Icelandic Thomas Saga. The passage that calls forth this comment is here appended, as it is probably derived from Prior Robert of Cricklade. It is further interesting for the curious statement that the Archdeacon of Canterbury was King Henry's Chamberlain for a short time, before he was made Chancellor.

"The King was still a youth, yielding an open ear to his councillors, who were both overbearing and not of the most righteous in their ways, froward withal, and nowise men of any great prudence. Now whereas there stand many ready to break the barge of St. Peter, the Archbishop was fain to find a man who might steady the craft somewhat, lest it should go adrift to utter wreck. But the craft of the elected ones for the Kingdom of Heaven is Holy Church, the which, it may well be said, was disabled by William Rufus, first of all men in England, but after his day things went on as if the kings went along hand in hand towards the fire,

KK

when as each dragged the right and the freedom of the Church headlong under the Crown. But for this place one so difficult to fill with a fit person to stand between the authority of God's laws and the grasping greed of the King and his men, the Archbishop seeth no one likelier than Archdeacon Thomas, he being proven in manifold wise a man of wisdom and good will. And to wise folk it will be clear enough that the Archbishop putteth a dissembling face upon his device when he setteth it forth to the King to take Thomas into his Court. And herein the Archbishop did rightfully, in that such is a holy craft which harmeth no one, yet increaseth the glory of God. Now it cometh to pass that the blessed Thomas betaketh him for awhile away from Canterbury and entereth the King's Court a second time. At this time it is recorded that by the tale of his age he was even thirty and eight years old, having been in the Archbishop's Court for fifteen winters. Thus for a time he putteth away the service of an Archdeacon and taken thereinstead to kingly attendance and courtly manners. And now it becometh his concern to keep watch of the King, when he sleeps as well as when he sitteth in his seat, with all heed and good will. No long time passeth by ere the King judgeth wisely this Thomas worthy of a higher honour than having this simple service to give his heed to, and therefore he leadeth this friend of the Lord into a station which is called the chancellorship" (pp. 45—49).

NOTE F (pages 195, 196).

ST. THOMAS IN FLANDERS.

Oye, a village three leagues and a half N.E. of Calais, and about a league from Gravelines, was in existence as far back as the Roman occupation under Julius Cæsar. In 1216 Renard Count of Boulogne ceded Oye to Philip of France, on occasion of the King's marriage to his daughter Matilda. At the request of the Duchess of Burgundy, daughter of the King of Portugal, two conferences were held at Oye to establish peace between France and England, which were followed by the truce concluded at Tours in 1446 and by the marriage of Margaret of Anjou with the King of England. In 1347, as a consequence of the capture of Calais by Edward III., the English took possession of the fort of Oye, and they held it till 1436, when the Duke of Burgundy took it, and it was destroyed by the Duke of Guise in 1558 (*Notice historique sur l'état ancien et moderne du Calaisis*. Par M. P. J. M. Collet. Calais, 1833).

Eldemenstre is the name that Herbert of Bosham tells us (p. 331) the inhabitants gave to a hermitage of St. Bertin. The place, now called St. Momelin, is a small village about four kilometres from Clairmarais and five from the town of St. Omer. It was there, on the little river Aa, that St. Omer in 626 established in the first instance the three saints, St. Bertin, St. Momelin, and St. Ebertian, and as St. Momelin was the oldest of the three, St. Omer made him the Superior. After the foundation of St. Bertin's Abbey, the beautiful ruins of which still adorn the town of St. Omer, the original foundation was known by the name of Vieux Moustier,

Vetus monasterium, and this is evidently the interesting Flemish word *Eldemenstre* preserved by Herbert of Bosham. The river Aa, in Latin *Agnio*, on which St. Thomas passed from Clairmarais to St. Momelin, was familiar enough in the seventeenth and eighteenth centuries to the students of the English College of St. Omer, as their country house called Blendecque was upon it, and so, lower down the river, was the village of Watten, on the height above which was the Novitiate of the English Jesuits.

Many places in the Low Countries claimed the honour of having been visited by St. Thomas, but it is not easy to see when such visits can have taken place. L'Abbé Destombes, in his *Vies des Saints* (Cambrai, 1852, tom. iv. p. 167), enumerates a long list. He begins with Bourbourg as having been visited before the Saint went to Clairmarais. Then he states that he left at the Monastery of Anchin a chasuble, a dalmatic, a little tunicle, and a cope, green in colour: while to Marchiennes he gave a pallium and a cross adorned with pearls and relics. It is plain that St. Thomas was not in a position to make costly presents, either on his exile or when he passed through the Low Countries again on returning to England. These however may well have been vestments that were used by him, which, on account of the veneration in which they were held, were brought to the great monasteries for preservation. At Marchiennes there was a manuscript Pontifical, which is now in the Public Library at Douai, No. 94, on the first page of which a librarian of Marchiennes Abbey has written, "Pontificale hoc ad usum ecclesiarum anglicarum recepisse nos a S. Thoma Cantuariensi traditione constanti habemus." At Arras in St. Anthony's there was an inscription in old characters, "Icy Saint Thomas célébra messe certainement." Near the Church of St. Mary Magdalene in the same town a fountain was called St. Thomas's, the water of which was regarded as a specific against fever. In the Church of St. Vaast in Arras a chalice of pure gold, said to have been used by the Saint, was long preserved. After Dixmude, where a chasuble and chalice still exist, St. Thomas is supposed to have gone to the Monastery of Auchy-les-Moines near Hesdin, where the religious had an especial veneration for their Abbot's oratory, as the Saint had said Mass there. At Blangy, where he is said to have gone next, a gold ring was kept in which a large topaz was set. The only reason for saying that St. Thomas was at La Motte-au-Bois is that an altar was there dedicated to him, in which some of his relics were enclosed. That he was at Lille is asserted in an inscription still existing on the front of No. 8, Rue d'Angleterre : " Sancto Thomæ Cantuariensi hujus ædis quondam hospiti sit laus, honor et gloria." In the church of Beaucamps-en-Weppes a wooden porringer was kept that St. Thomas had received from a countryman to quench his thirst on his journey. The religious of St. Nicolas-des-Près at Tournay had a tradition that they had been visited by the Saint. At St. Médard in like manner they claimed the honour of having had St. Thomas as a guest, and a dark red chasuble left by him there was afterwards in the Cathedral of Tournay. In the Cathedral windows the martyrdom of St. Thomas was depicted, and an altar was erected in his honour in 1171, which, if the date be correct, was before his canonization. Its place was between the columns in the fifth bay, and its three chaplains, Baldwin Hamdis, Arnold de Gand, and William de Vacques, are said to have founded it. Stephen the Bishop of Tournay calls St. Thomas in his letters *olim dominum et amicum.* All these details are taken from Destombes.

NOTE G (page 397).

THE EARL OF NORFOLK AND THE CANONS OF PENTNEY.

Hugh Bigod, Earl of Norfolk, and William de Vaux were excommunicated by the Pope, who by letter (*Materials*, vi. p. 550) dated from the Lateran, July 7, 1166, ordered St. Thomas to proclaim the excommunication with lighted candles. As the name of William de Vaux is not mentioned in the list of those excommunicated at Clairvaux (*Supra*, p. 310), he probably withdrew from his position and was absolved. On the 22nd of April, apparently of the year 1167, the Pope (*Materials*, vi. p. 557) empowered the Bishops of Winchester and Worcester to absolve the Earl of Norfolk under certain conditions, but if these were not fulfilled he was again to be excommunicated, and after a year of obstinacy his land was to be interdicted. That he did not amend is clear, as we find his name among the excommunicates of Clairvaux.

The cause of this censure was that the Earl and William de Vaux took possession of Pentney, which belonged to the Canons of Pentney. The Pope commissioned Gilbert Foliot, in the first instance, to obtain restitution. This he did, he says (*Ibid.* p. 548), with the help of the King's intervention; but the whole matter was brought as an action by the Earl of Norfolk before the King in person at Oxford, in January or February, 1166, and the Prior of Pentney, we may well imagine how, was brought to assent to a compromise which was very unfavourable to his community. Against it protest was made by the Canons, and both parties appealed to the Holy See. The Pope's decision was against the

Earl of Norfolk, and his obedience was enforced by sentence of excommunication, as we have seen.

The matter is memorable on account of two letters (*Materials*, vi. pp. 545, 553), one from the Bishop of London to the Cardinal William of Pavia, and the other from Pope Alexander to King Henry. The difference of principles between the two is very striking, and this was in 1165, when Gilbert Foliot would still claim to be a good churchman.

" I have received the Pope's command to straitly summon Hugh Earl of Norfolk, and unless on admonition he restores to the canons of Pentney the village of Pentney and all that they complain has been taken from them, to place him and all his land under interdict, and then unless he repent within forty days, to excommunicate him without delay. But in this we have been gravely opposed by the royal authority, for the King asserts that it belongs to the supreme dignity of his kingdom, that when he is ready to give full justice to any one who has a complaint about lands or fiefs against one of his earls or barons, neither the Archbishop nor any bishop of his kingdom may place him under interdict or excommunication. This he declares his predecessors have held up to the present time by assent of the Roman Pontiffs, and he reminds us that all the bishops of his kingdom have confirmed it to him by oath, so that he requires of us that we should stand by antiquity, and not diminish the privileges of his crown by leaving what we have sworn to. He supports by heavy penalties what his authority commands. We are therefore in straits, so that unless the Pope shall mercifully relax his mandate, we must either incur the peril of disobedience, which God forbid, or the King's reproach of perjury and breach of fealty. I had rather I had never been a bishop than have incurred

either one or the other.   Both swords are heavy, for
one kills the soul and the other the body; the first
is the heavier sword, but the second strikes more
heavily.   .And what utility will there be in my blood
to my dearest lord the Pope, if I go down into the
misery of being held to be a perjurer or of becoming
disobedient?—which again may Heaven forefend.
If I do not obey his Holiness it is death to me;
if I do obey him, nothing remains for me but to
quit the kingdom, the laws of which I break, fealty
to the King of which I desert.   If the cause were
one that merited death or exile, I should rejoice
that by my banishment or death I should show the
Pope good service.   But is the cause of six Brothers
of Pentney, living miserably without any observance
of rule or order, such that, because some few acres
have not been restored to them, a question on the
eminence of their dignities should be raised between
the Supreme Pontiff and his old friend—by God's
help his firm friend in the future—the King of
England?   Especially as in this cause each side
may easily have its rights, and this disturbance
may be brought back to peace and justice.   If the
King be allowed he will straightway determine the
cause by the counsel of the Bishops and other
prudent men.   If the Pope delegates judges, Earl
Hugh will not refuse to abide by their sentence."

Gilbert clearly shows how the Constitutions of
Clarendon practically worked.   A few sentences
from the Pope's letter to Henry will show how far
Gilbert Foliot's position was from that of the Holy
See.   "Though your filial devotion to us and your
mother, Holy Church, seems to have grown somewhat cold, we have never withdrawn our paternal
affection from you or the kingdom you govern.
Your Serenity knows that the blows of a friend
are better than the kisses of an enemy.   Consider

then more carefully and see, that as clerics are distinguished from seculars in life and habit, so the judgments of clerics are altogether different from the judgments of laymen. ⟨ If you upset that order and usurp the things of Jesus Christ, making new laws at your pleasure to oppress the Church and Christ's poor, bringing in customs that you call ancestral, you yourself beyond all doubt, in the Last Judgment which you will not be able to avoid, will be judged in like manner, and with the same measure that you have measured withal, it shall be measured to you. . . . We especially commend to your royal magnificence the Brothers of the church of Pentney, and their goods and possessions, which your lieges Earl Hugh and William de Vaux, laying aside the fear of God, have occupied, contrary to their own writings and concessions, and therefore we have excommunicated them by Apostolic authority and separated them from the Body of Christ, that is, the Church. By these Apostolic writings we pray, admonish, and exhort your Serenity, and for the remission of your sins we order you, for the love of God and the reverence of St. Peter and of ourselves, to maintain, protect, and defend these Brothers, the church in which they serve God, and their goods and possessions, and preserve them against the invasions of your subjects by your royal protection, that you may deserve happily to obtain an eternal reward from Almighty God and to be helped by the prayers of the Brothers and of all the other religious of your kingdom. And avoid the men who are thus excommunicated, for as leprosy spreads, so the same penalty extends from those who do wrong to those who consent thereto. And further, we greatly wonder that you unlawfully made the Prior of these Brothers, without their knowledge and assent, give over to the Earl in your presence the possessions of his church which were entrusted to him for improvement, not for injury, contrary to the authentic writings of the Popes our predecessors; for in this you have without doubt gravely offended God and have no little injured His honour and glory. This concession by the Prior, which by the Canons is void, we by Apostolic authority do altogether annul, and declare to have no force for the future."

NOTE H (page 398).

ST. THOMAS AND ST. GODRIC.

A monk of Westminster was on a visit to the holy hermit of Finchale, who asked him one day whether he knew Thomas, "the new Archbishop of Canterbury." The monk replied that he knew him, and added, "And do you know him, sir?" St. Godric's answer was, "With my bodily eye I have never seen him, but with the inward eye of my heart I have often seen him, and I know him so well, that if now I were to see his face, though no one were to tell me, and he were to be placed amongst many persons whom I did not know, I should recognize him immediately." The monk not making any remark, St. Godric continued: "I wish to send him some secret messages, if you will be my messenger." His companion expressed readiness, provided there was nothing wrong in the message. The old man smiled, and said that he hoped his injunction would be good. "When you see him," he said, "remember, I pray you, to salute him in the name of poor Godric, and say that he must steadily persevere in carrying out those things which he has resolved to do, for all the things he has resolved are most pleasing and acceptable to Almighty God. Yet he will suffer very great adversity, and he will very soon be driven into exile from England; he will for some time remain a stranger and a sojourner in foreign lands, until the period of his appointed penance is fulfilled. At last he will return to England, to his own archiepiscopal see, and he will then be loftier in dignity than when he left England. For that Archbishop and Malcolm King of the Scots, of all the rich men between the Alps and the furthest limits of Scotland, are the two who will be most pleasing and acceptable to God. And King Malcolm will receive from God the penny of the heavenly reward. Now, when you have told him this, I beg you to send me by some one his absolution of my sins, written and sent me by him." "Why do you ask his absolution," inquired the monk, "seeing that you are not of his flock?" "I know that it will benefit me," said St. Godric, "and therefore I ask you to send it to me." The monk marvelled at this conversation, for St. Thomas had not been very long Archbishop, and people did not think that he had seriously lost the King's favour. On his return he went with his Abbot to St. Thomas at "Warrennes Stanes," near Windsor, and when our Saint had heard St. Godric's message, he made inquiry from the Abbot respecting him. "I recommend you," said the Abbot, "to receive his message with gratitude, for he often foretells things to come." The next morning St. Thomas wrote to him, sending the absolution he had asked for, and recommending himself to his fatherly prayers. Within three months of the prediction, the biographer of St. Godric tells us that it was fulfilled by the exile of the Saint.

When St. Thomas had spent some years in exile, the same monk, being once more in the neighbourhood, consulted St. Godric respecting it. "The

Archbishop of Canterbury has now been a long time in exile, and there seems to be no possible hope left of a reconciliation, for we have heard that so many adverse things press upon him, that we are afraid he will never again return to England." "Yet a little while longer," replied St. Godric, "will he suffer his exile, for he has not yet passed his time of penance. Then the King will permit him to return to his see in Kent, with greater power and honour than when he went into exile."

This was the message of which St. Thomas was reminded on the day before his passion.

There is another similar narrative in another part of the same Life, which from the interest of being thus enabled to link two English saints together, we may be permitted to give at equal length. Reginald, the monk of Durham, who wrote the Life, speaks here in the first person.

"It was now mid-Lent, and the vigil of St. Cuthbert's day had come (March 19), on which his monks from all parts are accustomed to meet in chapter for the feast. And since I had kept half my Lent with the man of God (St. Godric), I spoke to him about it on the evening before, that I might get his leave to say Mass early the next morning and go home. As I was about to start after Mass, I knelt for his blessing, when he smiled and said, 'Though you are in such a hurry to go, it is possible that before you leave the gate you may come back again.' I went out, and immediately met some Cistercian abbots, who made me return, and asked to be allowed to speak to the man of God. I went in to him, and he said with a smile, 'See, how soon you have returned.' I then thought of his words, and when the interview with the abbots was over, I returned to ask his leave to depart: he gave it me with his blessing, but he added, 'If you go now, before you get out of the garden fence, you may be obliged, however unwillingly, to return again.' I did not give much consideration to his prediction, but I started for Durham as quickly as I could. But before I was clear of the place, a Brother in grey met me, who called upon me in the name of the Holy Trinity to stop and hear his message; and he commanded me in the name of the lord Thomas Archbishop of Canterbury, then in exile, that in virtue of the Holy Spirit and of obedience, I should tell no man what he was about to tell me, until I saw the end. This I promised. Having received the message of the lord Archbishop to the servant of God, I returned into his cell, and timidly and anxiously I began to consult him on some text of Scripture. He saw that there was something that I wished to say to him, and so he said: 'You always treat me like an unlearned person with your circumlocutions: say briefly and plainly what you are thinking of, and I will willingly answer you as God shall enable me.'

"Somewhat confused by this truthful and pleasant speech, but taking courage, I said that I wondered exceedingly why the long altercation between the King and the Archbishop had not been brought to an end by the mediation of some of the nobles. He answered: 'Because both of them did wrong in the gift and the receipt of that dignity, and therefore the Lord hath chastised them both with the rod of their own fault: but the Lord's clemency can bring good out of men's evil, and give a good end to evil beginnings.' Then speaking freely I told him all. 'Sir,' I said, 'a messenger from the exiled Archbishop of Canterbury is outside, and binding me by the authority of the Archbishop and by solemn pledges, he has told me that he has come here as his secret messenger, so secretly that scarcely any even of his

574 ST. THOMAS OF CANTERBURY.

domestics were aware of it, for if he were taken by the King's officials, he would certainly be punished with death. His lordship of Canterbury ordered him to give his precept in a secret manner to which-ever of the monks of Durham he found in attendance upon you. So in his name and as his messenger, and in the name of the Holy Trinity, he bade me secretly to go to you, whom he called the servant of God, and tell you his message. Three times you have sent to the Archbishop the knowledge of secret and future things, in each of which he has found you to be a true prophet in the Spirit of the Lord; for in each of them the end has come to pass as you have oretold. In the name of the Holy Trinity he ad-ured me to ask of you how long this dissension will ast, when he will be in accord with the King, and whether he shall ever return to England, or what the end will be; for on these points he is very anxious. Now he prays you as a father, he adjures you as a fellow-soldier, he asks of you as an ancient servant of the Lord, to tell him by me the end of all this calamity, for he has heard that you have predicted of him that within seven years his exile should have a happy end, and now those years have all but elapsed, and they have brought him sorrow rather than consolation.'

"After a long silence, he replied—'Three times I have sent him secret messages which the Holy Ghost revealed to me, and which I felt would come true in his regard; and now tell his messenger who is out-side, that when you came to me for leave to go home, I foresaw how your journey would be hin-dered. Tell him not to be troubled if for a little while he have much to suffer, for the longer the trial is, the fuller will be the crown, and the light burden of this tribulation brings forth an increase of ever-lasting beatitude. For within six months peace by word of mouth will be made between him and the King, but Godric will not then be living here; and within nine months his honours and possessions will be restored to him, and he will return to his see in Kent, where, not long after, an end shall come to him altogether and of all things—an end that shall be for his saving good, his joy and perfection; and to many men a remedy of salvation, a help and consolation. Tell these last words of mine frequently to his messenger, and repeat them again and again, for by the help of the Holy Spirit, as soon as he has heard them, the Archbishop will know their secret meaning. And there will be greater joy amongst all the English for his return than there was sorrow for his exile.'

"I then went out and told all this to his messenger, but nothing would satisfy him but that he should be admitted to speak to the servant of God; and when I had obtained this for him, St. Godric rehearsed to him over and over again what I have given above, and repeatedly told him that he must remember that in a little while the end of all was coming. Having received his blessing we departed together, and we understood nothing of the prophetic things we had heard. Once more I returned, after I had had his blessing, and he said: 'This morning you were in such haste to get to Durham; now you will not get there for the Chapter, but you will be there by dinner-time,' It happened as he said, and finding the monks going to the refectory, his prophecy came back to my mind.

"In about two months after this, the man of God departed this life, and before the martyrdom of my lord of Canterbury none of these words came to my memory; but after the solemn martyrdom of the Archbishop's death, then all the ambiguity of the prophecy was made clear. For all things happened as the man of God had foretold, and the end came as the Spirit of God had made known to him" (*Vita S. Godrici*, pp. 293, 297, § 27—280).

Fr. Stevenson, who edited this interesting volume for the Surtees Society, remarks that this prophecy was uttered in 1170, on the 19th of March, that St. Godric died on the 21st of May, that it was in October that St. Thomas of Canterbury was, "to all appearance," reconciled to King Henry, and his martyrdom followed on the 29th December. These dates show that Hoveden,[1] the chronicler, was mistaken when he says that the death of St. Thomas was revealed to St. Godric at Finchale, on the day on which it happened, for St. Godric, as we have seen, predeceased St. Thomas seven months.

Speaking of the connection between St. Thomas of Canterbury and the Saints of Durham, we are not aware whether any notice has been taken of a passage in the compilation of Thomas of Froimont, published by Dr. Giles under the name of Philip of Liège. Whosesoever it may be, it is certainly not later than the generation next after that of St. Thomas, and it contains this anecdote.

" When he raised from the earth to his shrine the blessed Cuthbert, the bishop beloved of God and venerable amongst men, and touched each of his limbs and his face and all the members of the Saint which had suffered no corruption, though six hundred years had passed, for he had lived a virgin from his childhood, famous for holiness and miracles, the King asked the Archbishop how he presumed to touch all the members of so great a saint; on which the man of God replied—' Do not wonder, sire, at

[1] " Eodem die passio beati Thomæ revelata est beato Godrico Anachoritæ per Spiritum Sanctum apud Finkhale, qui locus distat Cantuaria plusquam per (? ter) centum sexaginta milliaria" (Savile, *Scriptores post Bedam*, 1601, p. 522).

this, that with my consecrated hands I have touched
him, for far higher is that Sacrament which day by
day I, as other priests, handle on the altar, the
Blessed Body of Christ, which is committed to three
orders of priests, deacons, and subdeacons'" (*Anec-
dota Bedæ*, &c, Ed. Giles. Caxton Soc., 1851, p. 234).

———

NOTE I (page 416).

THE MARTYRDOM.

THE north transept, in which St. Thomas met his
death, has ever since gone by the name of the Martyrdom. The entrance from the cloister was then, as
now, in the south-western corner, adjoining which,
at the east end of the north nave aisle, was the chapel
of the Blessed Virgin. The eastern side of the transept consisted, first of the flight of steps leading up to
the north choir aisle, which St. Thomas was as-
cending on his way either to the high altar or to the
patriarchal chair behind it, when he was induced to
return to the transept by the voices of the knights.
Next to these steps upward were the steps that led
downward to the crypt. This arrangement remains
undisturbed on the opposite side of the church.
There was then a small space of wall between the
crypt stairs and an apse in which was the altar of
St. Benedict. It was with his back to this wall that
the Saint stood at his martyrdom, and it was here
that the altar "at the sword's point" was afterwards
placed. In the middle of the transept was a column
which supported a low vaulting over the corner of
the transept, and above this was the chapel of St.
Blaise.

William of Canterbury says that the Saint had a
LL

statue of our Blessed Lady before him as he stood
with his back to the wall. *Habens a læva præviam
crucem suam, a tergo parietem, præ se beatæ Mariæ Virginis
iconiam, circumquaque memorias et reliquias sanctorum*
(p. 132).   Grim, describing the Saint's position as he
turned to the right under the column in the midst of
the transept, says that he had on one side of him
the Lady Altar, and on the other the altar of St.
Benedict.   *Divertit in dextram sub columna, hinc habens
altare beatæ Dei Genitricis et perpetuæ Virginis Mariæ,
illinc vero sancti confessoris Benedicti* (p. 436).   The dis-
tinct mention of a statue by William of Canterbury,
who knew the place so well, seems to indicate that,
at the back of the altar of the Blessed Virgin in the
nave aisle, there was a statue facing across the transept, standing probably upon a column.   Of this
column we have apparently mention made by Leo
von Rotzmital, who came to England as Bohemian
Ambassador in 1446.   He speaks of *columna ante
sacellum Genitricis Dei, juxta quam orare, et colloquio beatæ
Virginis (quod a multis visum et auditum esse nobis certo
affirmabatur) perfrui solitus est* (Stanley's *Canterbury*,
p. 266).   He calls it a column *before* the chapel of
the Blessed Virgin, while a statue, to have been seen
by St. Thomas, must have been *behind* the Lady
Altar; but a visitor, standing in the transept, might
well speak of a column that was between him as he
stood and the altar, as *before* that altar.   The new
Lady Chapel, on the site of the chapel of St. Benedict, was built by Prior Goldstone I., between 1449
and 1468, just after Leo's visit, so that the Lady
Altar in the nave aisle had not yet been removed.
It is worth noting that Erasmus calls the little altar
at the sword's point an altar of the Blessed Virgin.
A column *behind* the old Lady Chapel would have
been *before* this; but it seems more probable that
Erasmus was mistaken in calling the altar at the

sword's point a Lady altar, and that the column belonged to the Lady Chapel in the nave.

Dean Stanley takes this view. " The site of the older Lady Chapel in the nave was still marked by a stone column. On this column—such was the story told to foreign pilgrims " (and here he refers to Leo von Rotzmital)—" had formerly stood a statue of the Virgin, which had often conversed with St. Thomas as he prayed before it. The statue itself was now shown in the choir, covered with pearls and precious stones " (*Canterbury*, p. 225). Dean Stanley was not acquainted with William of Canterbury, whose narrative bears out this part at least of the local tradition, that on that column there was a statue of our Lady. But Leo does not say that the *statue* had often conversed with St. Thomas, but that the Blessed Virgin had done so.

It may be well to remark that Dean Stanley, following Mr. Gough Nichols, attacks as a " mistaken tradition, repeated in books, in pictures, and in sculptures, that the Primate was slain whilst praying at an altar " (p. 103). And in a note he says : " The gradual growth of the story is curious—(1) The posthumous altar of the martyrdom is represented as standing there at the time of his death. (2) This altar is next confounded with the altar within the chapel of St. Benedict. (3) This altar is again transformed into the high altar; and (4) in these successive changes the furious altercation is converted into an assault on a meek unprepared worshipper, kneeling before the altar."

As to the attitude of kneeling, an artist might perhaps be justified in selecting that posture if he thought fit, as Fitzurse's third blow brought the martyr on his knees first, and then on his face. *Tertio percussus martyr genua flexit et cubitos* (Grim, p. 437). *Positis primo genibus, conjunctis et extensis ad Deum manibus* (Fitzstephen, p. 141).   *Orantis instar, junctis manibus et flexis genibus* (Herbert, p. 506).

Next, as to the "furious altercation" and the "meek worshipper," the only resistance St. Thomas made was at the attempt of Fitzurse to drag him from the church.   He did not so much as raise a hand to ward off a blow, and all remark that he met his end like a man in prayer.   *Ad modum prostrati in oratione jacebat immotus* (Will. Cant. p. 135).   *Recto corpore quasi ad orationem prostratus* (Bened. p. 13).   *Videns carnifices eductis gladiis, in modum orantis inclinavit caput . . . nec brachium aut vestem opposuit ferienti, sed caput, quod inclinatum gladiis exposuerat, donec consummaretur tenebat immobile* (Jo. Sar. p. 320).   *Genu flexo, et orantis modo junctis ante se manibus* (Herb. p. 498).   *Martyr insignis nec manum nec vestem opposuit percussori, nec percussus verbum protulit, nec clamorem edidit, non gemitum, non sonum cujuscumque doloris indicem; sed caput quod inclinaverat gladiis evaginatis immobile tenuit, donec confusus sanguine et cerebro, tanquam ad orandum pronus, in pavimento corpus, in sinum Abrahæ spiritum, collocavit* (Grim, p. 438).   Which do the descriptions of those actually present resemble the most, a man killed in a "furious altercation," or an "assault on a meek worshipper"?

Lastly, is it also a "mistaken tradition" that St. Thomas was killed "at the altar"?   Erasmus may have thought that the little wooden altar "at the sword's point" was in existence at the time of the martyrdom, but it would be hard to find any picture or sculpture representing it.   Fanciful pictures may represent the high altar; but the altar that might be represented with historical accuracy is that of St. Benedict, which was close by.   The Saint fell, according to Fitzstephen, *secus aram, quæ ibi erat, sancti Benedicti* (p. 141).   *In templo ante altare sacerdos obtulit seipsum hostiam vivam Deo* (Herb. p. 498).   *Coram altari inter consacerdotes et manus religiosorum* (Jo. Sar. p. 317). *Coram altari prostratus* (*Id.* p. 318). *Ante altare sancti Benedicti* (Lamb MS. Anon II. p. 131). *Inter crucis et altaris cornua.* This last description, in the letter of the Archbishop of Sens (Ep. S. Tho. ii. p. 161) is literally true, for his cross was on his left, and the altar on his right. As the Saint fell to the right, he must have been just before the altar.

NOTE J (page 419).

ISABEL COUNTESS OF WARRENNE.

"William, the King's brother," of whom Le Breton spoke as he dealt his blow on the head of the Martyr, was the third son of Geoffrey Plantagenet and the Empress Maud. He died at Rouen on the 30th of January, 1164. The grievance that Le Breton was avenging was therefore not a recent one. Indeed Isabel had married Hamelin the King's half-brother (*Supra*, p. 180) in 1163, her first husband William of Blois having died in October, 1159. The resistance of St. Thomas to the marriage of Isabel and William may therefore have been while he was Chancellor, and must have been before his rupture with the King at Westminster and Clarendon. If it was during the chancellorship, it will have been one instance the more of the care of the Chancellor for the observance of ecclesiastical law. Another uncanonical marriage hindered by him when Chancellor was that of Matthew Count of Boulogne and Mary of Blois (*Supra*, p. 198).

There are three views as to the relationship between the Countess Isabel and William, the brother of King Henry II. Isabel of Warrenne was the great-grand-daughter of Gundreda ; and the old and popular belief was that she was a daughter of William the Conqueror. If this were true, Isabel would have been in the third and fourth degrees of consanguinity, or, as we say, second cousin once removed, both to her first husband William of Blois, and to William Plantagenet, who wanted to be her second husband, for these two men were both great-grandsons of the Conqueror, the one by Adela and King Stephen, the other by King Henry I. and the Empress Maud. Hamelin, whom she did marry, though he was half-brother of Henry II., was not in the same kindred to her, as he was not the son of the Empress Maud.

The second opinion, started first by Mr. Thomas Stapleton in 1846, and accepted by Mr. Freeman and many recent writers, among others by Mr. Edwards (the Editor of the *Liber Monasterii de Hyde* in the Rolls Series, 1866, p. xcvii.), is that " Gundreda, wife of William first Earl of Warren and Surrey, was the sister of Gherbod or Gorbodo, the Fleming (first Earl of Chester after the Conquest), and therefore not the daughter of the Conqueror, but of his Queen Matilda by a former marriage." If this were so, there was no relationship between Isabel and either of the Williams, who were descendants of the Conqueror. So the question could not arise, why she should have been permitted to marry one and not the other, when the relationship was the same. She was related to neither, and therefore could have married either, but the laws of the Church would not allow her to marry both. William Plantagenet, the King's brother, was second cousin to William of Blois, Isabel's husband ; and therefore she was in that degree of *affinity* to him, and for that reason could not marry him. Hamelin Plantagenet, as we have seen, was not related to her first husband at all, and thus there was nothing to prevent his becoming her second husband. St. Thomas's opposition to the marriage of Isabel and William the King's brother is perfectly intelligible, and indeed was a strict and simple duty. This relationship is exactly described by Fitzstephen (p. 142) in the words: "This William [Plantagenet] by his mother the Empress Mahalt, and this William [of Blois] Earl of Warrenne [*jure uxoris*] by his father King Stephen, were the sons of cousins." I am indebted to Mr. Everard Green, F.S.A., for the reference that makes this matter clear.

The third opinion is that of Mr. Edmond Chester Waters (*Archæological Journal*, No. 163, 1884, p. 300) who regards it that "we may safely take it as proved that Gundreda was neither daughter nor near relation of Queen Matilda." The proof adduced by Mr. Waters brings in a second impediment into our case, and shows that Isabel de Warrenne and even her first as well as her proposed husband were really within the degrees of kindred, within which at that time marriage could not be contracted. The fourth General Council of Lateran in 1215, limited the impediment, which had previously extended to the seventh degree of consanguinity or sixth cousins, to the fourth degree or third cousins, which is the present law of the Church. Henry I. of England wished to marry his natural daughter to William de Warrenne II. who was the son of Gundreda. St. Anselm prohibited the marriage because the parties were related to one another in the fourth and sixth degree. St. Anselm would never have based the prohibition on their being third cousins twice removed, if they had been first cousins; and Mr. Waters reasonably concludes that Gundreda was not a daughter, nor indeed a near relation of the wife of the Conqueror.

But, in showing us that there was a relationship, according to the then existing law, between William de Warrenne II. and a daughter of King Henry I., Mr. Waters makes the conclusion plain that a relationship, still within the prohibited degrees, though very distant, existed also between Isabel, the grand-daughter of that William de Warrenne II. and William Plantagenet, the grandson of Henry I. They were in the sixth and seventh degree, or as we say fifth cousins once removed. The same relationship existed between Isabel and her first husband William of Blois. These very distant degrees seem to have been overlooked in the case, and we may be sure that the impediment that caused St. Thomas to prevent the marriage of Isabel with William Plantagenet was that of affinity, as he was her late husband's second cousin.

NOTE K (page 439).

THE MURDERERS.

" FITZURSE, Moreville, and Tracy had all sworn homage to Becket while Chancellor. Fitzurse, Tracy, and Bret had all connections with Somersetshire. Their rank and lineage can even now be accurately traced through the medium of our county historians and legal records. Moreville was of higher rank and office than the others. He was this very year Justice Itinerant of the counties of Northumberland and Cumberland, where he inherited the barony of Burgh-on-the-Sands and other possessions from his father Roger and his grandfather Simon. He was likewise Forester of Cumberland, owner of the

castle of Knaresborough, and added to his paternal
property that of his wife, Helwise de Stuteville.
Tracy was the younger of two brothers, sons of
John de Studely and Grace de Traci. He took the
name of his mother, who was daughter of William
de Traci, a natural son of Henry I. On his father's
side he was descended from the Saxon Ethelred.
He was born at Toddington in Gloucestershire,
where, as well as in Devonshire, he held large estates. Fitzurse was the descendant of Urso or Ours,
who had under the Conqueror held Grittlestone in
Wiltshire, of the Abbey of Glastonbury. His father,
Richard Fitzurse, became possessed, in the reign of
Stephen, of the manor of Willeton in Somersetshire,
which had descended to Reginald a few years before
the time of which we are speaking. He was also
a tenant in chief in Northamptonshire, in tail in
Leicestershire. Richard the Breton was, it would
appear from an incident in the murder, intimate
with Prince William, the King's brother. He and
his brother Edmund had succeeded to their father
Simon le Bret, who had probably come over with
the Conqueror from Brittany, and settled in Somersetshire, where the property of the family long continued in the same rich vale under the Quantock
Hills, which contains Willeton, the seat of the Fitz-
urses. There is some reason to suppose that he was
related to Gilbert Foliot. If so, his enmity to the
Archbishop is easily explained. . . .

" The murderers themselves, within the first two
years of the murder were living at Court on familiar
terms with the King, and constantly joined him in
the pleasures of the chase, or else hawking and
hunting in England. Moreville, who had been
Justice Itinerant in the counties of Northumberland
and Cumberland at the time of the murder, was
discontinued from his office the ensuing year; but

in the first year of King John he is recorded as
paying twenty-five marks and three good palfreys,
for holding his court as long as Helwise his wife
should continue in a secular habit.   He procured
about the same period a charter for a fair and mar-
ket at Kirk Oswald, and died shortly afterwards,
leaving two daughters.   The sword which he wore
during the murder is stated by Camden to have been
preserved in his time; and is believed to be the one
still shown in the hall of Brayton Castle,[1] between
Carlisle and Whitehaven.   A cross near the castle
of Egremont, which passed into his family, was dedicated to St. Thomas, and the spot where it stood
is still called St. Thomas's Cross.   Fitzurse is said
to have gone to Ireland, and there to have become
the ancestor of the M'Mahon family in the north
of Ireland—M'Mahon being the Celtic translation of
Bear's son.   On his flight, the estate which he held
in the Isle of Thanet, Barham or Berham Court,
lapsed to his kinsman Robert of Berham—Berham
being, as it would seem, the English, as M'Mahon
was the Irish version, of the name Fitzurse.   His
estate of Willeton in Somersetshire he made over,
half to the Knights of St. John the year after the
murder, probably in expiation—the other half to his
brother Robert, who built the chapel of Willeton.
The descendants of the family lingered for a long
time in the neighbourhood under the same name,
successively corrupted into Fitzour, Fishour, and
Fisher.   The family of Bret or Brito was carried on
through at least two generations of female descendants.   The village of Sanford in Somersetshire is still
called from the family Sanford *Bret*.

[1] "Now the property of Sir Wilfrid Lawson, Bart., where I
saw it in 1856.   The sword bears an inscription *Gott bewahr die
aufrichten Schotten*.   The word *bewahr* proves that the inscription
(whatever may be the date of the sword) cannot be older than
the sixteenth century" (*Dean Stanley's footnote*).

" Robert Fitzranulph, who had followed the four
knights into the Church retired at that time from the
shrievalty of Nottingham and Derby, which he had
held during the six previous years, and is said to
have founded a priory of Beauchief in expiation of
his crime. But his son William succeeded to the
office, and was in places of trust about the Court till
the reign of John. Robert Brock appears to have
had the custody of the castle of Hagenett or Agenet
in East Anglia.

" The history of Tracy is the most remarkable of
the whole. Within four years from the murder he
appears as Justiciary of Normandy; he was present
at Falaise in 1174, when William King of Scotland
did homage to Henry II,, and in 1176 was succeeded
in his office by the Bishop of Winchester. This is
the last authentic notice of him. But his name
appears long subsequently in the somewhat conflicting traditions of Gloucestershire and Devonshire,
the two counties where his chief estates lay. The
local histories of the former endeavour to identify
him in the wars of John and of Henry III., as late
as 1216 and 1222. But even without cutting short
his career by any untimely end, such longevity
as this would ascribe to him—bringing him to a
good old age of ninety—makes it probable that he
has been confounded with his son or grandson.
There can be little doubt, however, that his family
still continues in Gloucestershire. His daughter
married Sir Gervase de Courtenay, and it is apparently from their son Oliver de Tracy, who took the
name of his mother, that the present Lord Wemyss
and Lord Sudley are both descended. The pedigree,
in fact, contrary to all received opinions on the
subject of judgments on sacrilege, 'exhibits a very
singular instance of an estate descending for upwards
of seven hundred years in the male line of the same

family.' The Devonshire story is more romantic, and probably contains more both of truth and of fable. There are two points on the coast of North Devon to which local tradition has attached his name. One is a huge rent or cavern called *Crookhorn* (from a crooked crag, now washed away) in the dark rocks immediately west of Ilfracombe, which is left dry at low water, but filled with the tide except for three months in the year. At one period within those three months, 'Sir William Tracy,' according to the story of the Ilfracombe boatmen, 'hid himself for a fortnight immediately after the murder, and was fed by his daughter. The other and more remarkable spot is Morthoe, a village situated a few miles further west on the same coast—'the height or hold of Morte.' In the south transept of the parish church of this village, dedicated to St. Mary Magdalene, is a tomb, for which the transept has evidently been built. On the black marble covering, which lies on a freestone base, is an inscription closing with the name of 'Sir William Tracy—the Lord have mercy on his soul.' This tomb was long supposed, and is still believed by the inhabitants of the village, to contain the remains of the murderer, who is further stated to have founded the church. The female figures sculptured on the tomb—namely, St. Catherine and St. Mary Magdalene, are represented as his wife and daughter. That this story is fabulous has now been clearly proved by documentary evidence, as well as by the appearance of the architecture and the style of the inscription. The present edifice is of the reign of Henry VII.: the tomb and transept are of the reign of Edward II. 'Sir William Tracy' was the rector of the parish who died and left this chantry in 1322; and the figure carved on the tomb represents him in his sacerdotal vestments, with the chalice in his hand. But although there is no proof

that the murderer was buried in the church, and
although it is possible that the whole story may
have arisen from the mistake concerning this monument, there is still no reason to doubt that in this
neighbourhood 'he lived a private life, when wind
and weather turned against him.' William of Worcester states that he retired to the western parts of
England, and this statement is confirmed by the
well-attested fact of his confession to Bartholomew,
Bishop of Exeter. The property belonged to the
family, and there is an old farm-house, close to the
seashore, still called Woollacombe *Tracy*, which is
said to mark the spot where he lived in banishment.
Beneath it, enclosed in black jagged headlands, extends Morte Bay. Across the bay stretch the Woollacombe Sands, remarkable as being the only sands
along the north coast, and as presenting a pure and
driven expanse for some miles. Here, so runs the
legend, he was banished 'to make bundles of the
sand, and binds (wisps) of the same.'

"Besides these floating traditions, there are what
may be called two standing monuments of his connection with the murder. One is the Priory of
Woodspring, near the Bristol Channel, which was
founded in 1210 by William de Courtenay, probably
his grandson, in honour of the Holy Trinity, the
Blessed Virgin, and St. Thomas of Canterbury. To
this priory lands were bequeathed by Maud the
daughter, and Alice the grand-daughter, of the third
murderer, Bret or Brito, in the hope, expressed by
Alice, that the intercession of the glorious martyr
might never be wanting to her and her children.
Its ruins still remain under the long promontory,
called from it 'St. Thomas's Head.' In the old
church of Kewstoke, about three miles from Woodspring, during some repairs in 1852, a wooden cup,
much decayed, was discovered in a hollow in the

back of a statue of the Virgin fixed against the north wall of the choir. The cup contained a substance, which was decided to be the dried residuum of blood. From the connection of the priory with the murderers of Becket, and from the fact that the seal of the Prior contained a cup or chalice as part of its device, there can be little doubt that this ancient cup [now in the Museum at Taunton] was thus preserved at the time of the Dissolution as a valuable relic, and that the blood which it contained was that of the murdered Primate.

" The other memorial of Tracy is still more curious, as partially confirming, and certainly illustrating, the legendary account[2] of his adventure in Calabria. In the archives of Canterbury Cathedral a deed exists by which ' William de Tracy, for the love of God and the salvation of his own soul and his ancestors, and for the love of the blessed Thomas Archbishop and Martyr,' makes over to the Chapter of Canterbury the manor of Daccombe, for the clothing and support of a monk to celebrate Masses for the souls of the living and dead. The deed is without date, and it might possibly, therefore, have been ascribed to a descendant of Tracy, and not to the murderer himself. But its date is fixed, by the confirmation of Henry, attested as that confirmation is by ' Richard elect of Winchester ' and ' Robert elect of Hereford,' to the year 1174 (the only year when Henry's presence in England coincided with such a conjunction in the two sees). The manor of Daccombe or Dockham in Devonshire is still held under the Chapter of Canterbury, and is

[2] "According to this story, he reached the coast of Calabria, and was then seized at Cosenza with a dreadful disorder, which caused him to tear his flesh from his bones with his own hands, calling, ' Mercy, St. Thomas,' and there he died miserably, after having made his confession to the Bishop of the place " (p. 105).

thus a present witness of the remorse with which Tracy humbly begged that, on the scene of his deed of blood, Masses might be offered—not for himself individually (this, perhaps, could hardly have been granted)—but as included in the general category of 'the living and the dead.' But, further, this deed is found in company with another document, by which it appears that one William Thaun, *before his departure to the Holy Land with his master*, made his wife swear to render up to the Blessed Thomas and the monks of Canterbury all his lands, given him by his lord, William de Tracy. He died on his journey, his widow married again, and her second husband prevented her fulfilment of her oath ; she, however, survived him, and the lands were duly rendered up. From this statement we learn that Tracy really did attempt, if not fulfil, a journey to the Holy Land. But the attestation of the bequest of Tracy himself enables us to identify the story still further. One of the witnesses is the Abbot of St. Euphemia, and there can be little doubt that this Abbey of St. Euphemia was the celebrated convent of that name in Calabria, not twenty miles from Cosenza, the very spot where the detention, though not the death, of Tracy, is thus, as it would appear, justly placed by the old story " (Dean Stanley's *Historical Memorials of Canterbury*, 9th edition, pp. 70, 106).

NOTE L (page 469).

CHRIST CHURCH, CANTERBURY.

In Lanfranc's church the central tower was surmounted by a golden cherub, whence it obtained the name of "Angel Steeple." The nave had eight columns on each side, and ended with two lofty towers with gilt pinnacles. A gilded corona hung in this nave. The roodloft separated the central tower from the nave, and before it on the western side stood the altar of the Holy Cross. The roodbeam upheld a great cross and two cherubs besides the images of the Blessed Virgin and St. John. The Lady Chapel was at the eastern end of the north aisle. The two western transepts were alike, each having a strong pillar in the middle which supported a groining that sprung from the transept walls. In the south transept on the groining was the organ, and beside it in an apse the altar of All Saints; beneath in the same apse on the church floor the altar of St. Michael. Between this and the choir were two flights of steps, one that went down into the crypt, the other a longer flight that led to the upper parts of the church. In the south transept the lower altar was that of St. Benedict, and above the vault was the altar of St. Blaise. On this side also there were two flights of steps, leading down to the crypt and up to the choir aisle. Before Gervase wrote, the pillar in the north transept was taken away with the vaulting it supported, that the altar erected where the martyrdom took place there might be better seen, and where the vaulting had been a triforium or passage was made from which curtains and tapestry might be hung. From the transept there were steps up to the floor of the central tower, and thence again steps that led up to the choir.

The choir was built by Conrad, who was Prior under St. Anselm, Lanfranc's successor, and it was called his "glorious" choir. This choir was burnt on the 5th of September, 1174. There were nine pillars on each side of the choir, which ended in an apse composed of six of the pillars. In the wall over the arches on these pillars were "small and obscure" windows, above which were the triforium and the upper windows. Then came the ceiling, which was beautifully painted. It was here that the fire seized the church, by sparks from houses burning outside, which sparks were driven by a strong south wind under the lead roof.

A low wall between the pillars shut in the monks' choir from the aisles, and the enclosure embraced the high altar and the altars of St. Elphege on the north side of the high altar, and that of St. Dunstan on the south, where the bodies of those two saints rested. The presbytery was raised three steps above the choir, and the high altar three steps higher still. The patriarchal chair [of one stone, says Gervase; of great stones cemented, according to Eadmer] was immediately behind the high altar, looking towards it, raised on eight steps. At the eastern corners of the high altar were two wooden columns, decorated with gold and silver, which supported a large crossbeam over the altar. On it was a statue of our Lord in majesty, statues of St. Dunstan and St. Elphege, and seven shrines containing relics. Between the columns stood a cross gilt, adorned with sixty bright crystals. The choir was lighted by a gilded corona containing four-and-twenty wax candles. Under the high altar in the crypt was the altar of the Blessed Virgin, to whom the whole crypt was dedicated.

MM

There were three windows between Lanfranc's transepts and the eastern transepts, the walls of which were opposite to the fifth and seventh pillar of the choir on each side. Each of these eastern transepts had two apses containing altars, the southernmost of the two in the north-east transept being the altar of St. Stephen, with that of St. Nicholas beneath it in the crypt, the other being St. Martin's, the corresponding altar in the crypt being that of St. Mary Magdalene. The south-east transept had the altars of St. Gregory and St. John the Evangelist, with those of St. Ouen and St. Paulinus beneath them in the crypt, and St. Catherine's in front of St. Ouen's. Following the choir aisle eastwards, there was on each side a tower. That on the north side of the church had in it the altar of St. Andrew, with the altar of the Holy Innocents in the crypt; the tower on the south side, which had been originally dedicated to SS. Peter and Paul, had been called St. Anselm's, since the body of that Saint was placed behind its altar, and beneath it in the crypt was the altar of St. Gabriel. Between these two towers the chapel of the Blessed Trinity extended eastwards. Behind the altar on the right side was St. Odo, on the left St. Wilfrid of York; on the south side by the wall lay Lanfranc, by the north wall Theobald. Beneath in the crypt were two altars, on the south that of St. Augustine, the Apostle of England, on the north St. John the Baptist's. In this lower chapel in the crypt was a column in the middle that bore the vault, and on its eastern side was the place chosen for the tomb of St. Thomas.

Such was the church as St. Thomas knew it, Lanfranc's church with Conrad's glorious choir. When the choir was burnt, William of Sens superintended the work for four years (1175 to 1178) till he was disabled by a fall of the scaffolding. He was succeeded in the fifth year (1179) by his namesake William, an Englishman, who completed the north and south eastern transepts and the vault over the high altar. The chapel of the Blessed Trinity was then enlarged, the old chapel being pulled down, and the crypt beneath, where St. Thomas lay in a temporary wooden chapel, was rebuilt, eight columns extending beyond the old foundations into the churchyard of the monks east of the church. The altar of the Holy Trinity, where St. Thomas used to say Mass, was taken down on the 8th of July, 1180, and the altar of St. John, the northernmost of the two altars in the south-eastern transept, was made of it, which Gervase notes lest the memory of St. Thomas's favourite altar should be lost. As a temporary arrangement St. Odo was placed beneath St. Dunstan's shrine, and St. Wilfrid beneath St. Elphege's; and Lanfranc was transferred to St. Martin's chapel, and Theobald to that of our Lady in the nave. Ultimately (Cotton MSS. Galba, E. iv.; Dart, App. p. xlii.), St. Odo and St. Wilfrid were placed in shrines "at the Crown" on the south and north sides respectively, and St. Blaise behind the high altar. St. Andrew's and St. Anselm's towers were carefully preserved, but as they radiated from the original apse of the church, the space between them was narrower than the old choir, and the new chapel of the Blessed Trinity being made wider than the old one, the line of the pillars follows an unusual and strikingly beautiful curve.

Such is Gervase's account of Christ Church, Canterbury, as it was in the days of St. Thomas, and as it was rebuilt shortly after the fire that followed so closely on his death. Of Lanfranc's work not much is now remaining. His nave and transepts were rebuilt by Prior Chillenden between

1379 and 1400, and a turret stair in the north transept and perhaps some flagstones are all that were there at the time of the martyrdom. The descent to the crypt on both sides is however part of the old work. About 1450 or 1460 Prior Goldston I. transferred the Lady Chapel from the nave aisle to a new chapel which took the place of St. Benedict's altar. The central tower was built by Prior Goldston II. between 1495 and 1503, with arches between the piers to serve as buttresses, the arch however towards the Martyrdom being left open. A lantern above Becket's Crown was begun by the same Prior, but the work was abandoned when a few courses had been built, and in 1748 the fragment of a lantern base was finished off as at present, at the expense of Capt. Humphrey Pudner, R.N. (*Christ Church, Canterbury, a Chronological Conspectus of the existing Architecture.* By W. A. Scott Robertson, Hon. Can., 1881).

There is little therefore in the upper church that can be pointed out as having existed in the time of St. Thomas, excepting the outer walls of the choir aisles, the eastern transepts with their beautiful towers, and the chapels of St. Andrew and St. Anselm. But the grand crypt under the choir, built between 1096 and 1100 by Prior Ernulf, when St. Anselm was Archbishop, and the sculptures of its piers and capitals, added between 1135 and 1165, remain substantially what they were when St. Thomas was Archbishop.

NOTE M (page 475).

THE HEAD OF ST. THOMAS.

Mr. Gough Nichols in his Erasmus (p. 118) refers to a sketch of the coffer containing the relics of St. Thomas, given on the same page of the Cottonian MS. (Tib. E. viii. fol. 269) as the sketch of the shrine already given (*Supra*, p. 478). He reproduces the sketch very unfaithfully, and describes it as if the head of the Saint had been " exhibited on a square table, together with bones."

This error is very properly corrected by Dean Stanley (p. 232), who rightly calls it, " not a table, but the identical iron chest deposited by Langton within the golden shrine."

The inscription, which was injured by the Cottonian fire, is thus restored by Dean Stanley from Dugdale. " *This chest of iron* contained the *bones of Thomas Becket*, skull and *all*, *with the wounde* of his death *and the pece cut* out of his skull laid in the same wound."

Dean Stanley further says (p. 254), that in Henry VIII.'s time " the reputed skull in the golden ' Head' was treated as an imposture, from its being so much larger than the portion that was found in the shrine with the rest of the bones." But, in truth, no such assertion was made of the skull or of the crown *in the golden head*. The passage from the Royal Declaration of 1539 is given by Mr. Albert Way in his note to Dean Stanley's work (p. 285), that Becket's "head almost whole was found with the rest of the bones closed within the shrine, and that there was in that church a great skull of another head, but much greater by three quarter parts than that part which was lacking in the head closed within the shrine."

Now we know from Erasmus, who wrote about 1524, that "the perforated skull of the martyr" was shown in the crypt. "Hinc," that is from the "sword's point," "digressi subimus cryptoporticum : ea habet suos mystagogos : illic primum exhibetur calvaria martyris perforata ; reliqua tecta sunt argento, summa cranii pars nuda patet osculo" (Stanley, p. 284). The portion cut off, the *corona capitis tota amputata* of Fitzstephen, we have seen was kept in a gilt head or bust of the Saint in "Becket's Crown" in the upper church, of which Erasmus says, "Illic in sacello quodam ostenditur tota facies optimi viri inaurata, multisque gemmis insignita "—in fact, the costly reliquary made by Prior Henry of Eastry *pro corona S. Thomæ*. "Matthew Parker, in his *Antiquitates Britannicæ Ecclesiæ*, at the close of his Life of Becket, observes that at first St. Thomas was placed less ostentatiously in the crypt : 'Deinde sublimiori et excelso ac sumptuoso delubro conditus fuerit, in quo caput ejus seorsim a cadavere situm, Thomæ Martyris Corona appellabatur, ad quod peregrinantes undique confluerent, muneraque pretiosa deferrent '" (Stanley, p. 282). This would seem to be, not the *caput* but the *corona*, which was kept in the upper church. Then we have the narrative of the visit of Madame de Montreuil in August, 1538. "By ten of the clock, she, her gentlewomen, and the [French] Ambassador went to the church, where I showed her St. Thomas's shrine, and all such other things worthy the sight; at the which she was not a little marvelled of the great riches thereof, saying it to be innumerable, and that if she had not seen it, all the men in the world could never have made her to believe it. Thus overlooking and viewing more than an hour, as well the shrine as St. Thomas's head, being at both set cushions to kneel, and the Prior opening St. Thomas's head, saying to her three times, 'This is Saint Thomas's head,' and offered her to kiss; but she neither kneeled, nor would kiss it, but still viewing the riches thereof" (Nichols' *Erasmus*, p. 119). This may have been the head of St. Thomas in the crypt, as the Prior opened the reliquary that the head might be kissed, which is in accordance with the account given by Erasmus. Or, not improbably, the crown of the head in the upper church was also given to be kissed, called, like the other relic, " St. Thomas's head," as we have seen it was called by the Black Prince.

The very next month after this visit the Royal Commissioners for the destruction of shrines reached Canterbury. We may be sure that the first thing done was the removal of the precious stones and the gold and silver. The shrine was stripped till it was as plain as the sketch in the Cottonian MS., and we may be sure that the reliquaries of the head and of the crown did not escape. So far, however, the war was against the shrine rather than the Saint, and the Commissioners cared more for chests of gold and jewels, "such as six or eight men could but convey one out of the church " than for the bones of the saints. The head when taken out of its reliquary and the crown from the bust, were placed by the monks in the iron chest which was taken out of the shrine, This we learn from the sketch in the Cottonian MS.,

which must have been made after the despoiling of
the shrine, and Mr. Way finds a needless difficulty
" in reconciling the discrepancies " between the
preceding accounts and the inscription on the Cottonian sketch.   Dean Stanley's conjecture does no
seem probable, that the sketch was " not meant to
pourtray the actual relics (which were inside), but
only a carving or painting of them on the lid."   It
is much more likely that·the draughtsman desired
to place on record at once the appearance of the
iron chest and its contents.   If, a month before,
the head was shown in a reliquary apart from the
chest, why should it have been painted or carved
on the lid of the chest ?   As to the statement of
the Royal Declaration of the following year, that
the " head almost whole was found with the rest of
the bones closed within the shrine," this must mean
that it was " found " later, for earlier than the
despoiling it was not within the shrine.   Now this
might easily be, for it seems very probable that the
relics of St. Thomas were first buried in the iron
chest, and thus Harpsfeld comes to say, " We have
of late unshrined him and buried his holy relics "
(Stanley, p. 254) ; and Pope Paul III. declares that
King Henry VIII. " Divi Thomæ . . . ossa . . . *exhumari*
et comburi et cineres in ventum spargi jussit."   This
inference, that the bones of St. Thomas were buried
and before long exhumed and burnt, may perhaps
help to reconcile the conflicting statements that they
were buried and not burnt, burnt and not buried.
First, the shrine was despoiled and the reliquaries
taken away; then the iron chest, now for the first
time containing both parts of the head, with the
other bones, was buried; then it was exhumed, and
" the head almost whole was found with the rest of
the bones ; " and lastly, all were burnt.   This recon-
ciles every statement.

NOTE N (page 481).

ERASMUS' VISIT TO CANTERBURY.

The following extracts are taken from Mr. Gough Nichols' translation of the account (*Pilgrimages of St. Mary of Walsingham and St. Thomas of Canterbury. By Desiderius Erasmus.* Translated with notes by John Gough Nichols, F.S.A. Westminster, 1849, pp. 44—58) that Erasmus wrote, half or more than half in mockery, of his visit to St. Thomas.

"That part of England which is opposite to France and Flanders is called Kent. Its chief city is Canterbury. In this city there are two monasteries nearly contiguous, each following the Rule of St. Benedict. That which is dedicated to St. Augustine seems the older; the other, which is now called St. Thomas's,[1] appears to have been the see of the Archbishop, where with a few chosen monks he passed his life, as prelates still have houses near to the church, but separate from the houses of the other canons. For formerly almost all bishops and canons were alike monks. That is evidenced by clear remains of antiquity. But the church dedicated to St. Thomas erects itself to heaven with such majesty that even from a distance it strikes religious awe into the beholders. So now

[1] It is not true that the dedication of the Church was changed, but it is true that the universal phrase was "going to St. Thomas." "Though the Metropolitan Church, in which he suffered, bore the title of the Blessed Trinity, God yielded it to His Martyr, as though he had bought it at the price of his blood, and it began rather to be called by his name, so that any one would count it no slight fault if, on going to Canterbury or returning, he were not to say that he was 'going to St. Thomas,' or that he was 'returning from St. Thomas'" (Lambeth MS. *Materials*, iv. p. 142).

with its splendour it dazzles the eyes of its neigh-
bour, and as it were casts into the shade a place
which was anciently most sacred.   There are two
vast towers, that seem to salute the visitor from
afar, and make the surrounding country far and
wide resound with the wonderful booming of their
brazen bells.   In the porch of the church, which
is towards the south, are stone statues of the three
knights who with impious hands murdered the most
holy man.   Their family names are inscribed:
Tuscus, Fuscus, and Berrus.[2] . . .

" On your entrance the edifice at once displays
itself in all its spaciousness and majesty.   To that
part any one is admitted. . . .

" Is nothing to be seen there?

" Nothing, except the magnitude of the structure,
and some books fixed to the pillars, among which
is the Gospel of Nicodemus, and the monument of
I know not who.

" What comes next?

" The iron screens stop further progress, but yet
admit a view of the whole space from the choir to
the end of the church.   To the choir you mount
by many steps, under which is a passage leading
north.   At that spot is shown a wooden altar,
dedicated to the holy Virgin, but mean, nor remarkable in any respect, unless as a monument of antiquity, putting to shame the extravagance of these
times.   There the pious man is said to have
breathed his last farewell to the Virgin when his
death was at hand.   On the altar is the point of
the sword, with which the head of the most excellent
prelate was cleft, and his brain stirred, that he

---

[2] Dean Stanley says (p. 113 *note*) that in Hentzner's *Travels in
England*, 1598, it is mentioned that the names engraved in the
south porch, under incised figures of three soldiers, were Tusci,
Fusci, and Berri.

might be the more instantly despatched. The
sacred rust of this iron, through love of the Martyr,
was religiously kissed. Leaving this spot, we
descended to the crypt. It has its own priests.
There was first exhibited the perforated skull of
the Martyr; the forehead is left bare to be kissed,
while the other parts are covered with silver. At
the same time is shown a slip of lead, engraved
with his name, 'Thomas Acrensis.' There also
hang in the dark the hair-shirts, the girdles and
bandages, with which that prelate subdued his
flesh; striking horror with their very appearance,
and reproaching us for our indulgence and our
luxuries. . . .

"From hence we returned into the choir. On
the north side the armories were unlocked: it is
wonderful to tell what a quantity of bones was there
brought out. . . . We next viewed the table of the
altar and its ornaments, and then the articles which
are kept under the altar, all most sumptuous. . . .
After this we were led to the sacristy. . . . There
we saw the pastoral staff of St. Thomas.. It appeared
to be a cane covered with silver plate; it was of
very little weight and no workmanship, nor stood
higher than to the waist.

" Was there no cross?

" I saw none. A pall was shown, which, though
wholly of silk, was of a coarse texture and unadorned
with gold or jewels. There was also a sudary, dirty
from wear, and retaining manifest signs of blood.
These monuments of the simplicity of ancient times
we willingly kissed.

" Are not they shown to anybody?

" By no means, my good friend.

" Whence then was such confidence reposed in
you, that no secret thing was reserved?

" I had some acquaintance with the Reverend

Father William Warham, the Archbishop; he had given me a note of introduction. . . .

" From this place, then, we were conducted back to the upper floor, for behind the high altar you ascend again, as into a new church. There in a little chapel is shown the whole figure of the excellent man, gilt, and adorned with many jewels (*Illic in sacello quodam ostenditur tota facies optimi viri inaurata, multisque gemmis insignita*).[3] . . .

The Prior " opened to us the shrine, in which what is left of the body of the holy man is said to rest.

" Did you see the bones?

" That is not permitted : nor indeed is it possible without the aid of a ladder : but a wooden canopy covers the golden shrine, and when that is drawn up with ropes, inestimable treasures are opened to view. . . . The least valuable portion was gold : every part glistened, shone, and sparkled with rare and very large jewels, some of them exceeding the size of a goose's egg. There some monks stood around with much veneration : the covering being raised, we all worshipped. The Prior with a white rod pointed out each jewel, telling its name in French, its value, and the name of its donor ; for the principal of them were offerings sent by sovereign princes. . . .

" From hence we returned to the crypt, where the Virgin Mother has her abode, but a somewhat

---

[3] In an additional note (p. 245) Mr. Gough Nichols abandons the translation here given, and considers it "most probable that this was a portrait of Becket, painted in brilliant colours upon a gold ground." Far more probable is Mr. Way's conclusion that it was "one of those gorgeously enriched busts, of life size, covered with precious metals and jewels, a class of reliquaries of which remarkable examples still exist " (Stanley's *Canterbury*, p. 285).

dark one, being hedged in by more than one iron screen.

" What was she afraid of?

" Nothing, I imagine, except thieves. For I have never seen anything more burdened with riches.

" You are telling me of untold wealth.

" When lamps were brought, we beheld a more than royal spectacle.

" Does it surpass Walsingham in riches?

" In outward show it far surpasses her; what her hidden riches are she only knows herself. This is not shown except to men of high rank, or great friends. Lastly, we were conducted back to the sacristy: there was brought out a box covered with black leather; it was laid upon the table and opened; immediately all knelt and worshipped.

" What was in it?

" Some torn fragments of linen, and most of them retaining marks of dirt."

NOTE O (page 516).

MEMORIALS AND RELICS OF ST. THOMAS.

" Far and wide the fame of St. Thomas of Canter-bury spread. Other English saints, however great their local celebrity, were for the most part not known beyond the limits of Britain. . . . But there is probably no country in Europe which does not exhibit traces of Becket. In Rome, the chapel of the English College marks the site of the ancient Church dedicated to him, and the relics attesting his martyrdom are laid up in the Basilica of St. Maria Maggiore beside the cradle of Bethlehem. In Verona, the Church of St. Tommaso Cantuariense contains a tooth, and did contain till recently part of his much contested skull. A portion of an arm is still shown to inquiring travellers in a convent at Florence; another portion in the Church of St. Waldetrude at Mons; at Lisbon, in the time of Fuller, both arms were exhibited in the English nunnery;[1] his chalice at Bourbourg, his hair-shirt at Douay, his mitre at St. Omer. In France, the

---

[1] "The English Nuns do pretend that they have both the arms of Thomas Becket, Archbishop of Canterbury; and yet Pope Paul III. in a public Bull set down by Sanders doth pitifully complain of the cruelty of King Henry VIII. for causing the bones of Becket to be burned, and the ashes scattered in the wind: the solemnity whereof is recorded in our chronicles. And how his arms should escape that *bone-fire*, is to me incredible" (Fuller, *Church History*, book vi. quoted by Mr. Gough Nichols). Two things are worth remarking here: that Fuller should distinctly agree with Stowe that St. Thomas's bones were burnt; and secondly, that the English Nuns of Lisbon, the direct descendants of Sion House, now at Spetis-bury, have no such relics of St. Thomas and have no record that their convent ever had them.

scene of his exile, his history can be tracked again
and again. On the heights of Fourvières, overlooking the city of Lyons, is a chapel dedicated
to St. Thomas of Canterbury. Four years before
his death, it is said, he was walking on the terraced
bank of the river underneath, and being asked to
whom the chapel should be dedicated, he replied,
'To the next martyr,' on which his companion
remarked, 'Perhaps then to you.' The same story
with the same issue is also told at St. Lo in
Normandy. In the same province, at Val Richer,
a tract of ground, still within the memory of men,
was left unploughed, in recollection of a great
English saint who had there performed his devotions. In Sens the vestments in which he officiated[2]
and an ancient altar at which he said Mass, are
exhibited in the Cathedral; and the old convent
at St. Colombe, where he resided, is shown outside
the city. At Lille there is a house with an inscription commemorative of his having passed a night
there. In the magnificent windows of Chartres,
of Sens, and of St. Ouen, the story of his life holds
a conspicuous place. At Palermo, his figure is still
to be seen in the Church of Monreale, founded by
William the Good in the year of his canonization.
Even far away in Syria, St. Thomas was not forgotten by the crusading army. His name was
inscribed on the banner of Archbishop Baldwin, at
Acre. William, chaplain of the Dean of St. Paul's,
on his voyage thither, made a vow that, if he
entered the place in safety, he would build there
a chapel to the Martyr, with an adjoining cemetery

[2] The length of these vestments confirms the account of his
great stature. On the feast of St. Thomas, till very recently,
they were worn for that one day by the officiating priest. The
tallest priest was always selected—and, even then, it was necessary to pin them up (*Dean Stanley's note*).

to bury the departed. The city was taken and the vow accomplished. William passed his life within the precincts of his church, engaged as Prior in the pious work of interring the dead. King Richard, at the same time and place, founded an Order of St. Thomas under the jurisdiction of the Templars. And from these circumstances, one of the names by which the Saint henceforward was most frequently known was ' Thomas Acrensis,' or ' St. Thomas of Acon or Acre.'

" To trace his churches and memorials through the British dominions would be an endless labour In Scotland, within seven years from the murder, the noble Abbey of Aberbrothock was raised to his memory by William the Lion, who chose it for the place of his own interment, partly, it would seem, from an early friendship contracted with the Archbishop at Henry's Court, partly from a lively sense of the Martyr's power in bringing about his defeat and capture at Alnwick. A mutilated figure of St. Thomas has survived amidst the ruins of the monastery. In the rough border-land between the two kingdoms, no oath was considered so binding in the thirteenth century, as one which was sworn upon ' the holy mysteries' and ' the sword of St. Thomas.' This, in all probability was the sword which Hugh de Moreville wore on the fatal day, and which, being preserved in his native province, thus obtained the same kind of honour in the north as that of Richard le Bret in the south, and was long regarded as the chief glory of Carlisle Cathedral. In England there was hardly a county which did not possess some church or convent connected with St. Thomas. The immense preponderance of the name of ' Thomas' in England, as compared with its use in other countries, probably arose from the reverence due to the great English Saint. Next to

the name of 'John,' common to all Christendom,
the most familiar to English ears is 'Tom' or
'Thomas.'[3] How few of these who bear or give it,
reflect that it is a vestige of the national feeling of
the twelfth century! Another instance may be
found in the frequency of the name of 'Thomas,'
'the great Tom,' applied to so many of our ancient
bells. But at that time the reminiscences of St.
Thomas were more substantial. Besides the swords
already mentioned, probably of Moreville and of Le
Bret, a third sword, perhaps of Tracy or Fitzurse,
was preserved in the Temple Church of London.
At Derby, at Warwick, at St. Albans, at Glastonbury, were portions of his dress; at Chester his
girdle, at Alnwick or at Corby his cup,[4] at Bury his
knife and boots, at Windsor and Peterborough drops
of his blood. The Priory of Woodspring on the
Bristol Channel, the Abbey of Beauchief in Derby-
shire, were direct expiations of the crime. The
very name of the latter was traced by popular,
though probably erroneous belief, to its connection
with the 'Bellum caput' or 'Beautiful head' of
the slaughtered Archbishop.[5] London was crowded
with memorials of its illustrious citizen. The chapel

[3] William was, in St. Thomas's time, the commonest of Christian names among the Normans. Canon Robertson quotes a
story from Robert of Thorigny, saying that when the younger
King Henry kept the Christmas of 1171-2 at Bur, it was
ordered that no one who did not bear the name should dine in a
certain room; and that, when all others had been turned out, a
hundred and seventeen knights, all named William, remained,
besides many other Williams who dined with the King in his
hall (Migne, *Patrol.* clx. 514; *Materials*, i. p. xxviii.).

[4] Mr. Gough Nichols (p. 229 note) says that the cup at Corby
Castle is really of the early part of the sixteenth century.

[5] Pegge proves that the ground on which the Abbey stands
was called Beauchief or the *Beautiful headland*, prior to the
building of the convent (*Dean Stanley's note*).

NN

of St. Thomas of Acre, now merged in the Mercers'
Hall, marked the place of his birth, and formed one
of the chief stations in the procession of the Lord
Mayor. The chapel which guarded the ancient
London Bridge was dedicated to St. Thomas. The
seal of the bridge 'had of old the effigies of Thomas
of Becket [a Londoner born] upon it with this
inscription in the name of the city,

Me quæ te peperi, ne cesses, Thoma, tueri.'[6]

The solitary vacant niche, which is seen in the front
of Lambeth Palace, facing the river, was once filled
by a statue of the great Primate, to which the water-
men of the Thames doffed their caps as they rowed
by in their countless barges" (Dean Stanley's *Canterbury*, pp. 196—199).

[6] Howel, *Londinopolis*, p. 395.

INDEX.

the King 342; thanks the Pope for the canonization of St. Thomas 468.

Bath, Bishop of, *see* Robert and Reginald.

Bath, bishopric of, held vacant by Henry 326.

Battle Abbey, Chronicle of, referred to 47, 533 seq.; MSS. of Chronicle examined 548 seq.

Battle, Abbot of, *see* Walter.

Bayeux 53, 297, 329, 393.

Bayeux, Bishop of 272, 351, 440.

Beaucamps-en-Weppes 565.

Beauchief Abbey 609 and note.

Beaulieu, de, quoted 515 note, 523.

Beaumes, Richard de, Bishop of London 41, 99 note.

Beaumont, Rotrou de, Bishop of Evreux 152; Archbishop of Rouen 152, 231, 237, 337, 356, 373, 431, 432; present at the conferences of the Legates with St. Thomas 266, and the King 272; meets the Pope's envoys 329, 333; receives powers from the Pope 344, but is inactive 354; crowns Princess Margaret 439.

Beauvais, Bishop of 432.

Bec, Monastery of 271.

Becchetti family 509.

Becket, Gilbert 506; father of St. Thomas 5, 23; Saracen legend related of 3—5, 487, 523; citizen of London 5, 6, 525; a Norman 8, 12; native of Thierceville 15; Sheriff of London 8; personally acquainted with Archbishop Theobald 15; his property greatly reduced by frequent fires 6, 9; his death 10.

Becket, BB. John and Peter 507.

Becket, Matilda 8; mother of St. Thomas 5, 23, 525; Saracen legend told of 3—5; her dreams before and after the birth of the Saint 5, 6; her devotions 7; religious practice of 10; death of 10, 12.

Bede, Venerable 19, 526.

Beivin, William 397.

Bekker, Emmanuel 12 note.

Belet, William 455.

Benedict, *see* St.

Benedict, Prior of Canterbury 244, 514; Abbot of Peterborough (wrote "Passion and Miracles of St. Thomas") 391, 402, 418 note, 419 note, 454 note, 455, 456, 458, 459, 460, 465, 470.

Benedict XII., Pope 524.

Benedict XIV., Pope, quoted 230 note, 486.

Benevento 249, 263, 279, 280.

Berceto 509.

Berengar carried letters excommunicating Bishop of London 311, 312.

Berham, Robert of 586.

Berington, Mr., quotation from 523, 529.

Berkhampstead, Castle of 28, 161.

Bernard, *see* St.

Bernard of Grammont, Father, *see* Coudre, de la.

Beverley, Provost of 25, 39.

Bigod, Earl Hugh, *see* Norfolk.

Birchington, Stephen (monk of Canterbury), quoted 70 note.

Black Prince 471 note, 475, 476.

Blangy visited by St. Thomas 565.

Bletchingley 399.

Blois, Henry of, Bishop of Winchester, *see* Henry.

Blois, William of, *see* William.

Bohun, Engelger de 394.

Bollandists 510.

Bologna, St. Thomas studies at 24; Henry tries to bribe the citizens of 326.

Bonhart, William carried Archbishop's letters excommunicating Bishop of London 311, 312.

Boniface of Savoy, Archbishop 243, 470 note.

Borghese, Cardinal 485.

Bosham, *see* Herbert.

Pope 340; sent to meet St. Thomas 373; envoy to the Pope at Tusculum 429; made Bishop of Norwich 441.

John of Salisbury, afterwards Bishop of Chartres (author of *Life of St. Thomas*) 44, 55 seq.; 107, 194, 216, 234, 235 note, 249, 266, 382, 388, 392 note, 402, 529, 531, 557, 580, 581; quoted 47, 66, 138; writes the *Life of St. Anselm* 102; banished on account of St. Thomas 150, 151; promised help by Count of Flanders 201 note; writes to the Pope to remonstrate 258; writes to the Bishop of Thérouanne 261; advises St. Thomas to write mildly 264; very open with the Saint 265; account of the conference at Les Planches 267; goes to the King at Angers 283; writes to Master Lombard 288; sent to the King in Normandy 366; went to England to prepare for the Saint's return 372 seq.; present at the meeting with the murderers 402, 407; elected Bishop of Chartres 450 seq.; witness as to many miracles 462 seq.

John, Bishop of Séez 231, 237, 328, 337, 340, 351.

John, Count of Vendôme 125.

John, Bishop of Worcester 24.

Jordan of Plumstead 13, 14.

KENT 14; coast of 100; sheriff of 157, 158; *see* Gervase of Cornhill.

Knight, H. Gally, quoted 512 note.

LACOKE, Abbess of 463.

Lagny 35.

Lambarde quoted 496.

Lambeth Palace 609.

Lanfranc, Archbishop of Canterbury 20, 69, 232, 545, 554.

Langton, Cardinal Stephen 243, 470 seq., 498, 523.

Lateran, letters from 232 and note, 349.

Lateran, Second Council of 17, 18, 94.

Lateran, Fourth General Council of 583.

Laurence of Eynesford (cleric) 111.

Laurence, Abbot of Westminster 104, 106, 314.

Laval, Guy de (a noted freebooter) 38.

Le Bret, Richard, *see* Brito.

L'Egle, Richier de 8 note, 12; friend of the Saint 9, 137 note; anecdote of 9, 10.

Leicester, Prior of, *see* Aschetin.

Leicester, Robert Earl of, *see* Robert.

Leo IV., Pope 527.

Letard of Northfleet (a cleric) excommunicated 310.

L'Eveque, Roger de Pont, Archbishop of York, *see* Roger.

Liberius, persecution of 184.

Lichfield, Bishop of 342.

Liesse 515.

Lille, inscription at, commemorating visit of St. Thomas 564.

Limoges 35 note.

Lincoln 24, 57, 187; Bishop of 94, 101, 256 note; bishopric held vacant by Henry 326.

Lisieux, Bishop of, *see* Arnulph; Archdeacon of, *see* Nunant.

Lisle, Walter de 240,

Llandaff, Archdeacon of 328; Bishop of 94, 277.

Llewellen, Alexander ("the Welshman") 138, 139; crossbearer to St. Thomas 168; with St. Thomas at Pontigny 222, 223; and at Vezelay 246; and Les Planches 266; returns with him 388, 396; bears his last letter to the Pope 428, 430; becomes Archdeacon of Bangor 452.

Lombard of Piacenza, Cardinal Archbishop of Benevento 215, 258, 266, 288, 452.

William of Worcester quoted 589.

William (a priest) 389, 397, 506; brings relics of St. Thomas 390.

William (another priest) 456.

William (servant of St. Thomas) 387, 388.

William, *see* Beivin, Belet, and de Tracy.

Wimar (priest) 334.

Winchester, Bishop of, *see* Henry of Blois, Richard of Ilchester; convention of 23; city of 137, 384, 395, 405, 427.

Windsor 516, 609.

Wiscard (a falcon) 9 note.

Wiseman, Cardinal 514.

Witdeniers, Osbern (a relation of St. Thomas) 12.

Witsand, *or* Wissant, port of 374, 376.

Wolf, Christian, cited 452, 523.

Woodspring, Priory of 609.

Woodstock 126, 154, 156; Council held at Palace of 112.

Worcester, Bishops of, *see* Roger (de Melhent), John.

Wright 516 note.

Wrotham 389, 397.

Würzburg, Diet of 230.

Wycombe 103 note.

YORK, Archbishops of, *see* Roger of Pont l'Evêque, St. William; diocese of, not included in St. Thomas's legatine powers 232; province of, question of precedence 19—21, 68, 118, 126—128, 146; town 312.

York, Cardinal, Duke of 486.

Lightning Source UK Ltd.
Milton Keynes UK
23 March 2011

169738UK00005B/94/P